Just Enough

Tools for Creating Success in
Your Work and Life

Laura Nash and Howard Stevenson

Harvard Business School

WILEY

John Wiley & Sons, Inc.

Published by John Wiley & Sons, Inc., Hoboken, New Jersey.
Published simultaneously in Canada.

For general information on our other products and services please contact our Customer Care Department within the United States at (800) 762-2974, outside the United States at (317) 572-3993 or fax (317) 572-4002.

Wiley also publishes its books in a variety of electronic formats. Some content that appears in print may not be available in electronic books. For more information about Wiley products, visit our web site at www.wiley.com.

Library of Congress Cataloging-in-Publication Data:

Nash, Laura
   Just enough : tools for creating success in your work and life /
Laura Nash and Howard Stevenson.
      p.   cm.
Includes bibliographical references and index.
   ISBN 0-471-45836-8 (cloth); 0-471-71440-2 (pbk.)
   1. Success in business.   2. Success.   I. Stevenson, Howard   II. Title.
   HF5386. S8715 2004
   650.1—dc22

                                                      2003020252

Printed in the United States of America.

10 9 8 7 6 5 4 3 2 1

To the many from whom we have learned!

Contents

Preface

Cherie, Martha, Rosie, Trent, Sean, and Bill: Why are so many high achievers acting like adolescents?

—Headline in *More* magazine, April 2003

A senior executive at one of our sessions at Harvard Business School told us the following cautionary tale:

Long ago, in ancient China, the king wanted to reward a loyal citizen. The king gave this simple man the right to mark out as much territory as he wished, and that area would be his. All he had to do was walk around, marking off the boundaries of his desired reward, and then return to the king to claim this land.

The man set out, and on the first day he walked three miles. As he turned back to the palace in the far distance, he changed his mind. Perhaps he'd need a bit more, maybe just as far as the eye could see. A week later, he had finished walking this distance. But what if there was a drought or flood? Wouldn't it be better to mark out enough land for farming *and* fishing, and maybe a woods for hunting?

It took him a year to complete all of these goals. As he set off to return to the palace and complete the circle, he thought about his children. Would this be enough to pass on to them for 10 generations? Maybe they should have access to the ocean, in case they wanted to become shipping merchants. He walked further. By now he was quite tired, but on he went, inspired by the knowledge that each step was increasing his holdings.

Ten years later, he began his journey back, an old and tired man. Just as he entered the palace, he dropped dead. He never realized the ambitions he had continually adjusted upward. His children had no land. He never enjoyed even a fraction of the good life he sought because of his bondage to "never enough."

Sound familiar? Every culture has cautionary tales like this one, warning of the dangers of excessive ambition or the penalties for excessive sloth. Unfortunately, they give little guidance on what a more balanced approach might be for those who feel they want to make a mark in this world but have no framework for determining how much success is "just enough." To answer that question—for achievers in today's world—we embarked on the research for this book.

Recognizing "Just Enough" in a World of "Infinite More"

Success has always been an American preoccupation, but the definition of success takes on a new urgency today, when every conventional measure of success seems to have a faster burn rate than ever before. During the 1990s, we saw a dramatic rise in the rate of economic growth. Fueled by such radical changes as the Internet, measures of corporate and personal wealth became obsolete almost before the next quarter's performance results were reported. When the markets inevitably plunged, the paper billionaires and millionaires of the new economy took a haircut to the tune of several trillion dollars.

Overworked and undersatisfied in the boom, overworked and competitively vulnerable in the bust, traditional career paths suddenly seem pointless. What is success if you can't enjoy it? You mean I have to go out there and do it *again*? Even a once-simple idea like success in war is quickly shattered into a myriad of untidy problems in places like Iraq and Afghanistan.

Many people feel unprepared for this new world. It's not just about longer hours at work, uncertain job prospects, questions about retirement and health insurance, nor the newfound sense of peril we felt in witnessing the hottest stocks suffer market meltdown and once unsullied skies host a terrorist attack on New York City. It's about wanting to build something of lasting value in a world where the ground shifts daily. It's about wanting to make the most of your life.

At one time, success was a rich idea, representing a varied landscape of virtues, accomplishments, and rewards. Today, it has been reduced to a flat idea of riches. For that we are all the poorer. A few decades ago, a "two-comma" bank account (that's millions to you and me) used to be considered a mighty big success. But by the mid-1990s, there dangled the possibility of "three-comma" bank accounts by age thirty. As one interviewee told us, "Who wants to be a millionaire when billionaire is the new standard?" Like the simple man in the fable, the idea of success seems to have wandered far afield into an expectation of *limitless expansion:* getting more, doing more, being more. As author Michael Lewis stated, it's a world centered on "next" and "The New New Thing," a landscape of the infinite more. As the ante gets higher, our experience of success has been impoverished. Where there is no possibility of satisfaction, nothing is ever enough.

Which brings us to this book.

Why We Wrote This Book

When we began our research—just after September 11, 2001—we discovered that many people shared the concerns that inspired our project. More than ever, people were asking, "Am I making the most out of my life?" Whether it was a Harvard Business School reunion class at the top of its form, our survey of top executives, or someone downsizing his or her career, the message was refreshing: "Me first" is not all there is. Their problem was not an inability to imagine the good life in terms larger than money, but knowing how to go after it.

Whether your dilemmas are about uses of wealth or sources of pleasure, everyone struggles to some degree with when to go for more and when to say "that's just enough" and move on. Everyone faces conflicting desires between self-interest and being *part* of something that requires self-restraint for the sake of community. At one time, it was valid to ask leaders, parents, and workers whether they were doing enough for themselves *and* for others. Today these questions have nearly been washed away in the glamorous tide of celebrity ambition and celebrity crashes, from Enron to political candidates.

Like many, we've been discouraged by the moral failings of the past decade's success ethos. How to make sense of authority figures who one day seem to exude leadership legitimacy and the next are caught with their hands in the cookie jar or in the wrong bed? Such behaviors have led to a national crisis of trust about those whom we designate leaders. This situation presents a critical challenge not only to business and government as we identify successful leadership traits, but to individuals as they seek to define the terms on which they will pursue future prosperity and a good life.

In *Just Enough*, we take a fresh look at the foundational assumptions behind the idea of success, and provide a challenging but practical framework you can use to pursue and realize a success that you and others will truly value. **Our core message is that success is not about one thing nor an infinite number of things; it is about "just enough."** We found that reaching this state requires your active engagement in four very different kinds of goals: Happiness, Achievement, Significance, and Legacy. These form the basic structure of our success model, and with these tools you can construct your own unique profile. The framework can be helpful to people who are scaling back their career goals and those who are just starting out; to the promising leaders of great organizations and the breakaway seekers of a better vocation.

Our model is absolutely counterintuitive to the advice that tells you the secret to success is passion and focus, focus, focus. Interestingly, research in complex decision making suggests that it is actually possible to reach a constructive sense of limitation *more* easily in a complex landscape than when you seek one big, far-off goal. Judging by the way in which people seem to resonate to the four categories, it seems that we already have an adaptive capacity for this kind of complexity. The trick is not to kill this complexity in ourselves, but to make room for it.

Before we get to the model, however, a word about the research behind our conclusion is in order.

About Our Research

As educators and businesspeople ourselves, we've been studying all kinds of successful people and organizations for a long time. In over 150 Harvard Business School cases and more than a dozen books, we've dug into the factors that make entrepreneurs tick, the strategies successful companies employ, and the values driving great leadership. We realized that we had never fully addressed perhaps the biggest question of all, the one that drives all the others: What do we *really* mean by success?

We each bring somewhat different perspectives to this material. Howard Stevenson's work in entrepreneurship at Harvard Business School and as an entrepreneur himself has ranged from early stage investing to complex mathematical discussions of predictability. Laura Nash drew on humanistic traditions in the classics (in which she has a Ph.D.), sociology, and 20 years of research in business ethics and management. We found that some of the sharpest and most insightful findings of our research emerged from the interplay of our two perspectives.

The research for this book is composed of several strands. First, we conducted more than 60 interviews (over 300 hours) with successful professionals, a survey of 90 top executives attending Harvard Business School management programs, and informal observation of high achievers with whom we work and live. This formed the backbone of our study. We also held more than a dozen model-testing sessions with 50 to 110 executives per session to share our core findings and get further feedback. In nearly one-quarter of these sessions, spouses were also present. Most of these groups were drawn from Harvard Business School (HBS) graduates or current members of the Young Presidents' Organization and its affiliate groups (CEO and WPO).

We also conducted an extensive review of the problems that the general population reports around success. Our sources of information ranged from media coverage of this topic to conversations with friends, HBS colleagues, family, undergraduates, MBA students, and parents of our children's friends. We were assisted in this by having the good fortune to work with a number of great companies and business leaders over this period. We talked to people from all walks of life, at every level of the economy, in and out of business careers. Some are stay-at-home parents who had once worked full time, others were at the pinnacle of their careers.

We compared our findings with many new studies on work attitudes, happiness, and life satisfaction research; ongoing developments in the emotional intelligence and leadership field; and classic discussions of the good life in literature, history, and economics. Given the vast range of recent research in some of these areas, we've tried to keep the footnotes to a minimum and summarize this material.

Too often, success advice bifurcates into management tactics or psychological self-help. We felt both perspectives were critical. You cannot separate individual success from the success of the organizations in which we are imbedded: family, work, community, and the world. **Our goal is to enhance your ability to handle legitimate performance difficulties in today's business environment and to help you understand how this skill depends on deeper commitments to an authentic view of success.**

This led us to study the types of accomplishment that account for "real" success in people's minds—in and out of work—as well as how they proceeded to get there. We asked foundational questions and probed for concrete examples. We talked with people one-on-one and in groups about their experiences and their emotions. We discussed their values as well as their context. We were looking not only for technique, but for a critical point of view that would answer some of the deep concerns we hear voiced by our own students and that we ourselves share: Whom do you think your success should benefit? What is the purpose of business? At what point does individualism and the search for freedom turn into selfishness and social destruction? Where does happiness come in? How do self-reliant high achievers share their good fortune and transform their accomplishments into platforms for *other* people's success?

We believe that these are critical questions in today's society, when a culture of genius performance and winner-take-all repeatedly reinforces entitled behavior and short-sighted decisions. In the face of so many phony victories, we urgently need an understanding of success in a way that gets *real:* that provides satisfaction for people who don't have perfect knowledge and limited energy; people who are subject to the vagaries of fortune but still want to exert active control over creating enduring value in their own lives.

Who Sets the Benchmarks of Enduring Success?

From the outset we faced a serious methodological puzzle. Whose life would be a benchmark of success? We resisted the idea that mere achievement on some business scale would provide a foolproof example. If nothing else, the past decade has taught us the danger of drawing our success intelligence from the most recent superstars in business and politics. How many times did the experts on excellence have to recant almost before the ink dried? Our advice is not about how to become someone else's idea of making it, but how to effectively read and negotiate the many dimensions of *your own* aspirations—now and in the future.

We have not relied on celebrity to make our case for a deeper effectiveness—nor should you. You have to get real about success if you are to deal with its many challenges and rewards. From the outset, we were determined to honor the complex, diverse feelings that we have seen people bring to the questions of career, achievement, and the good life. We also believe that every individual has a unique profile of success that they should seek to fill in.

On the other hand, we weren't writing a values-neutral essay in self-esteem. Self-funded dabblers in manufacturing new forms of sealing wax were excluded from our research unless they had something else to recommend them. Instead, we applied a rough cluster of attributes that in our observation represent the successful alignment of personal satisfaction and success on multiple measures: high achievement, multiple goals in life, the ability to experience pleasure, the ability to create positive relationships, and a value on accomplishments that endure. In our experience, you can often find someone succeeding on two of these factors, but not necessarily all of them.

Selection Criteria

Our precise achievement threshold was variable. Our subjects include the high-achieving school teacher, the resourceful salesperson, the accomplished parent, housecleaners, and, of course, many business executives. We were not particularly concerned that they be at "the top" of the highest achieving organization in their sector, because in many cases that position was occupied by a person with a narrower horizon of success measures and personality traits than interested us. Factors that we considered were:

1. *Outward and varied success:* The selection criteria for *recognizable achievement at a high level* was that they had obtained a significant measure of outward success in comparison with their peer group—a category we came to call *the upper 1 percent.* We used this rough measure in the belief that although internal values are the ultimate guiding star, external comparisons are inescapable and essential to any useful model of success. **Our subjects were undeniably high achievers on some score that others were also keeping and felt was important.** Their success was plausible and theoretically desired by others. Their jobs ranged from screenwriter to

insurance executive, from facilities maintenance person to chairman of a Fortune 100 firm.

The variety of their accomplishments speaks to a fundamental assumption in this book: success cannot be limited to some extreme subset of activities in society. It is a domain in which all people participate to greater or lesser degrees. Some of the most admirable successes have occurred when people make a success out of dealing with a serious illness or family crisis. Some of the most revealing failures have occurred in the lives of those who temporarily occupied the top. Working on this assumption, we present a fascinating variety of observations from the ordinary-extraordinaries. People everyone can admire and emulate.

2. *Multiple goals:* Our second major criterion for research was *achievers who had multiple goals on their success horizon, driven by an acknowledgement of various emotional needs,* including the ability to experience pleasure across several domains: work, family, private time, in community. This is not the star who gives up family and friends in order to fulfill the demands of career, but the talented person who also works hard but has a life. It's the parent who cuts back on career for the sake of children but does not become lost in the mom role or dad role to forsake all other aspects of his or her identity. It's the CEO whose mission is to improve some condition in the world as well as increasing her own power and fortune.

3. *Positive contribution:* Our third criterion for research was frankly even more value-biased. We were not interested in just any achievement, regardless of its social value. We wanted to study people with the demonstrated aim of making a positive contribution to something besides themselves. When push comes to shove, they aren't always choosing their own interests first. As our surveys revealed, the most common measure of success among those we studied was "making a difference in the world"—whether directed at child raising, the arts, a customer group, employee relations, world peace, public health, nonprofit and political activity, or providing positive stock returns to total strangers who have placed their life savings in your firm.

4. *In it for the long term:* We also sought out companies and people who aren't in it for the short-term buzz. This is the bias you see in companies that are committed to staying financially healthy over the long haul and renew the community whose resources they are using up. You see it in people who reign in their appetites for endless consumption in favor of purchases or experiences that will continue to please; in institutional structures that provide opportunities in which people can grow for life; in families that seek to equip their children to be successful in their own right.

5. *Autonomy/empathy balance:* Success can make you a stranger to yourself. The great successes risk personal isolation even from those they love most. Our interest lay in those who overcome these dangers, who can be at the center of their own small mystery and yet be attuned to the worth of others. One word for this quality is humility. Another is humanity. We sought out people who, whatever their wealth or accomplishment, are not totally performance-driven or self-absorbed, who are able to experience intrinsic satisfaction from their activities. People who identify with others and still feel comfortable in their own skin. Call it a balance between autonomy and empathy, or in moral terms an I/We point of view (a term used in Amitai Etzioni's book, *The Moral Dimension*). We think it is a critical balance and a fundamental factor in a person's ability to live and work with integrity.

And this brings us back to the Chinese man's dilemma we confronted at the beginning of this introduction: How can we recognize when we have found just enough from success—for ourselves and others—in a world of the infinite more?

The Framework for Just Enough

In our interviews, an intriguing point kept surfacing: Approached in the right way, success can offer a rich palette of satisfactions of different emotional needs. **These findings offer a refreshing alternative to a frequently voiced view that high achievement is only possible for those with a neurotic sense of inadequacy.** We saw a very different picture and have developed a framework here that will help you do the same.

Shifting Targets Happen

The first challenge is to accept the paradoxical concept that although worthwhile and lasting success is dependent on a knowledge of what has permanent value in your life, this ideal will inevitably take the form of a multidimensional, continually shifting set of targets. Some targets are things you desire to have as pieces of your success, and you pursue them with vigor. Others aren't visible from where you stand, but you have to be ready to adjust your goals later. Some are unreachable—idealized or fantastically ambitious targets disguised in the language of greatness or charisma. Other targets are reachable but the prize is not satisfying, so you may want to pass them up in favor of something else. Ultimately, the pattern of targets that you seek to hit is yours to define, and they in turn define you. In the Zen of success intelligence, you are both the target *and* the shooter.

You probably have already experienced the dilemma of moving targets as you try to balance work and family needs, or when you have completed a difficult task only to feel slightly "empty" over the results. Success that creates a positive contribution for yourself and for others requires seeing this multiplicity as necessary and turning it into something *desirable*. People want to learn how to negotiate this complex landscape *and* feel the journey is worthwhile. **The good news is that we discovered many people who not only care about achieving a success that doesn't devalue their own deep values, they have learned to execute the complex challenges this necessitates taking on.**

The Four Categories of Satisfaction from Success

You can create your own stable base by applying a framework that brings order to this chaos. In this book, you will be introduced to four irreducible categories, which we discovered in every interviewee's ultimate understanding of success: **Happiness, Achievement, Significance, and Legacy.** These are things people want to establish about themselves and experience when they think of being a success. Even their external targets—such as reaching a certain financial goal—tend to expect these satisfactions, however much their activities may be aimed at one thing.

Knowing the distinctive features of these four categories helps you articulate what it is you are seeking in a certain activity, and we found this categorizing ability has its own power in motivating more decisive action. The categories also impose an important set of standards on success. **When you achieve these goals, success feels satisfying and worthwhile:** *Just enough.* Unlike achievements or pleasures that fade almost as soon as they occur, this kind of accomplishment endures. It represents time well spent, a life lived well.

We also found that the four categories work like a fractal pattern; they replicate on different scales of activity, time, and relationships. This "repeated constant" makes the framework particularly powerful in helping sort out the multiple targets of your life. You will see how using this framework as both a template and an ordering device brings an added richness to episodes that demand great commitment. That's no small sense of progress.

One of the great ah-has of our research was the realization that however much people might describe their activities in "collapsed" terms that imply you can have all four satisfactions at once, these same people were actually rapidly switching attention. They were applying various emotional and relational perspectives to their activities. The faster they could switch *and* link these accomplishments, the more often they created a sense of meaningful, satisfying activity.

The Kaleidoscope Strategy

The four categories will help you identify the nature of your success goals and the essential perspectives you must apply to each. But you must still actively compare and select among the many different possibilities. How do you keep the pieces separate and still hold the picture of your life together? We introduce the concept of the *kaleidoscope strategy* to address this fundamental problem. This strategy offers you a special kind of framework that allows you to hold your many aspirations up to the light and observe their changing patterns.

We found the kaleidoscope to be a great image because—like life—it is inherently about complexity, change, and relationships. If you think of the four chambers of a kaleidoscope as representing our four success categories in a coherent relationship, the colored chips that fill them are created by the things you accomplish that actually deliver these satisfactions. The intriguing patterns are formed by the goals you choose to pursue from all the moving targets on your path. With this organizing concept, you will begin to see how success does not have to be a lifelong chase after the biggest, most perfect chip, but rather a skillful interplay among the chips that makes the most satisfying patterns *for you*.

Some people seem to be under the impression that each time they tire of the pieces in their kaleidoscope, they can just throw it out and find another one. We saw just the opposite: Enduring organizations are built by people who choose wisely not just for today, but for the future as well. We'd like to help equip you to deal with this kind of complexity in your own pursuit of success. Not only will you be more likely to feel accomplished and fulfilled, the welfare of a nation's basic institutions depends on it.

A Reasoned Calculation of Just Enough

If success has an ordered, four-part complexity that arranges itself in shifting patterns, like a kaleidoscope, how can you capture the full spectrum within a reasonable time? How can you shift your attention so as not to go down with your one glorious and narrow win?

We found the answer in the concept of *a reasoned sense of enough*, a capacity that is particularly threatened in today's world of the infinite more, "bests," and maximized performance. Instead of trying to have it all and do it all, you have to learn to recalibrate to go after *just enough*. The critical level that gets you there is determined by a reasoned calculation of what will really satisfy your particular needs in one category for now, for tomorrow, and for the larger picture. Beyond that, you really begin to waste your energy at the cost of your opportunity to address your other needs.

Developing this capacity takes real skill. We walk you through both the signs of enough and ways to exercise it in the right proportions to achieve the full spectrum of expectations around success. At first hearing, enough may sound like a negative concept—as in, "That's it, Junior, I've had *enough*." In this book, we suggest a deliberate approach to enough that transforms the process of getting to enough from a negative state of *satiation* (that is, being so overloaded you now feel repulsed by a formerly desirable thing) to a positive state of *satisfaction*. Recognizing this state and that it differs from other kinds of satisfaction you may seek allows you to put that activity down, knowing it is enough for the moment.

When applied to the four categories of success, the concept becomes a powerful motivational tool. You give yourself permission to experience the rewards you seek and pace yourself to accommodate important emotional and energy needs. Yet you are able to return to a task knowing you have not done enough to satisfy your ambitions for the future. **This is the pattern on which lasting contributions are obtained without giving up a multidimensional life.**

Some people learn to deliberately cultivate this state of appreciation through nonrational exercises, such as meditation or philosophies of simplicity. We are not trying to replace such techniques, but rather to offer a rational set of decisions tools as well. When it comes to success, there are both emotional "enoughs" and pragmatic "enoughs" to be considered. These can and must be approached not only with emotional and philosophical intelligence, but with rational care.

The Components of Your Self-Definition

Enough in light of what? According to our model, in light of creating that larger picture of the four chambers in the kaleidoscope of success. A feedback loop is created with continual reference to your inner core and self-definitions that shape your goals: your values and beliefs, your own capacities development, multiple emotional needs, and the context in which you are placed. Each of these important drivers will be explored with surprising connections to achieving satisfaction in the four categories.

Toward a New Perspective

This book is about changing your perspective on the parameters of success in order to develop an organized set of tactics for accomplishing the very different satisfactions you seek. We assist you in the process by offering a model that helps people and organizations:

- Anticipate and sort the basic expectations of success (Happiness, Achievement, Significance, Legacy).
- Set limits on your desires so that you can regularly experience satisfaction along the way and make room for multiple kinds of success (the kaleidoscope strategy).
- Learn what shapes your goals (the components of your self-definition).
- Learn how to direct the right degree of resources toward each basic desire with the right timing (Just Enough).

The frameworks help you adopt the model in workable pieces, chapter by chapter. They offer a comprehensive, practical instrument for viewing your own attitudes and pursuit of success—or those of your organization. The kaleidoscope strategy offers you a special kind of lens through which you view your aspirations and accomplishments—past, present, and future. You don't have to hold your life up to the light of this model every minute. But by using it regularly to take a reading on how your pursuit of success is going, you can free yourself of many of the stresses, blind alleys, and addictions that can overwhelm even the most accomplished people and companies.

We especially direct our findings to the many talented people who are burning themselves out or turning their back on common causes in their desire to simplify the demands of "never enough." **Rather than discard or neglect your aspirations out of a sense of deep constraint, it is critical to tame them into a framework that reconnects you to sustainable achievement and the recognition that even when the going gets tough, you are engaged in something of enduring value.** We cannot and would not presume to tell you what you want in terms of success. We can give you a strategy for seeing it more clearly, anticipating the demands ahead of you, and knowing when you have achieved the satisfactions of "just enough" from success.

Acknowledgments

Were we to mention all the people to whom we are most sincerely grateful for the development of this book, our ecological conscience on paper consumption would be seriously violated. Our sources of information and inspiration have sprung from more than three hundred surveyed executives and interviewees, our back files of work with businesspeople and students over our own long careers, our unusual combination of educational perspectives, and the encouragement of our friends and families. Interviewees, many of whom wished to remain anonymous, were particularly patient with the process.

Life at Harvard Business School presents an unusual opportunity to test our ideas with incredible colleagues, alumni, and participants in the executive programs. We are grateful for their interest and their comments. We conducted several faculty research presentations as the study unfolded, and for those who barely recognize the final product, happy reading and thank you for keeping our thinking open-minded.

Specific mention should be made of the editorial and research support we received. Harvard Business School's Division of Research provided all funding for the research. Our unit research director, now unit chair Teresa Amabile, offered critical help with survey development at the start of the project. Gail Ross, with the help of Howard Yoon and Jenna Land at Gail Ross Literary Agency, helped us develop the proposal for the book and find the right editor, Airié Stuart at John Wiley & Sons supported by Jessica Noyes and Emily Conway. Special thanks goes to those who worked most closely with us on the final shaping of *Just Enough:*

Theresa Gaignard composed the chapter artwork and Nicole Chryssicas created the cover design. Naomi Lucks Sigal added her impeccable editorial insight and old-fashioned last-minute dedication to the manuscript completion. We hope they will all consider this book a concrete product of their joint efforts.

Most of all, we thank our families who taught us a great deal about the meaning of success while they suffered with us through the process of writing. Thank you Tom, Alexandra, and Corinna. Thank you Fredericka, Michon, Trevor, Devin, Cavan, Will, Charley, and Andy. Thank you to all the other friends who serve as great examples!

PART ONE

MOVING TARGETS

Chapter 1

Stress! Excess! Success?

Young Millionaires: What Do They Know That You Don't?
—Headline from cover of
Entrepreneur magazine, November 2002

"Jane" is an attractive, bright, 30-year-old woman with a passion for life. We met her completely by chance at an isolated bed-and-breakfast in the middle of the southern Utah desert, where she was taking some time off from work to think about her life. She and her significant other, Joe, were hiking the back country near Monument Valley, on a spiritual quest to resolve an important question with very practical implications: Should Jane quit her successful job in software to pursue a career in sacred music?

She was fully qualified to do either. Jane had majored in music and math as an undergraduate, and then put herself through music seminary by playing the organ in a local church. Afterward, she'd taken a good job at a startup software firm in her college city. It was a fun and intense team-oriented experience. Her boss was very supportive of her and the tasks were both challenging and lucrative. But after four years on the job, the money and success didn't seem to make up for the stress she felt in this position. How could something so good feel so bad?

As she and Joe talked about the future, the possibility of marriage and kids, and their mutual love of outdoor adventures, Jane found herself torn between competing desires. The software job was a real ego-booster, the people terrific, and the pay high enough to subsidize an apartment in the city. The long hours were tough, though, and she missed having more time for friends. She reflected on all

3

those concerts she wasn't attending, all those hours of problem solving at work that left her too tired to really enjoy her time with Joe. Her job was giving her a sense of real accomplishment, but something about it was wearing her down—especially when she thought about doing the same thing for another 20 years. Ironically, her problem wasn't that the job was wrong for her, but that it was right.

We asked Jane what bothered her the most about this situation. She fell silent, chewing on a piece of homemade bread to buy some time. Her face puckered, and she was clearly in distress. As last she said with a frown, "It's not just about time. It's about the whole picture—wanting to do different things and not knowing how to make it work." As we murmured encouragement, she suddenly said with dawning awareness, "There's an *emotional* element to this that the success books don't get at. I've done the right things. I already have 'success.' But it's not enough."

When Jane laid out all the pieces of her problem, we could see why she felt so troubled. Though she was succeeding at her job in software and had the right personality to become a star in her company, another part of her was longing to be involved in music, her true passion. Playing and listening to music provided a satisfaction that was very important and very different from what satisfied her about her software job. Jane missed the sense of contribution and significance that she'd had as a part-time church organist.

But realistically, as a person with high competitive standards, she believed she was actually more talented at solving business problems than as a professional musician. And what about her lifestyle? Her software job was financially lucrative. If she went into a career inside a church, she'd never be able to afford more than a one-room apartment in town. She did not want to live in the suburbs where she'd be isolated from her friends and the culture of the city.

She felt she had to have a certain amount of living space around her. In addition, nature was aesthetically and politically important to her, witness the hiking trip and her interest in the solar-powered hostelry where we conducted the interview—40 miles from the next town in the heart of a sacred space in the wilderness.

However she thought about these complaints, Jane couldn't seem to get control over the dissonance in her own makeup. Each aspect of her character generated a different but possible career or lifestyle. She felt as if she were wandering through a landscape of moving targets. Just as one goal seemed right and reachable, and she took aim to reach it, another popped up that seemed equally appealing and reachable. But try as she might, she could not make all of her interests and needs fit into one cohesive picture.

Intuitively, Jane knew this wasn't just a logistical problem of choosing the right job or recalibrating her financial goals. **Her anxiety centered on the larger question of success itself.**

Jane wanted to be a success, but not necessarily like the pumped-up entrepreneurs celebrated in the financial magazines and lionized at her fifth college reunion. However, she could find no magazines or models for the alternative success she was seeking. What did it look like? How did it *feel?* How could the choices she faced be framed to reflect the many aspects of her unique nature and still pave the way to success? What tactics should she use to achieve all the pieces of that puzzle? She felt in danger of becoming like the proverbial donkey who starved to death standing between two stacks of straw because he couldn't make up his mind which one to go after.

Too Many Choices

If Jane is ever going to leverage her talents into a positive outcome, she needs a base on which to stand. Before making a change, she needs a better understanding of where she is *now*. This process is partly associated with the domain of emotional intelligence that expert Daniel Goleman calls "self-awareness."[1] But Jane needs to develop more than her *emotional* baseline; she needs to assess the concrete trajectories of her current situation or she may not be *able* to get what she wants. Why is this so difficult for her?

Jane's dilemma is not unusual today, nor are her problems confined to her generation. In an era that proudly proclaims "no limits," it is commonplace to feel trapped between contradictory possibilities, paralyzed by moving targets and unable to accommodate or even order all the opportunities. Even retiring workers entertain urges to start another business, improve their golf, develop a long-neglected interest, or do something wholly new. Parents with careers hit many moments of reassessment in the course of raising children. Their decisions are not just about time management but about who they want to be in the deepest sense of the word. Some use this self-awareness to reposition their careers toward family needs. Others transform their nurturing inclinations into positions of greater responsibility in their companies.

Such moments of personal reinvention can be liberating, but without some disciplining framework, they can quickly deteriorate into a sense of bondage to the evolving "more." For example, consider two young friends who seek financial wealth by starting a public relations firm. They vow to each other that they'll consider themselves satisfied when they have a $1 million in the bank. The first has a meteoric success and moves his stopping point to $10 million. The other, also successful, has spending habits that delay him from reaching his original goal. Neither is able to develop a sense of mastery over the many possibilities that they see for themselves: things, jobs, relations, fun, status. As a current MBA student put it, in thinking about what his ideal life would be 10 years from now:

> The truth of the matter is that I have no idea how I will make all of this work. I want to be a superhero—to run a company, have children, keep a beautiful home, and have a loving spouse. I want to take a grand vacation in Italy. I want to be a leader who contributes to the well being of society. I want to sit on boards of nonprofit and for-profit organizations.
>
> I want to be the boss. I want to win. I want to be recognized in the newspaper and to be the recipient of numerous accolades and awards. . . . As a result, I have a hard time stepping out of my fantasy world to predict what will truly happen in the future. But the one lesson that I have learned from the past is to be careful of what you wish for, because it just might come true.

In this poignant moment of truth, we see a person excited about having many targets but self-mocking because it is so unlikely that he'll be able to reach all of them and also because he's not sure where to go first—and clearly, that's not the typical platform from which greatness is achieved. **He has no conception of a middle ground where multiple steps could be taken in pursuit of the things he thinks he might want out of success.** He wants many things on a grand scale; but unlike his cohorts who eagerly signed up to kill themselves on a predictable fast-track position after business school, he hasn't yet chosen to pursue even one of his ambitions. Dripping with irony, he puts a good face on the prospect before him: enduring the path to a success he's not sure he wants.

When Success Feels Just Out of Reach

When we looked at the future goals of an entire MBA class that was about to graduate, we were struck by how frequently these students accept the idea that they are destined to be two entirely different people in life: the one their cohorts know, who will find a lucrative position in a Hobbesian world of self-interested accomplishment, and the future self whom no one knew: the person who would make a larger contribution to society, be a surprisingly good parent, and maybe even master the guitar. It's as if they are standing on the edge of a cliff, sure of their footing now, and planning a future leap to the other side. Except that there is no bridge between here and there.

You may think of this as a choice to be made later, when you have the time, but for most people that idealized future self represents values that are being put on the line *now*. Some will keep moving fast enough to ignore the signs when they become hardened to their own best impulses. Others, like Jane, will be so sensitive to the trade-offs and sense of loss that they jeopardize their chances of reaching any goal in the face of their own indecision.

At one time this problem would simply have been described as the cost of success. But we've become accustomed to entertaining simultaneous, multiple meanings about ourselves and our environment.

We accept incoherency as normalcy, preferring to hope for it all rather than make a choice. We accept that focus is good *and* bad (as when it keeps you from going home at night). Our educational systems frequently don't prepare us for this complexity, especially for the problem of resolving noncomparable choices. When you're practicing to make the varsity soccer team, you're feeling guilty about not doing your all for your grade point average.

Success Isn't a Tease—It's a Moving Target

When William James famously called success a "bitch goddess" that the world gives and takes away,[2] he was referring to that peculiarly powerful combination of desire and dread that money and making it provokes in our culture. You see an ad in the subway that proclaims: "An Acme Diploma will help you achieve the success you deserve!" What can this be about but financial success, the American dream of the one sure path to personal transcendence? Raise your material circumstances and great things will follow—unless, of course, you lose your head and your conscience. In which case, your meteoric rise to the top, complete with stock options, may end up in a perp walk. Or, like a recent editor of the *New York Times*, your lifelong dream to create a great newspaper goes up in smoke after you bend the rules to meet your other organizational goals. Or, through no fault of your own, you simply experience the first really unstable negative market in 20 years and you become one of the 175 formerly hot Internet firms that went out of business in 2000, or one of the bottom 80 percent of today's dot-coms predicted to fail within the next 12 months. Reality strikes everyone: One member of the Young President's Organization attending a Harvard session estimated that he and his friends in Silicon Valley collectively lost $150 billion in market value in the previous year.

Bring that down to human scale and it's about young college kids and long-term professionals suddenly discovering that the success talents that were clear winners just a few short years ago are now considered *incompetencies*. Corporations and people are told they must constantly "reinvent" themselves, which raises a really interesting question: When do you get to enjoy and thrive on who you are *now?*

The escalating choices in all our lives—at least as suggested by what others seem to have or do—has also escalated the instability relating to knowing what you should actually pursue and be satisfied in completing. The last week of May 2003 was one of those moments when it became particularly clear that we all live in a world of moving targets and that they are changing at an ever more rapid pace. In that week, two important sports events took place: the fiftieth anniversary of Edmund Hillary and Tenzing Norgay's ascent of Mt. Everest, and the entry of Annika Sorenstam in the Colonial Country Club's LPGA tournament. Scores of climbers raced to break records at the top of the world, while Sorenstam moved out of women's competitions to challenge the longstanding male markers of golf success. Both events featured only the most experienced and talented athletes. Success couldn't be simpler, right?

Well, not quite. In fact, the markers kept changing. Whereas only a few days earlier *winning* the Colonial was the measure of success, once Sorenstam entered, it was about making the final cut or even just getting through the opening rounds without becoming spooked by the media attention. Meanwhile, on Everest, a number of records were made and broken with lightning speed. In one week new targets were set for oldest, youngest, fastest (set again a few days later), and most frequent climbers.

But it's not happening just in sports. Everyone seems to be struggling with the *Tantalus effect.* This mythological character was punished with an eternal, raging thirst. To make things worse, he was placed in the middle of a magic lake whose waters receded every time he tried to take a drink. So, too, just as you seem to reach a tantalizing success or goal, your position of competitive dominance is snatched away—or you change the target yourself! We break up 30-year marriages to start life over; we abandon successful careers to take time for ourselves. In such an environment, it's natural to wonder whether our past 30 years were really a success or an illusion of success.

When Do We Get to Declare Victory?

There is an inherent bias in Western and Eastern value systems toward linking what we value with that which endures—whether it is someone's character in the face of temptation, a religious belief in the face of hardship, or the truth of a great piece of literature. In his classic essay on the genius of Shakespeare, Alexander Pope called this kind of enduring knowledge "literary truth." However many other plays are written, the truth of *Hamlet*'s insights will not be replaced by these other creations. He contrasted this type of truth with what he called "scientific truth," which he noted is more temporary. A new discovery of scientific truth can *replace* old discoveries, as the discoveries of Galileo replaced the truths of Copernicus only to be superceded by Einstein.

Success straddles each of Pope's types of truth. Like scientific truth, it is a journey of constant change and replacement. One goal or desire replaces another and demands a shift in attention. But to feel authentic, the past episodes must also have something of lasting value, the equivalent of "literary" or moral truth. Something that endures and is meaningful. This latter kind of value is harder to determine for yourself when the external measures of success are constantly readjusting on the paradigm of "scientific" truth. It is not that shifts in success measures are wrong, but rather that constant shifting without some lasting value to balance it feels meaningless.

Given our deep-seated association of value with the enduring, it's difficult to view today's rapid-fire disruption of success with dispassion. Like Jane, the more our targets shift and move, the less settled we feel. So many targets surround us that we can lose all power to move forward effectively. Success takes on a flat, collapsed dimension that gives little satisfaction. The climb to success begins to resemble an Escher drawing of a staircase that goes nowhere.

You wouldn't think so, however, when you read the celebrations of money and achievement touted in the press or at motivational seminars. We live in a culture that glorifies, lionizes, and simplifies the presentation of success. **Time and again we are all exposed to** top achievers who are admired for their current wins—the entrepreneur who's founded three groundbreaking corporations in a row, the person in your firm who got a bigger promotion, the child who makes the all-state soccer team. In our research we learned to be alert for "the rest of the story" as we studied people's accomplishments and their models of success. When we probed further, we found that many were not necessarily doing very well with their other targets: family, long-term business health, building a place to work that people actually value, developing a personal character that holds up when they got out of the public spotlight. As they themselves discovered, no matter how much money they have made, there's always someone out there who's richer or more powerful. Even Bill Gates has his Sultan of Brunei for comparison!

What Is the Enough You Want from Success?

Part of the problem for us all is not knowing what we want from success—what is *just enough*. To escape the buffeting of every new choice out there, you have to be prepared to go beyond generalities and really assess what it is you are seeking:

- What will challenge you?
- What will make a difference in the world?
- What will attract you?
- What will endure even after you've moved on?

We found that on first pass, many people say they "just" want happiness from success: things, family security, self-esteem, membership in an elite group. Oh, and maybe a sense of accomplishment. (Wait for it.) Oh yes, and perhaps a certain degree of variety and challenge . . . yes, but it's all ultimately about doing something of use in the world.

Such generalized statements are typical. On the one hand, they make sense. Even Aristotle noted that our happiness was composed of many desired ends and not just one. On the other hand, the glamorization of success doesn't prepare you for the push-pull of having quite so *many* contradictory claims. People go mad seeking success—and many go even madder once they possess it. We suffer angst over *not* being a success, and we fear being a success and losing our soul. In 1967, the writer Joan Didion observed that the most publicized self-doubts in America were *Vietnam, Saran-Wrap, diet pills,* and *the Bomb.*[3] In 2003, the most publicized self-doubts are *Iraq, SUVs, Dr. Atkins' diet advice,* and *financial success.* They summarize our collective sense of what we *should* seek to do or acquire even as we feel dread about the possible side effects.

And yet what's the alternative? Even if you hate thinking of yourself as baldly pursuing success, would you seriously suggest that this is the wrong object of universal quest as long as it's *real* success as you define it? Isn't it rather like the holy grail—dangerous but impossible to resist? If you succeed in securing success, you possess a powerful talisman against want and rejection, like the Yiddish observation that the man who has money is a good singer—and he can dance, too! But like any grail, this one causes the informed seeker to entertain second thoughts. What price will the quest exact? Will the grail really deliver the dazzling but vague blessings we expect from obtaining it?

We Search for Glory and the Good Life

The perplexing glory and pain of success is an age-old moral problem and not just an American anxiety. In Homer's *Iliad,* the Greek hero Achilles has his fate laid out before him: If he stays to fight at Troy, he can become the greatest warrior ever known, but he will also be fated to die before the war ends. He is in love with a woman and adores his father—how tempting to leave the battlefield and enjoy the happiness of home for many years to come. Achilles agonizes over whether he should fulfill his semi-divine potential as a warrior and die young or go home and grow old. As he reflects on the choice before him, neither target fully eclipses the other. Homer compresses all the tragic implications of this dilemma in a single line: "And yet I must choose."

Sometimes the inescapable choices around prosperity are downright funny. The Roman satirist Horace comically describes a feeling that could be said of New Yorkers today: "When the Romans are in the city, they long for the country. Then they immediately tire of the simple life, and want to rush back to the city." The difference now is that the explosion of information places more and more of the rewards of success before us: People of any income can comfortably imagine the most exotic vacations just by watching a TV ad or reading a popular magazine. Regular working stiffs can buy $6 worth of coffee at Starbucks and take a flyer on an IPO. Whereas the most fashionable fashions and furniture used to be the reserve of the well-traveled frequenters of Fifth Avenue and Via Scala, now anyone can find these items on the Internet or even at their local mall. You can even get the "private" skinny on the favorite travel spots of the really upscale traveler in *Andrew Harper's Hideaway Report*. Despite an era of supposed downsizing, the *average* price of a wedding in the United States is now $20,000. The more we buy into the luxuries of the supposedly leisure class, the harder we're really working. According to the Bureau of Labor Statistics, Americans are averaging only two to two-and-a-half weeks of vacation, while Europeans take five.

Scientific advances make our choices even more numerous. The extension of life expectancy and basic biological functions such as fertility logically invite a youth-oriented population to adopt a no-limits strategy in their youth-like search for novel experiences. Daily reports of yet another twenty-something "making it" (see the quote that begins this chapter) only increase the sense of possibility and anxiety. Define it as growth and it is exciting. Watch it in real time and, for many of us, life is overextended and undersatisfying. So many targets. So little time.

This is especially true for those who have already experienced success. As one head of a publishing division put it: "I can *want* to be fit, fulfilled, and have time to tuck my kids in bed each night—and I do want this. I also want to be at the head of everything I do: board of directors, soccer coach, deacon at church. But that doesn't take care of the stack of work on my desk and the need to pay my kids' tuition. I stay until all hours, love my job in the abstract, and know I'm crazy for living this way."

It's easy to sympathize with this editor's dilemma. Most people could understand if he were just a bit fearful of considering any other job strategy lest he lose his position to more competitive individuals. Even if these are not your personal fears, they might crop up in thinking about how to encourage your children's success. Today there is widespread concern that children are being pushed too fast, too far, too early. But if you refrain from pushing your child on a prodigy track (intense training and achievement expectations from an early age), can he or she ever be a success when the competition for college is so intense?

Like many, this editor is gripped by an optimistic, wholly American assumption that has been touted for centuries in the success literature of Benjamin Franklin, Horatio Alger, Norman Vincent Peale, and many of today's success gurus. **You should want to have the good life even if you know you'll never fully get there. You have a moral obligation to strive to be all you can be—even if it kills you.** Not obtaining these ideals is a sign of personal failure or a tighter economy or something else that is temporary and possible to overcome. Success Version 21 (for the twenty-first century) has dramatically increased the volume of the static between people's desires, counterdesires, and capacities.

Some individuals have no trouble with this picture. They simply zoom full speed ahead on a course that will maximize one or two of their talents—and hope that the rest will follow. Others see the problem in ambition and materialism and try to exercise a moral sense of restraint in the face of so much pressure. Some people—including ambitious MBAs—told us they were sick and tired of today's success worship. They wondered about whether it wouldn't be preferable simply to drop off the fast track of high achievement. As many in the business school class that was surveyed indicated, the real question is how to exercise control over your options and still remain a contender.

Success Has a Deeper Structure
Than Winning—Just Like Our Needs

It would be easy if we could simply do triage, sorting out good and bad targets of success and then focusing on those that felt most important. But in a world of moving targets, our sense of what is most important is constantly changing. In our view, the problems around success today—stress, burnout, personal disappointment, and indecision—cannot be solved in a one-stop either/or choice between excess or asceticism, lion or lemming, president or parent. **Like Achilles, we face difficult questions about whether to push the limits or accept them.** For sustained success, you have to do both and on many different dimensions. Success is such an overworked, oversimplified theme that it is easy to underestimate this complexity and therefore the nature of the problems people are confronting.

Success Is Multidimensional

To realize your visions, you have to approach success as representing many important psychological and metaphysical quandaries:

- To the degree that it signifies accomplishment, it represents notions of mastery.
- To the degree that it signifies luck, it represents powers that are larger than human ability and shape our destiny.
- To the degree that it signifies reward, it represents justice and other moral obligations.
- To the degree that it signifies things that are admired by society, it represents belonging.
- To the degree that it brings pleasure, it represents happiness.

Success helps us articulate what we believe are the core boundaries of human nature, the parameters of the universal search for pleasure, and the moral components of what it means to live well.

It is a definer of purpose, a rudder for social organization, a maker of meaning.

Success Is Not Just Winning Big

It's important to review the potential richness success can represent in your life, especially since much of the success advice today is written without a view to these meanings. Success has been reduced to winning big. Often, discussions of success, especially in business, are based on people who don't acknowledge the pull of multiple desires out of an overwhelming passion for one thing. Their focus may be a result of being emotionally immature or literally being young, like the twenty-year-old millionaire featured on the cover of *Entrepreneur* magazine. Or they may have silenced their inner struggles with a robust air of self-confidence.

Such approaches are creating a crisis of leadership and personal complaint in our society. Businesses choose profit as the only measure of success and then fail to grow. Stay-at-home parents choose family service as the only measure of success and then wince at their own self-worth in a larger universe. Narrow success is, ultimately, narrowly rewarding. It holds up neither for individuals nor for society.

Our surveys revealed some very important information about success and its attributes.

Success Is Not a Platitude

When we surveyed 90 executives attending Harvard Business School programs about how they measured success, they tended to state broad, nonspecific measures ranging across many different domains of life. Their top indicators of success were:

- Making a difference.
- Having family happiness and harmony.
- Being involved with a business with significant achievements, that is solid.

- Being spoken of with respect, as a person of integrity.
- Having children who share your values.
- Making a contribution to society.

Many of these executives expressed the hope that their time at Harvard Business School would equip them to achieve the mix of all these goals more skillfully. On the other hand, they showed a distinct bias for simple and uncomplicated explanations of success. When asked if they had any special maxims about success that presented their views, typical answers were:

- Be true to yourself ("I am the captain of my soul").
- Teamwork and respect solve most problems.
- Luck is where preparation meets opportunity.
- All success comes from failure.
- He who does not risk cannot win.
- The process is just as much fun as the result.

Despite our admiration for these people, their generalities were of limited help. They read suspiciously like a lukewarm audiotape of the latest motivational book. Our chief concern was with "the rest of the story." If people really measure their success by multiple standards and desires, how do they reconcile these targets with the simple road maps of advice they encounter in books and business courses? On what basis did experienced achievers make decisions about the parameters of what they regarded as the good life, and where did their pursuit of success fit into this picture?

"Perfect Success"

When we dug deeper, we discovered that most people experience many stages in their understanding of success and that no one event in this process is purely about a single goal. Even for those who felt that money and power were hugely important at first, upon acquiring these things, most sought something more in terms of personal happiness, family health, and the social value of their business contributions. Those who are able to sustain such complexity alter their measures and actions around success accordingly. We found that we were drawn to certain types of successful achievers by their paradoxical ability to *retain* a complex intuition of what would be truly enduring in their eyes even as they skillfully shifted their attention from need to need.

By contrast, some of the successful entrepreneurs we interviewed—like many other people—adopted many simplifying strategies to make all the pieces work together but they lost the richness of their dreams in the process. They believed a single habit (such as focus) to be the secret to success, or devised personal rules that collapsed all their goals into large encompassing synergies: Success is not about selfishness but about win-win. It's not about having it all but being all you can be. Be true to yourself and you'll always succeed.

We've all heard these neat formulations before, and who would deny their motivational power? But the very charm and superficial plausibility of such statements can actually be very misleading if you adopt a "one-hit-gets-all" assertion as your model. When we looked behind the veil of good intentions, most of the targets they depicted as having a good "fit" with their overall values actually only fit periodically. The rest of the time they demanded trade-offs and sacrifices. You can be a top executive and know you care about family, but even if you go to a therapist to change your workaholic habits, your time in therapy is going to be a drain on the family's other needs for your attention. You can look for a win-win solution with your customer, but if you don't distinguish between their needs and yours, you will soon be out of business. You can feel a deep obligation to be generous, but chances are you won't be giving *all* your money away to the point where you lead a life of poverty so that others can be more prosperous. On what basis do you decide what is enough for yourself and what is enough to give to others?

Learning from Public Figures

Many people underestimate the calibrating measures they are really applying to their lives. Today's worker is far more aware of the choices and costs of success, but still people are often unprepared for the moral and practical ambiguity this presents. We tried a little thought exercise in our executive classes. We prepared four *Doers' Profiles* of obvious public successes—Jimmy Carter, Katharine Graham, Donald Trump, and Bill Gates—drawing from their own writings to get as close to their thinking as possible. What was it, we asked, that accounted for their success? Every class discussion ended in a very mixed review. Strengths (such as focus and passion to win) became weaknesses under certain conditions and yet were essential to success. Jimmy Carter was a great ex-president but not a success as a president. Katharine Graham had exhibited great and lasting leadership as a publisher, but no one wanted to replicate the tragedies of her married life and childhood, which seemed to fuel this great strength. Donald Trump was no doubt an innovative triumph at branding buildings and himself, but there were doubts about the ultimate value of his tactics. Bill Gates was simply unreal, revealing little of his inner self beyond pride in mastering many kinds of problems. As the flaws emerged, many participants in our classes objected that although these figures exhibited successful habits, *none* of the people we studied were real successes in their eyes.

We pressed further. If that was the case, then come up with an example of what you consider *real* success in light of your reservations. The executives tended to go to the other extreme of wealth and worldly power, citing one-dimensional examples of self-sacrifice such as Gandhi or Mother Theresa. Why was it, then, that none of them chose to go to Calcutta? Were they aware of Gandhi's own family problems, or Mother Theresa's occasional personal soul sickness from overwork? If they took these moments of unhappiness or neglect of important values seriously, what did it say about these leaders' success?

The only surprise here was their surprise that choices in one area of leadership and success seemed inextricably linked to

failures to achieve other things valued as good. The positive-negative aspects of success have been one of the most lasting puzzles of great literature and history: What are the characteristics of true leadership, and why can't one person of great talent do it all? Agamemnon was the most powerful leader at Troy, but sacrificed his own daughter to get there. Lear is both deservedly noble king and deservedly abject slave to his dissatisfied court. Lincoln implicitly tolerated Sherman's brutality even as he fought against the intolerance of slavery. Not one of our interviewees (though we admired them all) was totally uncontroversial in terms of family devotion or self interestedness. Many historical "great man" theories would suggest that these very contradictions occasion greatness. As the Greek philosopher Hippocrates once explained, "*Polemos* (war, conflict) is the progenitor of all things."

What do these conflicts represent to us, not just in practical terms but in moral and emotional responses? When is the pursuit of conflicting targets a legitimate feature of real success, and when is it simply success at the price of higher values? Is there a success model that actually helps manage these conflicts in a way that gets you more, if not all, of what you and others desire? The short answer is yes—but you have to be prepared to do more than "lock and load" on one idealized target.

The Rest of the Story

When we entertain success stories in which heroic Doers blast through all obstacles in the pursuit of One Great Goal and afterward "have it all," we are likely to hitch our stars to something that does not really represent the full spectrum of what we really expect—and can get—from success. As we discovered, there usually turns out to be more to the story, and this raises the kind of reservations our students had about the four Doers' profiles.

Take, as one example from many you could find, Bernie Ebbers, the former CEO of WorldCom, and Scott Sullivan, WorldCom's former chief financial officer. Not so long ago, WorldCom was on everyone's success list, a real value in a competitive marketplace. The lives of these leaders were envied and emulated. But by 2002, Ebbers was in personal debt to his company to the tune of $408 million and in no position to pay. His wealth was largely in WorldCom stock, which plunged 97 percent over three years. Meanwhile, WorldCom's former CIO Scott Sullivan was accused of the largest accounting fraud in U.S. history, and in April 2003 was hit with new charges of fraud and lying on financial statements to help the company secure more than $4 billion in credit. Yet, many people had previously seen these men as successful. According to Mitchell Marcus, who worked for WorldCom for 14 years, these two "were considered near genius, if not saints, by the majority of company employees,"[4] They're not the only idols being torn down these days.

We concluded that the search for a balance of good things from success cannot be achieved through the emulation of a perfect success example, much to the disappointment of many. Nor can we promise to reveal the sure-fire secret strategy or personality type that makes it all work seamlessly. By now everyone should be wary of these stories, like the archetypal working mother who wraps up a multimillion dollar deal during her twelfth hour of labor, returns to work two weeks later, sends her kid to Harvard, and is universally loved by her family and feared on the squash court. Do you know this woman? Neither do we. Either these people live on a different planet, where time and physical energy have no meaning, or their romanticized success stories are delusional. In either case, they don't really help the rest of us mortals cope with our relentlessly moving targets. Even if you could secure enough wealth, power, and good health to buy a ticket to this planet, you would still hold different expectations about success that reflected your unique values and needs.

Embrace Conflict

Instead of trying to reduce your many desires around a good life to a common denominator like your company's stock price, it is important to embrace the idea that diverse, sometimes conflicting impulses are not only inescapable—they are also *a positive resource* in think-ing about what success really means and how you will pursue it. It is possible to achieve a more balanced, well-rounded, contributing form of success, but to do so, you have to be able to manage a vision of success that is inherently multifaceted. For business people who have learned to prioritize quickly, it can be hard to take this step back and give credence to the whole picture.

What we (and those who depend on us) really need is a better understanding of the process of complex choice in the pursuit of success:

- How do we identify and evaluate the many changing targets that pop up?
- How do we aim effectively at both opportunities and obstacles?
- How do we shift from a lock-and-load rigidity to an adaptive set of goals?
- How do we hone in on the right targets when presented with conflicting alternatives?
- How do we order the chaos of these demands so that every choice is not an occasion for regrets about the road not taken?
- How do we choose the right ammunition for each target?

Our research uncovered a critical skill that we've not seen fully identified before. The high achievers who were able to handle success and make positive contributions in the lives of many oth-ers not only recognized multiple goals in their work and life, they managed to retain a deep sense of commitment to whatever they were engaged in, in spite of having these multiple targets. They accomplished this through a special kind of adaptiveness to com-plexity that involved both intense focus and lightning abandon-ment of one mode of experience for another. (We call this strategy *Switching and Linking,* and we discuss it in detail in Part Three.) They could attend to family. They could act in their own interests

but also in the interest of others. Instead of chaos, they created a coherent sequence to their goals around success.

You might expect that they did this by radically reducing or eliminating the complex ambitions that are causing so much confusion
for people in real time. Indeed, the media often depict some of our
interviewees as having a meteoric success that brooks no side-tracks.
We discovered that the reason they weren't being side-tracked was
not that they'd set only one goal for themselves, but that they *regularly* "nailed" different aspects of their aspirations in the here and
now. As they chalked up a victory, their aspirations and their abilities
were increased as was their sense of satisfaction. Instead of feeling
cheated out of not getting it all, they were renewed by a sense of just
enough and could move on to the next challenge.

To develop the same ability, you have to change the way you understand the landscape of success. Whether shooting for the moon
or trying to get to your friend's birthday party, you have to become
an expert at the ballistics of moving targets.

Hitting the Moving Targets

Effective and rewarding pursuit of success requires changing your
fundamental vision of what you are aiming for and how it relates to
what *else* you may want now and in the future. The question is not
about how to seize on the perfect balance between work and family.
**Success is not a static target you choose to shoot at or not. Rather,
it is an expanding landscape through which you move throughout
life, picking and choosing among the many possible targets that
you choose, or that choose you.**

Traversing this landscape is a sophisticated process. It requires
multiple frames of reference. Like the air you breathe in and out,
success is both an externally determined and internally generated
standard. Some of your measures of success are unique to you, but
others are dependent on the cooperation and approval of outsiders.
You want to make a profit, but to do so you have to serve others so
that these others recognize you as deserving reward. You want to

put your customer first, but not if your customer wants you to give the product away. Jane wants to make money, play in the church choir, have children, and enjoy urban culture. Her boyfriend wants to support her in her goals *and* go hiking.

If each goal is something you have to aim for, then success is rather like a shooting gallery—various kinds of targets are always popping up from one direction or another, at different speeds and in different combinations. Hitting one gets you a score, but others are still out there, and there are always more to come. Some targets, like finishing an educational degree or enjoying a moment in the day, allow the opportunity for a straightforward win. You hit them, and you get a point. Other targets come in the form of obstacles: they may not be intrinsically important to you, but they get in the way of your aim and you've got to shoot them down in order to reach your goal. Power inside an organization can be this way: It is something you need but is not necessarily an intrinsic desire.

Many targets are simultaneously obstacles *and* goals, depending on the context. Family, for instance, can feel like an obstacle to work, but it can also be your most important goal in the larger picture. Two careers can seem the ticket to a more leisurely and affluent family life, but according to Juliet Schor's research, the demands on dual-career families have added almost an extra month of "work" to fathers' and mothers' schedules.[5] For the 9 million-plus people in the "sandwich generation" today, caught between caring for both beloved parents and kids *and* working at careers, the desirable-obstacle target is particularly stressful.

Mark Twain's Tom Sawyer had a much simpler set of measures: "Work," said Tom, "consists of whatever a body is *obliged* to do, and play consists of whatever a body is not obliged to do." It's a comfortingly simple thought, but success with any form of achievement is not so simple. Success can turn your emotions upside down. Work you love can feel like play, and play can become real work as the new targets that come with success throw you off balance. Take, for example, the two young men fresh out of high school who started a software games business. When their business really took off, they suddenly felt they had to buy into a new lifestyle to match the appearance of success. Formerly flannel-shirted slobs, according to their father, they now deferred to the way they thought wealthy dot-comers lived and were made happy: new cars, new clothes, new condos. But instead of joy, they'd taken on a set of worries about appearances, caring too much about what the house looked like rather than how to continue to have fun with their friends. Their targets of leisure had actually turned into what they felt they were "obliged to do," using Tom Sawyer's phrase.

When "Never Enough" *Is* the Only Good Life

One of the most classic examples of success failure rests on the problem of retreating targets. Each time you seem about to hit your mark, it moves farther away again, like the amount of money you want to make or time with your family or how much power you need. Nothing is enough. The elusive, "never enough" quality of such targets both inspires and frustrates. **To the degree these goals or targets are associated with the rewards of success, success itself becomes an elusive, frustrating target.** No matter how many times you hit the target, it moves back or gets larger, and tempts you to go for it again. Whether you keep up this pursuit will affect your ability to pursue other targets as well.

This was Jane's problem. She had wonderful targets for her future and lots of skills to hit any one of them, but they didn't line up neatly so that she could aim to hit all in one shot. She didn't *think* she was just being shallow and materialistic in finding it tough to commit to a career in music, but so far she hadn't found a solution that would give her everything she wanted. She'd tried to develop a sequence for herself that would put the organ music at bay until she could afford it, but like most live targets, this one wasn't going to sit still or stay out of sight till she had time to go for it. It kept popping up in her emotional landscape. Meanwhile, her software job was clearly a success, but one that seemed a betrayal of some parts of her makeup.

There is a generous confusion to the complexity of Jane's moving targets, perhaps because they capture an inescapable impulse to go after a success that is essentially *true* to her sense of what is important. To paraphrase Oscar Wilde, the search for such truth is never pure, and rarely simple. You have to be prepared with more than one kind of ammunition, and you have to know how to assess what it is you really want.

You can't really do this until you abandon the idea of success as a carnival game. It's not about hitting all your targets, eliminating them, and walking out with the prize. What is sadder than the person who deliberately stops growing because they've "made it"? Or the CEO who can't make way for the next generation because being at the top of the company is the only target he or she has? How many people decide to scale back their careers in favor of family, only to feel over time that something is missing?

Even those who've been decisive about what they want are forced to reconsider from time to time. We call this the "wince factor"— that feeling that although you willingly chose to turn your back on some target, you wince when you see someone else hit it and think, "I could have done that, too." Just because you turned your back on something, it does not mean this prize will conveniently disappear, never popping up to tempt you again. **You have to be prepared for these moments with a sense of enough. You have to be able to recognize the full range of your criteria around the good life to evaluate how any one activity really fits into that framework.**

Where Do You Set Your Targets?

What is the good life to *you?*

- How will your success look if you achieve this life, even if imperfectly?
- Which targets will you go after?
- Which targets do you want your organization to pursue?

- Will your goals be driven by a deep sense of needing to make a contribution and needing to express your most creative talents?
- If you score high on actions but fail to meet your aesthetic needs, will this really feel like success?
- How will you approach the inevitable costs either course demands—costs on your attention, costs on your ability to achieve your other desires?

Too many people don't allow themselves the time to think these questions through. Many businesses favor new hires who never hesitate in their drive to achieve, and then wonder why the organization fails to reach greatness.

You could go for the simple solution: You could simply try to make your multiple desires conform or defer to One Big Goal, such as money. But this won't get you the things that money ultimately represents in your eyes: self-esteem, control, freedom, belonging, admiration, happiness. One big goal will not erase the prospect of multiple targets, nor will it prevent the multiple dissatisfactions of not hitting them squarely. One big goal, such as maximized shareholder value, will not build the kind of organization or relationships with the public that mark the kind of success that lasts.

Alternatively, you could conceive of success as a long-term process of multiple choice and change, one in which you fulfill your own deepest drives and receive some measure of reward from external sources. We call this latter ideal *enduring success*, enduring because it does and gives things that having lasting value.

An Overarching Target: Enduring Success

What is *real*, enduring success? The most succinct definition we could muster, given the personalized nature of the concept, is:

Enduring success is the collection of activities that will be viewed affirmatively by you and those you care about—now, throughout your life, and beyond.

To get there, you need to regularly cultivate episodes that give value on the many measures you and those you care about consider important. Some of these fortunate or meaningful moments will last longer than others in the eyes of the world, but their *value* to you and society will be, without question, part of the fabric of what you consider a good life. What you get and put into success will be worth it.

Forms of the enduring can be as grand as the Constitution of the United States or as personalized as the lasting satisfaction you received on the day you graduated from college. It can even be about a yard sale, as we will see later in this book. Episodes of enduring success come in many forms and sizes: a long-established business that continues to create new and fulfilling products and jobs; parenting that results in thriving children who can find their own success; an experience that so stretches your sense of what you can do and who you can be that you never forget it. It is the combination of achievement, pleasure, and growth that marks that unforgettable first step of a child. It lasts, but you also need to address new targets. Who would be satisfied if this were the only success their child experienced? Enduring success doesn't get rid of the paradoxical challenges that changing targets impose; in fact, it thrives on movement and growth.

In some ways, enduring success is very similar to the definition of entrepreneurship that we use at Harvard Business School: the pursuit of opportunity beyond resources you apparently control. Success is essentially about bringing to accomplishment the goals shaped by your changing awareness of new opportunity through the wise marshalling of your resources. Creative dissatisfaction has its place, but today's culture of envy threatens to take the dissatisfaction too far—stressing novelty and personal reinvention without the flip side. It skips from target to target without ever experiencing lasting satisfaction, lasting contribution. For the latter, you need to have a sense of *enough*—which is, after all, the original definition of satisfaction, from the Latin root, "to make or do enough."

Being Prepared for the Right Opportunities

Whatever your parameters of success may be, as long as they involve growth and your own emotional engagement, they will inevitably involve moving targets. One of the greatest difficulties today—especially for successful people—is in finding a satisfying level for any one goal. Sheer stoicism or a philosophy of simplicity can be an exhausting and insufficient approach to this task. **For lasting success in business or in life, you need the skills to manage the sum of your targets effectively.** You need to anticipate and adapt to instability in its many forms with a strategy that captures achievable goals you can savor forever. This is an approach we saw operating in the high achievers who seem to "get it all" on many levels, and which is confirmed by a rich body of theoretical research on appetite and will. While we don't believe in simple formulas or a one-size-fits-all metaphor, a few ground rules will help you develop this capacity more fully in yourself and in your organization:

- *See the big picture and be prepared to embrace the irreducible variety of what you seek from success:* You have to approach the multiple parts of your conception of the good life as part of a coherent but rich and growing pattern. There is no end point, but the moving targets can be more easily selected when you know how they "fit" into basic categories of aspiration around success: Happiness, Achievement, Significance, and Legacy. (These categories will be presented in greater detail in Part Two of this book.) The mere act of labeling and sorting your needs gives you a much greater sense of control.
- *Order your aspirations:* When your environment is chaotic, you have to *order* this mix. Ordering the components of success helps determine what is really enough for each. Save the rest of your energy for something else. You don't have to take every activity to the max to ensure it satisfies your criteria of success. You don't have to plan a trip around the world after retirement to relax. Sometimes simply understanding that your attraction to the here and now may

allow you to experience a moment of rest and pleasure that adds to your happiness quotient makes it easier to put down the problem-solving of achievement for the moment.

Taking an inventory not only helps you see if you are putting too much effort into things that are already satisfied by something else, it helps you rebalance the parts of your picture that are "thin" in a timely way. Labeling the "type" your goals represent helps you understand more deeply what it is you most want from the many opportunities around you. It helps you understand when a supposedly terrific job offer is wrong and what you should be aiming for instead.

• *View the targets as opportunities rather than threats:* Moving targets are in fact a powerful resource in the landscape of aspiration. A strategy that simply tries to dispose of your desires actually cuts you off from the potential to increase your felt experience of the good life. When you hit these targets, that success must be savored in the here and now. **This can only be achieved by knowing what specific kind of satisfaction you can and cannot expect from a given category of activity.**

There is a pragmatic aspect to immediate fulfillment as well. According to decision experts, when you actively *engage* in the possibilities that life offers, you not only grow, you acquire good predictive powers.[6] You are more prepared to address not only your aspirations but those targets that are forced upon you, like attending to a grown child who was just diagnosed with cancer on the day you thought you were going to nail down a new business deal or suddenly refocusing your customer service strategy in the aftermath of the market crash or figuring out a solution to a demanding and ethically questionable accounting proposition from your key investor.

A Brief Illustration in Real Time

This approach to moving targets is the difference between putting out a fire and creating a new source of energy. We saw it in the long-term decisions around diversity that were made by current PepsiCo chairman, Steven Reinemund.

Early in his career as president of Pizza Hut, a big target suddenly blocked his way. Reinemund's division became the subject of a bitter lawsuit by a franchisee and attracted public criticism by the Hispanic community. He could have simply concentrated on disposing of this litigation, making his only target winning the case. Driven by his own values, however, Reinemund was uncomfortable with the "enemy" attitude this seemed to be engendering. He met at length with his critics, face to face and with the help of Ron Harrison. He became more aware of a broad horizon of issues that the Hispanic community was facing, and quickly saw that many of them were relevant to the future of a company like PepsiCo. In this process, his overall goal was transformed. Instead of simply focusing on settlement of the legal problem, he radically recalibrated his targets around diversity.

That was the beginning of a comprehensive series of decisions by Reinemund and others that have increased PepsiCo's employment and marketing to Hispanics, consulting on special health and nutrition issues among the Hispanic community, and expanding its operations in Spanish-speaking countries. These efforts have been part of a substantial commitment to many other kinds of diversity and inclusion at PepsiCo. Reinemund's decision to expand the targets at his company has not only led to positive business results but to the creation of a very different and richer profile of success for PepsiCo. In 2003, the company was acclaimed by a number of organizations for its minority record, from appearing in the #9 slot of *Fortune* magazine's minority employer list to being honored by the Lawyers' Committee for Civil Rights Under Law.

Understanding Your Own Landscape of Success

The models in this book will help you understand the nature of *your* values and desires amidst the turmoil of today's moving targets, and provide a coherent framework for making choices that are both controlled and expansive of your own life profile. They will help you understand what measures to apply to these problems, and over what time frame. They will give you the baseline to determine what rewards will make the sacrifices and costs worth it. They will also help you anticipate and manage a constructive openness to your next set of moving targets.

But, like Jane, you have to be prepared to make choices. You have to be prepared to anticipate costs as an inevitable part of the process and something over which you have some control. You can do this if you know how to select the targets that are right for you now, and for the you who expands in experience and capability over a lifetime. Few of these problems have one-step solutions. Enduring success means seeking goals in a way that allows you to hit your targets and move on to the next set. The secret is in knowing the basic dynamics of the kinds of targets you associate with enduring success, and in being able to define *just enough* for each one.

As Henry Thoreau asked in *Walden*, "Why should we be in such desperate haste to succeed, and in such desperate enterprises?"

Quick Points: Stress! Excess! Success?

Why conventional success advice is failing us:

- We have too many choices.
- Our targets shift and escalate as more choices and obstacles appear.
- Enduring success is not just about "me."
- Enduring success is not one simple thing: It is the collection of four kinds of activities that will be viewed affirmatively by you and those you care about—now, throughout your life, and beyond.

Chapter 2

The Dangers of
Going for the Max

It's supposedly next to impossible to do leveraged buyouts of technology companies, but this nobody made a quick $1 billion doing just that.

—Headline from an article in *Forbes* magazine on
Tom Gores, who founded Platinum Equity at age twenty-nine[1]

One of the most ironic aspects of the fiftieth anniversary of Sir Edmund Hillary's scaling of Mt. Everest was how ephemeral the standards of climbing success turned out to be. As the world observed Hillary's lasting mark 50 years after the event, the statistics that marked extreme achievement on Everest were blown away as new records for the oldest, most often, and fastest climbs were logged in over a one-week period.

Excelsior! It's an exhilarating standard, to be sure, whether the score is the highest mountain in the world or how many zeros you tally up in your portfolio. New levels of human performance take us closer to the gods and set the stage for what we hope is excellence in our own DNA.

These moments also make good copy. Rocketing success markers that are already fueled by marvelous heights of new achievement are further escalated by the glamorized treatment they receive in today's media-centric world. The elements of celebrity—spectacle, "bests," charisma, and any form of novelty from the latest in consumption to a sexy new organizational culture—have vaulted popular ideas of success over the top. You may be immune to the grosser forms of celebration—how many really believed Dennis Koslowski's financial excesses at Tyco were a sign of good business leadership?—but culture is a strong shaper of worldview. **These patterns are leaving a deep footprint on the ground assumptions people and businesses bring to success.**

We are so hyped up on the eternal "higher" that we are tempted to believe that that's all there is. We can think we have to be (or appear to be) the almighty to be anything at all. One thirty-nine-year-old fellow we interviewed cashed out his startup software business for a cool $19 million in 1999 and felt ashamed to tell his peers he hadn't made more! When records break at such earth-shattering speed, being all we can be doesn't just get tougher, achieving multiple desires becomes *impossible*. If we value achievement and adopt celebrity standards, we will certainly fall victim to our own excess. Nothing will be enough, and success will never satisfy. If we're high achievers, we may be plagued with self-doubt, feeling that we've never done quite enough.

When Reaching for the Stars, Why Think about Limits?

To achieve multifaceted, lasting success in a world of moving targets, it is not enough to soberly reject celebrity as the only leadership style. **You have to understand the baseline assumptions behind celebrity, and how deeply they undermine the way you might measure and plan your choices around success.** In addition to the moral difficulties that are posed by celebrity's narcissism and materialism, there are seeds of self-destruction in the celebrity approach to high achievement. Many people and organizations under appreciate this problem and hence bring a self-defeating paradigm to their pursuit of success. They assume they have to anchor their aspirations on some celebrated form of the "best," an essentially limitless standard, to meet even a minimal standard of success. And yet they seek many ends in life.

You cannot maximize two things if they are tradeoffs, by the very definition of maximizing. Unless you see the fallacy of this approach and are sensitive to how many cultural and economic reinforcements are making it seem inevitable, you make yourself all the more vulnerable to the moving targets phenomenon. You are unprepared to find the satisfaction of "just enough."

It's a classic dilemma. The ancient Greeks pondered the same question at the height of Athens' artistic and political strength in the Periclean Age of the fifth century B.C.E. The tragedian Sophocles, in his famous "Ode on Man" in the *Antigone,* marveled at humankind's resourcefulness and success: The chorus notes that without gills, man has devised ways to travel on the sea. He has invented speech, and plows for the earth. With these accomplishments he secures good things such as food, shelter, the rule of cities, and complicated forms of reasoning. But, argues the wise chorus, "from death alone he still cannot escape . . . Limitation is built in to the human condition. You need to bend to higher laws."

Limits? Tell that to today's college graduates, more in debt than ever before and with the prospect of sudden wealth still a recent possibility if they can just be the next genius. Limits are about *failure,* about being inadequate as a contender. Even if your goals are not necessarily about record-breaking, today's shoot-the-lights-out standard of success seems totally plausible. And for many, all this feels totally out of control. We're not just referring to the ousted CEOs who are contending for the highest S/E ratio (severance package/earnings losses during their tenure). In 1965, Intel's Gordon E. Moore astounded the world by asserting that the number of transistors on a silicon chip would double annually. Although he had to refine that prediction downward to every 18 months or so, his words received celebrity status and came to be called Moore's Law. Drawing on Moore's Law, technological innovation and billionaire wealth took on an obsessive pace in the go-go years of the 1990s, and not just among the Silicon Valley dot-comers. This seemed to be *everybody's* idea of success.

A Nation Rethinks Success

After the market crash in 2000, there was talk that Moore's Law had reached its theoretical limits and perhaps the pace of innovation needed reining in. Then came September 11 and a new spirit of self-examination caused many to ask whether they were making all they could of their lives. Author Po Bronson struck a newly exposed nerve with the book *What Should I Do with My Life?* His message is about a good life measured by peace and fulfillment rather than scale alone. For some, these trends have led to a new questioning of extreme consumption, a dissatisfaction with being overworked. And yet these intimations of other targets are constantly being cannibalized by new celebrity treatments of the desire for "simple living."

You have to be prepared to question the sure success even when it seems to be about simpler values. Like the upper-middle-class living room featured in sitcoms, many depictions of a simple life today cost more than you might think. Our collective fixation on "the best" and what the best means is an open invitation to be deceived by the latest success fairy tale. Today's featured record-breaker is often tomorrow's letdown.

And we're not just talking about all those millionaires doing the perp walk—like Martha Stewart, Bernie Ebbers, Sam Waksal, and Dennis Koslowski. It's also true for some of the most admired in business. Here's a familiar success pattern that should give pause, but instead seems to shed all possibility of providing "sticky" lessons: After a meteoric rise in his company's earnings during the boom, a captain of industry caps his reign as a celebrity CEO with a guru book of success lessons. Almost before the ink dries, the same CEO is mired in notoriety, a celebrity failure as it were. The reasons trace back to fundamental imbalances in the mix of beneficial or self-serving aspects of his lifestyle and perk package. Some people feel tricked as the details of all this glam are revealed to have been funded at the company's expense. Others shrug it off. After all, he got the job done for the shareholders. Why shouldn't he get his reward? Surely it is more than possible that the fabulously performing winners are really just ordinary decent people who got lucky.

However you might admire his achievements, would you really want to be the *total* celebrity CEO or just the parts about wealth and winning? Is there a single model out there that can make these distinctions for you, to which you can securely hitch your star? Is there any more effective motivator than the *Absolute Best?*

The Best Is Not Necessarily the Highest Score

For many people trying to piece together the best parts of the best performances they see out there, success has mutated into a series of irresolvable contradictions. Needs for achievement, ethics, family life, connection to others, and faithfulness to yourself seem doomed to vie in a terminal contest for your exclusive attention. It's easy to feel stupid when you compare yourself to the celebrity successes, easy to feel inadequate if you don't command great wealth, or your family doesn't resemble the Brady Bunch. It is hard to understand how other people find the time. And yet these models also raise doubts. You may wonder whether it is ever possible for a Bill Gates to be a "regular guy" at his scale of wealth and power. Can families survive the effort to grow this far this fast? Are business schools right in buying into a method of scoring the game that threatens to reduce their diversity of intellectual and social capital? All for the sake of a best list ranking? Are these really the right signposts on the road to a success that endures?

In its addiction to "best," today's culture trivializes or ignores the age-old human struggle between striving toward that which brings us ever closer to godlike power and voluntarily accepting limits. Then, once in a while, we are offered the gift of reexamining our measures of success in light of a more nuanced and meaningful standard.

In the same week that Everest was being littered with trash by one group while another band of hikers was organizing to pick it up, a different kind of record was being broken. Golfer Annika Sorenstam had beaten out 40 other players—all men—in the opening round of the men's PGA tournament at Colonial Country Club. Ultimately, she didn't make the final cut, but her victory as a woman competing successfully in a male tournament carried so much interest and credibility the conventional measures of golfing success— winning the PGA—were suddenly called into question.

Since Sorenstam didn't win, what measure *would* capture the sense of success that the public and this athlete clearly felt? There were many scores out there: David Owen of the *New York Times* summarized her success in terms of beating out 40 of her competitors, which "turned the men's C-minus into an F."[2] She beat the Las Vegas oddsmakers over-under by eight shots. She won on the publicity scale: Blasted by media attention that would have undone many a new player, she emerged from the relative obscurity of women's golf to dominate public attention. She herself had another standard: to see how much better she could go by competing with better players. In her eyes, she'd achieved success, even if she didn't win the final prize. Far from being demotivated by the recognition that she'd hit a limit, Sorenstam seemed to find satisfaction in knowing that limit was still an amazing stretch for her and women's golf as a whole. She had achieved *just enough* for now. Instead of defeat, she got energy.

Maximization Does Not Work as a Measure of Success

What is the right measure of success in your eyes? What is it for your company or school? Is being *really* successful inevitably a matter of being the best, highest, youngest, richest, smartest, and prettiest on every scale you know—that is, celebrity winner-take-all? Such standards are *maximized* forms of accomplishment. Simply put, maximization is any form of going for the extreme—genius intelligence, superhuman effort, the best house, the unique lifestyle, and the most profit possible. Pick up any magazine and you can find a glamorized message of "making it" that assumes not only extreme performance but maximized reward: great wealth, drop dead attractiveness, *all* the attention, and possible omnipotence.

Maximized measures begin to start counting success at the limits, only after you've gone further than most other people. This leaves individuals and organizations facing a very large territory of failure and a very small sweet spot in which they can actually feel they've won. And the spot changes with each new competitive achievement— moving targets. No wonder we're stressed out. Maximized versions of success are more than superficial presentations. They have the power to *coopt* our innermost standards of expectation, however insecure they may make us.

Undoubtedly, goals calibrated to maximization have the power to inspire. "Be all that you can be" sounds more like a virtue than a vice. "Go further than humankind has ever gone." Who would argue the opposite as a rule for success? But even if you are drawn to the positive aspects of maximization as your standard, most people's sense of success demands high scores in many differing categories. Sometimes these goals contradict each other: Wealth *and* best friends who love you for yourself, not your money. A generous nature *and* being in the top position. Leading a team *and* being able to do everything your way. Not to mention being best at every activity of your life, from tennis to cooking to managing your portfolio.

For this kind of mix, maximization will not work as an operating paradigm. How can you maximize four things? Can you really base your idea of success on super-effort times four? Would you want to? Before you anchor your ambitions on the outer limits, think of the Roman and British empires. Rome continually pushed its borders in a political philosophy of limitless power—only to discover it had to build a wall to keep the invaders out before it could really build and protect its roads. The British set up a legal and bureaucratic system in each of its colonial territories, but the idea of limitless exploitation became the empire's undoing.

If life were lived in a fixed time frame, where success was measured only in the instant you hit the peak, maximized measures would work. But the only fixed time frame we know for sure is death. Everything else is subject to moving targets. If you wish to live with a continually renewing sense of success that really seems worthwhile and lasting on all your success targets, you have to give up the standards of maximization.

Cultural Pressures to Maximize

Giving up on maximization is hard. Today's businesses, schools, families, and especially public messages are so oriented on maximized behavior that a powerful paradigm has been created. Think back to the last person you saw or heard portrayed as a real success. Chances are their persona was artificially enhanced to star status and their abilities assumed to be extraordinary in a single area that somehow implies an express ticket to the good life. As in, "Jack Welch did fantastically. He increased General Electric's market cap $250 billion over the time frame, became number one market cap in the world, and led the most admired global company for five years in a row."[3]

Such over-the-top figures are very seductive. Who wouldn't want to match or beat the best? But then, what does that really mean? What went into that leap from market cap to most admired? Such labels can quickly lose their luster in the aftermath, and yet this formula of celebrity is repeated again and again in our interpretation of today's events.

There is a certain futility in attempting to mass merchandize the unique, but illogic never stopped the media. Even after the market meltdowns and revelation that so many of our leaders had clay feet, our popular benchmarks of success have continued to stress prodigy performance, record-breaking, hero worship, and hype. On the one hand, we are witnessing a much less hierarchical organization in business, especially in connection with technology. You might expect a flatter paradigm of success as well. But actually, the stories of wealth at the peak continue to proliferate, even if lucrative stock options turned out to be in the cards for only a few people in the hot companies.

If anything, the new patterns of economic wealth have exacerbated the maximization paradigm. It's as if everyone feels at the fringe, seeking success in highly individualistic, meteoric, record-breaking feats. Take Michael Lewis's visionary profiles in his book *Next* that features in-depth studies of the stars of the pancake world (his term) we live in. He argues that flat, upside-down sources of authority and expertise appear to be equalizing the playing field. Thirteen-year-olds can get on the Web, offer legal advice, and create their own successful business services. When Lewis asked one such teenager what he wanted from all this, the youth said he wasn't doing it for the money—but he did rather hope he'd be bought out so he could start his own band and become a rock star.

You have to believe that our current presentations of success have gone to a dysfunctional extreme, creating a set of measurements that are too narrow, too fickle, too tailored, and too out-of-reach to provide a stable platform on which you and others can achieve success. **Celebrity success takes the already powerful vision of maximum performance and turns it into a glamorous spectacle, thereby giving success nearly magical power.** Performing at the peak, being on top, giving 110 percent effort, winning on a single bet in a lottery economy, having it all—do this and you stand apart. You're special. You have charisma. The more novel your spending habits—that is, the better copy they provide a hungry media—the stronger your success.

All of these messages are variations on the idea of perfection, a particularly American point of reference and yet another form of maximization. Oprah Winfrey rises to *Forbes*'s list of billionaires, and her picture is perfect. We admire Oprah, but doubt she herself is comfortable with this image of perfection that the hungry press demands. Thus it was when Enron declared its intention to become the biggest the fastest by maximizing return in newly deregulated markets and financial instruments. It looked like the perfect strategy.

As the Enron example illustrates, maximization and celebrity status aren't just attractive, up to a point they are economically logical. Even if you resist the idea that you can do it all and must have it all to feel personally satisfied, the marketplace may demand maximum return or put you out of business. As actor Michael Caine remarked in a refreshingly farsighted view of his success, "Actors don't retire. The business retires them."[4]

The Effects of Celebrity Success Thinking

The effects of this paradigm are more pervasive than many realize. The footprints of maximization can be seen in many of our fixations around the good life today, from the desire to be perfectly self-actualizing to the longing for lifestyles associated with extreme wealth even if you are a high school student on scholarship. In a mutation of America's widely vaunted Protestant ethic, success has become a grueling search for individual perfection frosted over with consumption habits that reveal an un-Protestant-like rejection of self-denial.

Writes demographer Annetta Miller, college graduates in the 2010s are destined to be "the 'linked decade,' defined by a busy, mature ethnically heterogeneous group of consumers who are confident in their ability to read anything, buy anything, and experience anything."[5] In thinking about the good life it's not unusual to expect a perfect stock pick, perfect spouse, perfect wedding, perfect kitchen, perfect vacation, perfect education, blockbuster funeral service. Even the most mundane office presentation is now expected to be a spectacle of perfect visuals on PowerPoint. When life turns out to be not so perfect, a culture of complaint is the predictable fallout.

Or just try harder. We constantly pump up the volume on self-improvement and peak performance and assume we're better off for dancing to this tune. The romanticized success tales have painted opportunity in the marketplace as seemingly limitless to those with an optimistic, *unique* vision. As a society, we are afflicted with what Harvard professor Marjorie Garber calls "an infatuation with superlatives."[6] She, like Malcolm Gladwell, author of *The Tipping Point*, notes society's over-reliance on another form of maximization, the extreme expertise of "genius solutions," a form of achievement that has taken on its own kind of celebrity status.[7]

Test Your Baselines of Success for Hidden Celebrity Elements

To open your thinking to the process of a more fulfilling and reachable success, it is critical to understand how approaches stressing the features of maximization and celebrity can distract you. What do they look like and where do they come from? Everywhere. Just think of all the "bests" that confront you daily. The best coffee, the best deal, the best colleges, the best dressed, the best foods followed by the best diets. Even failure submits to this paradigm: better to be in the best place on a list of the worst dressed, or the best company in the worst industry than not to be superlative at all.

If you swallow all this, you may fall prey to believing it takes a genius or some other form of superhuman intelligence and ability to compete, to win, to be a success. You and the social dynamics of your organization may become overwhelmed in assuming that everyone has to be the smartest and the fastest. That anyone with ambition has to have the best. If you are not naturally endowed with such genius, then you may believe the guru promise that all you need to do is maximize the leveraging of your own potential: leverage your time to the max, same with your energy.

Levers aside, that still takes a *lot* of effort. You probably need a concierge lifestyle to fit in all the pieces: a money manager, a personal trainer, a cook, a nanny, a spiritual advisor and so on. Even the newly revived quest for simplicity has quickly been transformed by the gurus into a quest for getting the *most* from your time and money so as to live a magazine-worthy lifestyle. Ask yourself:

- Am I formulating my ideal performance, consumption and relationships on a perfect or best outcome?
- Do I assume I have to work at my max all the time to achieve success?
- Do I believe the people in my organization should also believe this?

Backing Off without Dropping Out

Unless you believe what so many are urging—that continuous improvement in effort and rewards is a limitless possibility—it is ridiculous to endlessly recalibrate your own peak upward. Such strategies of one-way success almost always fall apart from entropy. They stretch the system so far it breaks down under its own weight. How versatile is being at the peak in terms of multiple targets in your life? If you aim for being at the peak, don't you have to come down to address your other needs? According to MIT psychologist Dan Ariely, who does happiness research, too high a peak can actually be a setup for gloom. He draws on research by Nobel prize winner Daniel Kahneman, who developed what he called the Peak/End rule: Most people tend to assess their experience by two points—how it felt at the peak and where it ended. Even a mild trend toward improvement in the overall pattern can make any experience seem better—and vice versa.[8]

But you have to set up the right assumptions if you are to map the steps of this journey. One is the ability to change directions, despite your large ambitions. **At some point you must be prepared to go down your particular mountain, if only to climb the next one.** Doing this shouldn't leave you feeling a failure. Think again of Michael Caine and his self-awareness about the rhythms of success. He observed that while he doesn't want to stop starring in movies, there may be a time when the acting opportunities reduce in size. He's ready for this challenge, deliberately refusing to standardize those features that are most appealing to his audience today. As he says, "I specialize in imperfection."

It's More Pervasive than You Might Think

As our research progressed, we became interested in the effect that celebrity success has on the framework with which people analyze and pursue their multiple targets of success. Sure we know it's hype, but we seem to think that as long as we know the way the media works, it won't have any real effect on our deeper assumptions. That is apparently not the case. However media-savvy the public might be, the fact is, celebrity star success presentations continue to sell well, no matter how often the celebrity successes fail to live up to their press. Even today *Forbes* magazine continues to run its "Midas List," and top ten lists still regularly frame public standards. **We like this stuff. As some level these dreams seem plausible for our lives.**

The spillover into social norms has been acute. Whether sports stars or ultra-entrepreneurs, many celebrity successes today have embraced a degree of wealth that isn't just out of the ordinary—it's out of the extraordinary. Between 1970 and 1999, the average real compensation of the top 100 U.S. CEOs went from $1.3 million to $37.5 million.[9] In the 1950s, the average CEO salary was six times higher than the president of the United States. In year 2000, it was 350 times higher. In 1979, the average compensation of the top 100 CEOs was 39 times the average worker. In 1999, it was 1,000 times. Instead of appearing to be what it was—namely an exceptional reward for an exceptional few—income creep among the successful began to look inevitable. Few eyebrows were raised, for example, when former General Electric Vice President Gary Wendt demanded a $45 million signing bonus to become the CEO of Conseco. One year later, Conseco was bankrupt, the third largest bankruptcy in U.S. history. We might laugh at such nonsense were it not for the constant comparison of salaries we overhear among MBA students.

So, too, celebrity has been factored in mainstream assumptions about leadership. Harvard Business School professor Rakesh Khurana has noted that the ubiquitous portrayals of success today place a particularly strong emphasis on charisma, which is a key feature of celebrity.[10] His research questions whether we are truly right in placing such a high value on this quality when there are so many counterexamples of "quiet" leadership that stays the course. We see an additional problem: Charisma contributes to the leadership philosophy that leaders deserve it all.

The very factors that create celebrity promote an unexpectedly attractive view of *maximization*. Not only does this increase the confusion between net worth and self-worth, but it makes it harder to anticipate the idea of valuing anything less than the best. These forces run deep. Even in the post-September 11 reevaluations of what life was really about, one of the most common phrases heard was, "Am I making the *most* of my life?" For many, that question is so extreme it becomes paralyzing.

Don't Drop Out, Just Understand Why
Celebrity Lets You Down

You don't have to go to the other extreme and choose a life of poverty and cynicism as the alternative to celebrity. You don't have to drop out. Most people want some degree of prosperity and the challenge of making a mark in this world. Even Charles Darwin wrote in his journals that his success was born of a mixture of "pure love . . . of natural science and the ambition to be esteemed by my fellow naturalists."

The cultural dominance of the celebrity paradigm is puzzling, but given its ubiquity, it is important to critique its many flaws. In assessing the degree to which celebrity presentations are supporting or undermining your ability to formulate a vision of the good life and go after it, it is important to bear in mind some cautions about celebrity success.

Celebrity Success Stresses Self-Absorption over Social Connection

The irony of today's lionization of celebrity performance is that it actually is *reducing* the quality of life for most people. With all that glamour supposedly just within reach, it's no wonder people feel as if someone is speeding up the treadmill. They not only find themselves unable to manage multiple targets for themselves, they encounter difficulties in implementing their *social* ideals.

Celebrity reinforces public acceptance of highly individualistic values. Like other forms of narcissism, celebrity substitutes priority on the self for the give and take of belonging to a real community. It is essentially a very self-centered concept, justified by a perverse belief that my interests should bring you joy because you identify with me. You can hire a retinue of a hundred people to help you get through an airport with your favorite latte in hand, but that won't buy the experience of sharing in the lives of others in a way that makes you mutually important to one another.

An important question to ask yourself is "Why do I like this image?" What really attracts you to it? Chances are that a variety of other unselfish impulses such as social acceptance and aesthetics also figure strongly in what it is you seek.

You Cannot Go after It All

Ironically, to reach a sky's-the-limit achievement, you have to impose serious limitations on your targets, *restricting* them to a very few or even one goal. Having it all, as the celebrity success implies, cannot hang on maximization. You cannot go after two things to the max. When you take one thing to an extreme, it exacts a cost from your other talents or emotional strengths.

If, for example, you really believe that a successful company must maximize its stock price, you cannot also be the best corporate citizen, best place to work, and best long-term value—unless you operate in a monopoly position. If you really want to win a competition against other maximizers who start practicing for success when they're five years old, you'd better get on the same focused track. You can't be an ideal mom and give 100 percent at work, despite the celebrity reports of the women executives who delayed labor until they could get their business plans in. The same is true for being an ideal dad and a celebrity executive; being both just isn't possible.

Celebrity Success Is a Snapshot, Not a Full Picture

Celebrity success doesn't tell the whole story, only the fairy tale parts. Typical are the daily profiles of top athletes whose dedication is celebrated, rewards reported, but the messier parts of their lives, like how they behave in a limousine or at home, are edited out. One interviewee reported being threatened with a thrown coffee mug by her celebrity boss. Later that same day photographers at a big benefit caught him presenting a very benign and glamorous picture of philanthropy and success.

The next time you see a picture that incites envy, ask yourself: "Does this profile include the rest of the story?"

Celebrity Success Is Frozen in Time

Because it is packaged for immediate consumption, this is a success with no future. In a celebrity world, novelty, the latest new thing, replaces long-term gains. When you read of a 20-year-old like Gene Kan (one of the people whose programs for the file-sharing Gnutella protocol was bought by Sun Microsystems for $10 million), the picture of empire building is usually compressed into a few sound bytes. But as the postbubble market demonstrated, many of those instant millionaires lost their fortunes within a few years (if not months). In the same way, most cultures have some variation on the saying, "rags to riches to rags in three generations." The high achiever who was motivated by a poor background to become a huge success in one generation in turns fails to produce children who can succeed at the same extreme level.

The Peak Is a Precarious Perch

Celebrity success is about catching the wave. It is a vision most appropriate for a nineteen-year-old bungee jumper with fantasies of making three commas (that's a billion dollars to you and me). Celebrity success includes the wunderkind geek with the world's biggest purple yacht whose company has gone out of business and whose employees are without jobs. There seems to be such freedom and power in celebrity. Surely it should be secure. But being at the top is a ruthlessly precarious place: no one sustains this kind of position for long, and don't expect help in staying at the top. The presenters of celebrity seem able to find a constant source of new material. What you don't often see is the story of the has-been who has come down from the pinnacle but would still be regarded by many as a talented, successful person. Celebrity success is not a vision that presumes enduring value.

Celebrity Success Is Morally Hazardous

And then there's the E word. Some of our celebrity successes, especially in business, have been notoriously lax about the basic rules of ethics. It seems that many people have forgotten that maximized expectations are built on breaking the limits. They *depend* on an absence of restraint. Or, as one executive from a now-defunct Wall Street firm assured us, "We motivate on greed. As long as you can keep it within bounds, it's the best motivator around." When his company went bust after being discovered to have built its empire on insider trading, it was too late to moderate their no-holds-barred approach.

Even those who stayed within the law seemed to have bought into a disturbing ethic of one-upsmanship. Listen to the reunion conversations, the panels on success: My job is perfect, our investment strategy cleaned up when all others failed, the corporate team is motivated by mutual respect and passion, my spouse's outfit is a "most original," my philanthropy tops Bill Gates. There's now even a top 50 list of sports philanthropists, with a list of their foundations, showing that doing good has as much celebrity potential as any other success activity in America.

Celebrity Success Can Be an Empty Promise

There has been a great deal of moral disappointment and general confusion about those who have embodied success in the recent past, whether it's the student who got into a top university by cheating, the bad boy athletes, or business crooks who had enough to go around and still had to have it all for themselves. Success was once for the person who had paid his or her dues: the struggling young Rockefeller who saved dimes and invested in oil wells; the hoofer in the back row of a Broadway musical who got a lucky break; the dedicated scientist, like Bill Hewlett or Edwin Land, who turned a new discovery into a mass-marketed product. These people struggled and gave back. They stayed with their companies when they could have retired.

By contrast, maximized standards have led to an all-or-nothing approach to the world. In February 2000, just before the crash, *Wall Street Journal* columnist Carol Hymowitz summed up the spirit of the times in this headline: "The New Fast-Trackers Work Like Maniacs And Then Take A Walk."[11]

Today's presentations of success trace a fast and unstable trajectory. They promise a lot, but will they prepare us for a September 11, an April 2000 market meltdown, or even our own children's questions about what it is we exactly do all day at work? Will they prepare us to help *them* succeed?

The Source of This Myth's Power

Common sense and a media-savvy public know at some level that celebrity success has caught us in a powerfully attractive fantasy. Why do we swallow the myth when it is so unreachable and so many of the celebrity examples have failed to stand up to the test of time? Two factors seem to be particularly responsible: the unprecedented growth of the free market and the explosion of the media through new technology (meaning information industries in general) in the 1990s. The fact that they gained dominant power together made these forces particularly influential in our thinking about success.

With the breakup of the Soviet Bloc in 1989, capitalism essentially had no serious competitors. At just about the same time, the commercial uses of information technology exploded. In April 1994, Netscape was born. Seven months later it was Amazon.com, triggering a host of powerful new applications of Internet commerce that rested on access to information. Soon new laws allowed the media to be both content provider *and* delivery system. Throughout the 1990s, laxer regulations on derivatives and other "alternative" financial instruments opened up fast new sources of capital to fuel this growth.

Information technology and free market capitalism were now released from the bonds of typical corporate bricks and mortar. Either one on its own was a powerful force; but in this case they reinforced each other, gaining increasing dominance in the

economy in tandem. In the 1980s and early 1990s, about $2 billion in venture capital was raised each year in the United States. In 1998, that figure had risen to $28 billion, and $103 billion at the time of the bust in 2000, according to National Venture Capital Association.[12] Forty percent of this money went into Internet business. The media quickly became information providers and deliverers in this marketplace, creating new stories about the successful in celebrity magazines like *People* while using the new technology to create additional highways for dissemination.

"Success" Has a Shorter and Shorter Life Cycle

As a result of these forces, a powerful feedback loop was created: the economy fed on information and information businesses fed off a particular kind of celebrity worship of economic wealth. The ingredients of celebrity success were particularly hot as long as they could remain novel enough to keep the public entertained. One of the fastest growing segments of the media—financial information—particularly capitalized on this approach: best lists and star personas proliferated even in such formerly staid news outlets as the *Wall Street Journal*. Most major newspapers increased their financial coverage with sections on business and entrepreneurial celebrities. Pushed in the media and fueled by a boom economy, the calibration for "best" rapidly notched upward even as the time frames for achievement narrowed.

A few decades ago, Andy Warhol predicted that in the future, everyone would have their 15 minutes of fame. Well, as anyone who has been on network news can tell you, 15 minutes of fame is now a *long, long time*, more even than the celebrities profiled on *Entertainment!* can expect. Technology, especially the explosion of new technology in the information industries, has cranked up the velocity of success to nosebleed speed. The paradigm today is faster and cheaper so you can offer and get *more!* Standing in the onslaught of proliferating channels and choices for the consumer, businesses and individuals find their success is inextricably hitched to the next new thing.

We are currently exposed to a continuous spectacle of new bests, from the way we interpret new book production (bestseller lists) to the ways in which we judge the success of businesses (quarterly returns with stock price hitting new maximums) to the way we evaluate education. Success stories have been transformed into byte-sized, juiced-up hits of sudden fame and wealth. Most of these stories are like the end of a fairy tale, that brief, delicious moment when the prince finally asks for the maiden's hand and they live happily ever after.

The point is not simply to excoriate the media for pushing the greed button. They wouldn't be publishing this stuff if there wasn't a hungry audience willing to put out hard cash for it. Rather, it's important to understand how far the success norm has tipped toward instant wealth and expectations of peak performance—and what the effects of that tilt have been on normal people's expectations around success.

Beware the Midas Syndrome

In today's environment, no story of extreme wealth—however outrageous—seems implausible. One example out of thousands would be *Forbes* magazine's Midas List, a medley of the year's top 50 venture capitalists. When it was launched in 2001—just about a year after the March bursting of the stock market bubble—the list seemed a perfect example of what the rewards of success should be. Like Midas, these venture capitalists carried the optimistic message that there was plenty of gold to be minted for a small down payment, as long as you still had "the touch." Everyone naturally either wanted to be a Midas—or have one at his or her disposal by taking a flyer on an IPO with hard-earned savings.

We found many people in our own circles deeply influenced by the 1990s' Midas syndrome. We had to look hard for a young person who *doesn't* assume that the number one foundation of a successful career strategy is the possibility of cashing out by age thirty-five or forty. (Where they go from there varies enormously, depending on their other values.) So, too, we found talented entrepreneurs at

Harvard Business School who judged themselves against the Midas standard and actually felt poor for having generated less than $100 million in personal assets.

By 2002, of course, the job market looked very different, but the underlying success paradigm still appears to be alive and well. In 2003, after two years of horrendous losses for shareholders and a drop in available venture capital from $107 billion to $17 billion,[13] you would think the *Forbes* Midas List would have discreetly disappeared. On the contrary. *Forbes* continues to root out the successful Midases for its list, and the story is essentially the same: thirty-four-year-old Rob Soni puts $10 million into a computer networks firm and comes out with three times that within a year. Forty-four-year-old Jay Hoag (number 39 on the list) puts $35 million into a new company called Altiris, and within a year finds his firm's stake worth $110 million.[14] At least one of your own cohorts is making triple your income.

As individuals adopt these perspectives, they may be only partially conscious of how extreme and contradictory their ideas of success have become. In particular, the landscape of moving targets begins to feel wrong, even though these needs are widely shared, if not universal. Maximization says it should be *one* target at which the well-trained person aims. Then all the rest you want will flow from success.

There is a disturbingly familiar lack of self-protection in those who believe in the Midas syndrome, and an alarming lack of awareness of what the "Midas touch" implies. In the past, the tale of King Midas served as a warning against the desire for extreme wealth, especially unearned wealth. Midas gets his wish, which is essentially based on a maximization strategy: He wishes that everything he touches will turn to gold. He ends up unable to experience any of things he'd hoped to enjoy. Everything he touches—his food, even his daughter—turns to gold. All he desires does *not* follow.

Moral suspicion was largely removed from Midas Version 2000. Then, as a number of the wealthiest executives and stars in America were found to have engaged in wrongdoing to get their share, the public was confused. That didn't stop us, however, from drawing on the same stale paradigm. Now we get our standards from demonizing celebrity failures!

Beyond Celebrity Success

In an environment such as ours, the idea of enduring success is almost incomprehensible. After a decade of speeding up, the past, present, and future have all been compressed into the here and now—and it is a now with particularly high-energy demands. **How will we couple achievements measured in nano-seconds to the less evolved emotional needs of human beings?**

You could cope with the new environment by imitating the celebrities of media and technology. You could constantly reinvent yourself and adopt all the new ways of defying your biological makeup. But in our observation, constantly going back to square one becomes exhausting over time. It's an exhilarating game for kids, but not a recipe for a life well lived. To escape the nightmare of being washed up at forty, either you have to radically change your notion of yourself, or you have to change your notions of success. Multifaceted success cannot be reached through one extreme, single-facet activity.

Celebrity Success versus Enduring Success

First, it is important to compare the essential conditions of real, enduring success with the packaged assumptions of celebrity success, and to be aware of the flaws and contradictions between them.

Celebrity success presents:

- An obstructed view (much of the story is left out).
- Self-centeredness.
- Cost-free rewards.
- No sense of limits.

- Freeze-framed universe.
- Unidirectional movement: one *big* win after another.
- Novelty without variety.

Enduring success, by contrast, sets you up for a:

- Multiperspective view.
- Ability to care and share.
- Trade-offs and juggling.
- Benefit in limitations.
- Rhythmic momentum: a lifetime of accomplishments that wax and wane.

Real Success Is Always a Mixed Picture

Second, it's important to study the actual measures by which any success is celebrated, and be prepared for a mixed picture. To return to our Doers' Profiles discussion, we found that when our students really studied the lives of Jimmy Carter, Katharine Graham, Bill Gates, and Donald Trump, the picture was decidedly mixed. Their strengths were like double-edged swords: they cut both ways on the goals of enduring success.

Jimmy Carter's passion and self-confidence about his role as international peace keeper (he titled his first autobiography *Keeping the Faith*) has made him a great ex-president, but these same success characteristics fed his tendency to hoard information and be too self-reliant, which got in the way of his effectiveness as chief executive of the nation. His determination and intellectual skills helped him broker critical solutions to human rights conflicts around the world in the years after his presidency. But this same passion and focus clearly interfered with his family's ability to thrive, and led him into an obsessive state about certain problems, such as the Iran hostages. Up to the very last hour of his presidency, a time when many would be contemplating their accomplishments, he waited by the phone in the hope that the call would come saying the hostages had been released.

Trump's personal qualities seem even more extreme in terms of self-confident drive and passion. He doggedly pursued success in the face of considerable obstacles, breaking into the top ranks of real estate entrepreneurs. Some criticize his street-fighter values—the very qualities often touted in success books as long as they appear in a more "refined" package. Others admire his pioneering achievements in real estate. The idea of branding had never been extended so imaginatively or with such financial success in real estate until Trump did it.

Gates, too, received mixed reviews, even though he scored high on competitiveness, passion, and focus. Even Katherine Graham, a superficially less self-confident leader, shared qualities of resiliency, passion, and focus with the other four Doers, and yet her essentially disquieting unease over power caused one to wonder if she ever *really* felt herself a success by achieving so much in publishing. Even if she appears on Collins' list of the Best 10 CEOs.[15]

Instead of considering these reservations a fatal blow to our Doer's potential as success models, we should interpret these nuanced, multi-faceted profiles in a more positive light. Success is not a one-liner or a headline, it's a novel you write over time. Even though we have few current literary works that actually explore the deep nuances of business success in its many aspects, we need to remember that no person, however talented, escapes a reckoning on multiple measures.

Remember: Success Is about More than One Thing

Even those who seem to do it all turn out to have mixed goals—which is part of what makes them more enduring successes. **The mix, however, is not just about layering one set of upscale must-haves over another.** Sometimes the simplest pleasures provide the greatest satisfaction—as in the CEO who told us his best conversation of the day occurred during a cab ride when the driver and he shared baseball statistics.

Margaret Loesch, former CEO of Odyssey Channel and the U.S. Hallmark Channel, provides a particularly upbeat example of the difference between empty glamour and enduring achievement. On the surface, Loesch seems to have it all and have done it all. Starting as an office assistant at ABC Network, she eventually became founding president and CEO of Fox Kids Networks Worldwide in 1990. She left Fox to become head of Jim Henson Television Group, where she contributed her expertise to a new partnership resulting in the purchase of Odyssey and subsequent formation of the U.S. Hallmark Channel. Loesch has earned four Emmy Awards, along with the honor of a George Foster Peabody Award and is serving her second term as vice-chair of the Academy of Television Arts and Sciences Foundation. She recently co-founded a new entertainment company, The Hatchery, LLC, and produced a new motion picture "Benji Returns." You might think these credentials were Loesch's key measures of success, but they're only part of the story. While she's proud of her success, she also knows that getting there has been a mixed bag. She's had to make sacrifices in terms of family, and also renegotiate her goals on several well-publicized occasions when she's seen a very different vision for her company than top management.

We spoke with her right after she left Hallmark to strike out on her own for the first time in order, as she put it, to be able to put what she really most wanted into programming. She talked about her own modest start as an office assistant. One of her greatest moments of success was in just getting hired. She couldn't type and the supervisor who reviewed her application decided to give her a chance anyway. The supervisor told her, "I see something special in you. You're going to go far."

Later when Loesch was leaving Hanna-Barbera to become president and CEO of Marvel Productions, she wrote a letter to the supervisor to thank her. Those words of support had stayed with her and she liked to think they had made a critical difference in her success. The supervisor wrote back, obviously not remembering Margaret. "Oh," the woman declared breezily, "I used to say that to *all* the girls we hired."

If you can tell that kind of story on yourself with real pleasure, you have a humble perspective on success that opens you to really appreciating those moments of victory. Instead of falsely implying that you made it totally on your own, your measures take other people into account. (Here's a little test: How often do you know the names of the other people in a celebrity CEO's organization? Is this a realistic view of what it really took to create that kind of success?)

It's a particularly critical point of view to be prepared for a world where there are many different peaks defined as "the top," and the highest won't necessarily be the best. You have to have your own set of standards. You need to thrive on a bit of mystery rather than the expectation of getting to some point that grants you all your wishes. **No aspiration is quite what it seems to be from afar once you get there. You can view this as constant disappointment, or you can enjoy what is enough at each stage.** The satisfaction is in knowing you've made it on a scale that is important to you, in comparison to people with reasonably comparable talents and contexts.

What It Means for Jane

Even though she had no ambitions of being a celebrity CEO or musician, our interviewee Jane suffered many of the symptoms of maximization stalemate. In honestly believing "to thine own self be true and thou can'st be false to any man," Jane was caught in the cross currents of her own multiple talents and opportunities. There wasn't one self to be true to, but many. **There isn't any one action she can take to actualize these different aspects of her nature—she will have to see them as functions of many actions. That means she cannot maximize.**

Until Jane abandons her hope to maximize her potential on every measure she holds dear, she will not break out of her indecisiveness. There is no perfect balance that gets it all in one picture. Until she sees that not only is there a cost in every action, but that maximized efforts exact *higher* costs on your other activities, she will not find a way to balance her time and keep the multiple goods she seeks alive and satisfying. Referencing her dilemma on the most superficial aspects of lifestyle is only leading her further astray. She will have to find a framework that will not only give full appreciation to the many things she desires but will help her see them *in relation to each other*. As we will argue, there is such a framework, but instead of maximizing, it calibrates on the idea of Enough. Instead of a no-cost celebrity narcissism, it sees giving value to others as an essential piece in the pattern of success.

We began this chapter with an account of the extreme record-breaking mentality that dominated the events around the fiftieth anniversary of Sir Edmund Hillary's scaling of Mt. Everest. All the pieces of celebrity success were in place: extraordinary people going to the max, scrambling to reach new heights, and when they succeeded, they were celebrated with instant fame—only to see the records broken again. But what about Hillary himself? The man whose endeavor was being celebrated? He, too, was offered the chance of fame and spectacle in the form of dining with Queen Elizabeth to celebrate the day. While reportedly quite grateful, he had other goals. He returned to Nepal and spent the anniversary with old friends. (Tenzing Norgay died in 1986.) Some climbers that week saw themselves as continuing the two hikers' important legacy. Appa, a Nepalese Sherpa, completed his thirteenth ascent up Everest, more times than any other human.

To complete this climb, Appa followed the east route that Hillary had originally taken—as part of the group that was picking up the trash.

Quick Points: The Dangers of Going for the Max

Why going for the max is not only dangerous, but impossible:

- There is no maximum, there is always "more."
- Real success requires skill at breaking and accepting limits.
- You cannot maximize two goals.

(continued)

Why celebrity success works against real success:

- It stresses self-absorption over social connection.
- It stresses benefits not the costs.
- It stresses now, even though life moves on.
- It stresses the peak not the aftermath as new idols are created.
- It stresses the positive but not the complexity of the embedded moral hazards.
- It stresses fame and not the ever shorter life cycle of fame.

Why enduring success is the real thing:

- You can care and share.
- You understand and benefit from limits.
- You realize multiple kinds of satisfaction.
- You deal with the waxing and waning that is a part of real life.

Chapter 3

The Satisfactions of Just Enough Success

He was the man who . . . had the largest and most comprehensive soul. . . . He is many times flat, insipid; his comic wit degenerating into clichés, his serious swelling into bombast. But he is always great, when some occasion is presented to him.

—Dryden on Shakespeare[1]

Competing scores and mixed records are inevitable for anyone who seeks more than a paycheck out of life, but our responses are not so rigidly programmed. On the one hand, moving targets can lead to endless frustration over the short-lived, unrewarding nature of each "win" you may achieve. Aware of what beckons or threatens, high achievers and nonachievers alike can fall into a compulsively dissatisfied state, always needing to do and have "more" than they have already accomplished. Success, in this light, is at best a series of temporary highs and at worst a difficult slog through an endless string of quick solutions that never quite satisfy complex desires.

That was Jane's problem. She couldn't get to a career and lifestyle solution that reflected enough complexity and meaning to give her lasting and thorough satisfaction. Each of her many accomplishments felt satisfying only temporarily, but were quickly undone by her sense of loss in other areas of her life as she set her sights on a specific target. Her own confusion threatened to secure her a life she didn't really want.

Still, targets are exciting—they make you stretch, grow, contribute. They challenge and organize groups of people. **We don't know anyone of accomplishment inside or outside business who** doesn't have a fine-tuned aim at something. Our interest lies in how to cultivate this skill and not let it work against your pursuit of many things. In this chapter, we'll profile some people who personify an alternative yet recognizable sort of success, one that is very different from celebrity and maximization.

Peter Ueberroth: One Approach to Enduring Success

Another of our interviewees was Peter Ueberroth, the well-known organizer of the Twenty-Third Olympic Games in Los Angeles, *Time* magazine's "1984 Man of the Year," former baseball commissioner, and a highly successful entrepreneur. Though surprisingly unknown to the general public, Ueberroth has built a legendary string of successes where others fear to tread.

In the early 1970s, after putting himself through college, Ueberroth joined Kirk Kerkorian's Trans International Airlines as an operations manager. Several years later, he started his own successful air service and then a travel reservations company, First Travel. By 1978, his company was the second largest travel agency in the United States after American Express. Ueberroth sold First Travel for $10.4 million when he accepted the position of heading the 1984 Los Angeles Olympic Games. There he revolutionized the structure of corporate sponsorship by wildly increasing the fees and making sponsorship into an "elite" activity. Instead of running in the red, as many predicted, Ueberroth set off a bidding war that made the games financially successful—this in spite of the Soviet boycott and the city of Los Angeles' condition that not one cent of municipal funds be spent on the Games. Before it was over, terrorists' threats and television network animosities taxed Ueberroth's energy and dedication to the max. Even the lighting of the torch required Ueberroth's single-minded will to get it done. He refused to accept former Olympic winner Rafer Johnson's message that he might not be able to make it up the final steps due to an injured hamstring. (Johnson eventually did light the flame.)

By any measure, he has had a good run. Yet the public picture of Ueberroth throughout the Olympics and for most of his career has been half tyrant and half miracle worker, calling into question our very measures of success. What disturbed us after meeting with him was the lopsided press he had gotten. It was as if success were only measurable on a single dimension, which he passed or failed, depending on which dimension a writer adopted.

Reality, of course, is always more complex. When we spoke with Ueberroth, he was deep into his next set of business ventures, operating a venture capital firm out of a modest office in Newport Beach, California. When we asked him what most pleased him about his career so far, he replied:

> Funny. It's not the biggest deal I ever did, but the time I put into establishing a downtown renewal project in Los Angeles, called Rebuild Los Angeles. On any measure you'd have to say this project was only partially successful, and we'll probably never get to where we hoped to be in terms of economic revitalization of the area. But still, that was my greatest and most satisfying accomplishment. This was a community that was absolutely dysfunctional after the Los Angeles riots. Absolutely. We started with no resources and were never able to raise as much money as was needed, to my disappointment. But the people on that project have been extraordinary. The progress that was made, at least there's something there now.[2]

Ueberroth has a decidedly disciplined urge to achieve. Demanding of himself and those around him, quick to take charge when something's not right, he has drawn his fair share of fire for being ruthless and many accolades for being wonderfully inspiring.[3] What brought him admiration is not the definitive nature of his style or even the final score various people put on his important accomplishments, but the *lasting* nature of his commitment to achievement, to society, and to family. His projects endure for others. His businesses created new value out of collections of underperforming assets. Unlike the freeze-framed snapshots of success we studied in the previous chapter, Ueberroth's career is *not* a portrait of maximized behavior, nor does he exhibit the self-absorption of the celebrity. He's seen dark times and bright occasions, and through it all he seems prepared to address *each* of the major commitments in his life. Twenty years after his success with the Los Angeles Olympics, he is still building, always taking time out to be with family, insisting his employees do the same, still engaged in community projects, still passionate about golf.

We define real, enduring success as *a collection of activities that will be viewed affirmatively by you and those you care about, now, throughout your life, and beyond.* By any measure, Ueberroth's career certainly qualifies. Parts of it resonate with many other people in the cities and businesses and communities he cares about. Others are particularly personal to him. Not everyone would want to be or could be Peter Ueberroth, and he would be the first to say so. Rather than try to collapse all the visions of enduring success that we garnered in our research, we looked for the key factors that seemed to be particularly distinctive to the process of achieving this ideal.

Multiple Goals with Multiple Beneficiaries

The critical factor in the success profile of someone like Peter Ueberroth is something both important and underarticulated in today's culture: **He presents a complex picture that is about no final victory, no one reward, no single secret of success. His performance over a lifetime has occurred in multiple realms of his life; his achievements have supported his own prosperity and that of others on many dimensions beyond money.**

We've had the privilege to observe many such leaders in the course of our teaching and research, and we realize how difficult it can be to capture the complete picture in a way people are receptive to hearing. Take today's popular profiles of that complex character President Bill Clinton. In his postpresidential position, he wants to establish his legacy as a progressive leader by fostering the growth of a number of nonprofit organizations. He also appears to want to have some fun. And he may want to achieve even more politically than he already has. **Some part of the public scolds back whenever he fails to maximize his experiences in any one of these areas.** As the bon vivant, he may not be enjoying the successful life unless he's making naughty headlines. As the do-gooder, his enjoyment of a party on a yacht is suspect. But what if he, like the rest of us, wants a bit of it all?

The idea of having multiple goals frustrates many people, yet we found it is a key feature in the success strategy of those who make large and lasting contributions, and who find career and life deeply fulfilling at a personal level. Enduring successes are people who are actively engaged in hitting moving targets all the time, and yet they do it in such a way as to create a coherent set of satisfactions for themselves—and for others. This was Ueberroth's skill: knowing the multiple pieces of what he regarded as a good life and being able to discipline himself to score hits on each of them repeatedly. Success for him was a constant and exciting journey, not a static endpoint of "making it." On the other hand, he is known to be capable of intense focus on the goals he sets.

That takes not only versatility but also adaptability. Each of the targets of a good life requires a different set of qualities, conferring different benefits on yourself and others—which may explain why people like Ueberroth and others attract such contradictory press. Family man or ruthless CEO? First in his dedication as citizen and backer of new businesses, or opportunist? Confident and self-fulfilled or impatiently intolerant of himself and others?

These contrasts and interruptions in the neat chain of achievement are not just for those at the top of the economic or power food chain. The same conflicts between enjoyment of the here and now, achievement of something larger, toughness, and compassion are there for most people. We were struck by how much Ueberroth and our interviewee Jane shared in terms of their desire to negotiate the good life on many playing fields, not just one. **Enduring success isn't about one set of values, it's about knowing how to apply values to multiple goals.**

Four Markers of the Enduring

What makes targets of success enduring? What turns an episode of accomplishment from a successful dabble in the next new thing to an experience whose meaning lasts even beyond its assumed practical impact? Like the discovery of the telephone, or the first date with your future spouse? We found the answer from several sources, including people's discussion of their emotional sense of fulfillment, the concrete scale of their accomplishments, how their accomplishments were viewed by others after the fact, and the ways in which their success left some sort of legacy that was actively influential on others.

Enduring success generates four important outcomes, scalable but consistent:

1. *Growth toward the extraordinary in some form:* Innovation, personal stretch, expanded capacity beyond that of your competitors, an ideal of excellence, and so on.

2. *Importance to you:* Fulfilling some aspect of what you regard as necessary and meaningful to a good life.

3. *Social significance:* Contributing something valued by society and the people you care about.

4. *Sustained impact beyond present effects:* Not a flash in the pan but having an impact that carries on in the lives of others.

Ueberroth's reflections on what he regarded as the enduring success of the Los Angeles Olympics, for example, stressed the revolutionary change his marketing strategy represented (outcome 1), the personal satisfaction he had taken in proving his financial and athletic goals could be accomplished under conditions that significantly stretched his abilities (outcomes 1 + 2), the value his nation had placed on the results (outcome 3), and the positive changes it wrought on Los Angeles far beyond the summer of 1984 (outcome 4).

All of Ueberroth's successes can be replicated in your life on a different scale and with different particulars. Enduring success can be found in organizations that are "built to last," which started with revolutionary new products or business approaches and continue to create a positive impact on society. It can be found, for example, in the lasting success of one of our interviewees, entrepreneur Ken

Hakuta's "Dr. Fad," a children's television character who introduced science and the marketplace to youngsters for over a decade.
(In Chapter 9, we show how Hakuta built on the multiplicity of
success factors over his career.) It can also be found in MBA grad
Dennis Pemberton's first job experience, when as a young manager
in Atlanta he reengineered the entire client account service system
at his firm in a way that outlasted his position there. That accomplishment was the first of many, but he said it *lasted* for him in terms
of its satisfaction, importance, and contribution—as it did for his
former place of business, which is still using the system.

What about Jane, our troubled young software engineer on a
walkabout in the desert? Her feelings about her successes were not
so enduring, despite her achievements. Each of the factors that
would contribute lasting parts of her desired ends were being un-
dermined by her own mixed feelings. She worked hard and enjoyed
life, and yet she was deeply uneasy that this was not the platform
for the kind of success that she really wanted, that would be worthwhile and lasting. Her career milestones held little satisfaction for
her; she worried about whether she was really contributing enough
in the software field, and how much of a player she would feel as a
church musician compared to her peers in business. She wondered
how long she could stay committed to either career if she had to
live in a too small apartment or give up her music. **None of these
questions could be answered by the hedonistic calculus that
many of us try to put to such worries about success: What
makes you happy?** Jane's sabbatical rested on a search for something beyond happiness: it was the search for growth, personal
mastery, enjoyment of life, giving, and leaving something behind.
As she remarked, this wasn't just about logic, there were deep emotional needs involved.

Enduring success is only as strong as it is able to provide these
personal and social satisfactions, and they are of multiple types.
Howard Stevenson's mother used to say, "success is getting what you
want. Happiness is wanting what you get." If success is "getting
what you want," you have to be very aware that it is not just for now,

but for tomorrow, and for a lifetime. You also have to have happiness along the way. They're not the same, but they *are* related.

Clint Eastwood: Example of the Complex Mix

Enduring success is a complex mixture of renewal, growth, satisfaction, timelessness, and contribution. Clint Eastwood—actor, director, musician, and politician—is a good example.

Eastwood's accomplishments over his nearly 50 years in the film industry stand out for their continued creativity and change. At seventy-two, we would call Eastwood an enduring success.[4] He's acted in or directed over 40 films, many of them memorably path-breaking, from his unorthodox cowboy roles in early spaghetti westerns to the controversial *Dirty Harry* series in the 1970s, to the drama *The Bridges of Madison County*. In 2003, he was given the Screen Actors Guild for Life Achievement award.

Not only do his films endure, Eastwood personally thrives. **Unlike the quick, lucky rise to stardom and equally quick personal decline that many of his peers have suffered, Eastwood appears to have earned and enjoyed his good fortune. He's taken risks, scored many wins (not only in acting, but in politics, music, and real estate), continues to grow, and brings many others along with him.** Meanwhile, his enjoyment of the process, whether in the music, the people, or the landscape, has been noted by any number of interviewers. Norman Mailer once described an Eastwood set as a group of professionals "drunk on the wealth of their own people." Most recently, Lillian Ross noted in a profile for the *New Yorker*, that during Eastwood's time on the set "he seemed to be oblivious to the frantic pressures that usually overwhelm key figures in an imminent big-time movie production."[5]

The setting for Ross's observation amounted to a quintessential portrait of skillful marksmanship in the landscape of moving targets. Eastwood was directing a movie, *Mystic River*, to be shot in Boston. But just before shooting, he turned his attention to the creation of a public television documentary on the blues, being produced by Martin Scorsese. Ross accompanied him to this event at his Mission Ranch property in Carmel, a for-profit inn he created out of a decaying dairy farm and officers headquarters during World War II. It's not far from Pebble Beach, another of Eastwood's projects—now complete with his pet pig and various farm animals. Eastwood appears in this thoughtful profile as a complex and yet essentially human-scaled success. He is someone who can jam with legendary blues artists like eighty-nine-year-old Pinetop Perkins, check the water bottle for the pet pig, and take a phone call from his mother. As Sean Penn noted, "He's the least disappointing icon in American film."[6]

Eastwood's career could not have come to fruition without a strong measure of restless dissatisfaction and desire to reach new heights. These qualities took him into areas that repeatedly provided lasting wins, but they were also offset by something that every interviewer notices: his ability to keep things simple, go his own way, tease the best out of those around him—and always enjoy the journey. "If it weren't fun, I wouldn't be doing it," quips Eastwood to Ross.[7]

Our Search for Enduring Successes

People like Eastwood, with multiple talents and interests, can find it challenging to judge their moving targets. Some try to adopt a simple formula: put your achievement first and the rest will follow. But how does that help you choose between conflicting opportunities (a question faced by people like Jane) and figuring out what to do when you reach a goal but don't find it nearly as fulfilling as you'd hope? What distinguishes the pursuit of genuine success from survival after a series of shallow or even destructive victories?

To answer these questions, we studied hundreds of success patterns of high achievers and the attitudes they had about the process and rewards of success. We surveyed over a hundred attendees of Harvard Business School executive programs. We observed venture capitalists who, despite having created several *Fortune 500* companies, had few friends and multiple alimony payments. We listened to MBA students discuss their priorities as they sought new jobs, noting who and what they compared themselves to and where this was likely to take them. We heard parents ruefully describe their children buying into false personas of affluence after "making it." We talked to successful film producers and wanna-be writers, software designers in startups, and about-to-retire accountants in real estate. We read and discussed the autobiographies and approved biographies of obviously important public successes. Not to mention the cases we had written in the past. We also interviewed and surveyed seasoned executives and workers of high accomplishment who had made a mark that was positive for themselves and others in the course of a career.

Bill Oakley: Extending an Established Success

One such person was Bill Oakley, former head writer and then executive producer of *The Simpsons*. After working up from freelance script writer to co-head writer with his friend Josh Weinstein, Bill joined Matt Groening and Jim Brooks as executive producer of the show in its seventh season. At the time, he worried that *The Simpsons* might have already peaked, or even worse, that it was about to take the familiar celebrity fall from creative and commercial success to simply commercial. Would *The Simpsons* suffer the fate of many other TV successes? Just as it reached its apex, would it degenerate into a short-lived fad? Or could it endure on terms he and the public whose opinion he cared about would value?

These were high and complicated standards. As a Harvard graduate and former president of the *Harvard Lampoon*, Oakley was following in a humor legacy that ranged from former members Robert Benchley and John Updike to Doug Kenney (co-founder of the *National Lampoon*). This legacy not only included creative writing, but commercial success with a personal element of *fun*. The context for today's media hit, after all, is business.

Oakley had to keep the creative edge of the writing team alive, partly by resisting the complacencies of success. The writers' working space was kept small and informal—artwork in progress rather than a showplace of glitzy product was displayed on the walls. (At least, he didn't admit to wearing a Bart tee shirt when we met with him.) The season's stories were mapped out at a hotel down the street rather than some fancy retreat. Change was critical. Predictable pressures from the network to formularize whatever had gotten the previous good laugh were strongly resisted. Oakley knew that if you didn't build variety and surprise into the script, you'd lose the comedy game. (Fortunately, cartoons are particularly adept at changing characters and scenery.) And because an episode can take up to 10 months to produce, all this had to be accomplished for up to two seasons worth of material at a time.

In many ways, the revitalization of the *The Simpsons* will be an enduring success in Oakley's mind, to the degree he will use the word at all. But in the late 1990s, other targets began to press. *The Simpsons* required him to commit his whole life to produce it. It was more of a success with fraternity boys and girls than family people. And Oakley's family was planning a child. His wife, Rachel, had already cut back her writing and editing career. Oakley and Josh Weinstein took the leap. They formed their own production company and began to piece together several new projects.

The first "lesson" we learned from observing the style of Oakley and others like him was that the "secret" of their success went well beyond the traditional characteristics of focus, passion, hard work, or risk-taking: **One goal is not enough and one success does not constitute a lifetime.** Though very different on the surface, all of these people shared the following personality and style traits: dynamic equanimity, realism, resilience, integrity, self-pacing, enjoying the process, family oriented, concerned, versatile, humility, and sharing. Let's explore each of these qualities in more detail.

Dynamic Equanimity

Perhaps the most startling observation we had was right in front of our face. One of the things that intuitively drew us to certain unusually talented achievers was their seeming ability to be intensely engaged and then rise above the fray, to move amidst the targets like a panther or a bumble bee, depending on their style. Oakley could step back from *The Simpsons* at the height of success and realign his playing field. Ueberroth could sell his business to head the Olympics.

Contrary to most success advice, enduring successes do not invest limitless passion and focus in their work, despite the fire in their belly. Rather, they create the conditions for *punctuated* moments of response and achievement. **These moments are bolstered by their very ability to step back, view the big picture, plan, build resources, and especially, to renew themselves with rest, companionship, or simple random curiosity to explore the perimeter.** Several of our interviewees were described by others as "cool under fire," or "always able to make you feel like you're the only person in the world when they're talking to you." Others had a more restless composure, literally scanning the spot behind your head even as they answered tough questions. Behind the personal style, each subject exhibited an unusual ability to rise above the noise of the many demands they confronted every day to go for the next target.

The source of this adaptability became one of the key questions of our research. Did it have a distinctive pattern? What drove this ability: calculation, perspective, intuition, or just luck?

Realistic Dreamers

A greenhorn will run after every cow that crosses the road. An amateur will fall for a sucker punch. The only way to effectively negotiate moving targets is to exercise control over what you aim for. Enduring successes don't go for a "sky's the limit," "I-can-do-anything!" approach. Resisting the bravado of this week's market or media darlings, they pick and choose difficult but achievable goals. And in many cases, like Peter Ueberroth, they felt their most memorably enduring moments of success were not necessarily what the world would call their highest achievements.

This kind of skill depends on realism. The ideals of enduring success can be formed on fairytales or be based on real examples. One of our interviewees, who had been a skyrocket at a major financial firm, confided that in his early days he was always picking out those he most admired around him and watching them closely:

> I'm constantly aware of what's making somebody successful or ineffective in that meeting. How are they getting what they want? How are they describing their position? How is their behavior? Are they picking up their cell phone at a meeting? You know, just little things that go on in a meeting that influence how somebody's position is perceived. And again, it all comes back to self-awareness and how you think about your own personality and how you can become a more effective representative of the firm, a more effective negotiator, or more effective leader.

However naturally charisma may come to you, it's still important not to be lulled into complacency about what it really takes to the get the job done. Leadership, by one definition, is getting other people to do that which they might otherwise not be inclined to do, but which you want done. Enduring success requires such leadership—few significant successes occur without help and cooperation from others. To acquire this skill, you have to resist relying on the seductive power of charisma and celebrity measures to charm people into cooperating. That requires a realistic self-assessment. As we discussed in the last chapter, charisma is highly overworked in today's media success stories, where someone somehow—through sheer ego, guts, and attractiveness—appears to get it all for themselves. Or their business "cleans up" the market. Get real. Even the best have failures and setbacks some times. The darling companies of Wall Street experience down cycles in their market dominance, Eastwood's hair is thinning, and his first 27-year marriage didn't survive, but he's still a success. What Eastwood doesn't appear to do is try to live a fantasy of half-lies about his own abilities and pleasures in life. Witness how he delivers on new ventures time and again.

The companies that create enduring successes are similar. When the market changes and their vulnerability is imminent, they don't try to ride on a glossy press image or their past victories. They take a fresh look at what's really out there. When Ford first confronted its quality problems way back in the early 1980s, then-chairman Philip Caldwell reported that taking this honest look at the product was one of the hardest things he and his board had ever done.

In emphasizing the importance of setting your sights on a success that is real, on people who have not lost their humanity even as they push for new levels of achievement, we faced a difficult choice concerning the success of our book. On the one hand many of the high-powered executives we work with seemed to feel that the only authoritative insights on success were those based on people who had demonstrated *maximum* achievement: the ones who'd made the most money, had the biggest homes, proved themselves the smartest and toughest in the marketplace. At the same time, they were looking for a more meaningful set of success measures that took into account personal happiness, giving back, the health of society. We felt we couldn't honestly describe how people get to the latter if we based all our examples on the formulaic winner of the best sellers.

Our message here is that you cannot get truly close to ambitions of enduring success unless, ironically, you engage in realism. That can sound crushingly dull unless you are seriously looking for an alternative to maximization models. **Realism will get you closer to your dreams than the bravado tales of limitless power, happiness, and love that often accompany reunion profiles.**

One of the enduring successes we most admire is Rosie Eduardo (not her real name), a Salvadoran housekeeper in Washington, D.C. Eduardo is a single mother of two who started her own housekeeping business after getting divorced. Five years later, she was employing more than 100 people, mostly Salvadorans in the neighborhood, for a thriving housekeeping business. And recently, she has begun to expand her services to include home hospice care for the Latino community. Few people have created such distance between their starting point and their current prosperity, and yet Eduardo kept her sense of who she was and her real capabilities. Though extremely smart and attractive, Eduardo did not strive to be Jennifer Lopez or a Vanderbilt. She did not become bitter about what she could not do or be. Nor did she sell herself short by sticking just to her own housekeeping.

Resilience

As exemplified by Eduardo's journey from extreme poverty to thriving businesswoman, every one of the enduring successes showed *resilience*. None had escaped setbacks or defeats in their lives, and many felt that those moments were the ones they learned the most from. That's easy to point out, but as we learned, many talented people who get stalled on their success goals fail to bounce back, going from a bad situation to worse.

Some studies of depression suggest that people may have fairly fixed levels of optimism or despair in the face of trouble,[8] but even so, there are many ways to nurture resiliency. A key factor relevant to our model is the ability to look at *the entire picture of your success and that of others.*

In the 1980s, high-performing investment banker and Harvard MBA Betty Eveillard faced the tough choice of whether to support and follow her husband on a three-year stint in France just as her career was taking off at Lehman Brothers. She and her husband had to consider the possibility that leaving her firm would undoubtedly set back her career. By her own admission, this was a very hard test. She knew that if she left New York, her assignments would not be the hottest ones around. Would she be perceived as not serious enough to succeed? By taking the long view, Eveillard was able to absorb and grow while overseas. Three years later, several partners took her aside and said that if she wanted to have a career in the firm she should go back to New York. On proposing this move to her husband, he replied, "You gave up something for my advancement. I'm ready to do the same for yours."

On her return, she picked up the industry niches where there was less blood sport and a longer time line to the payoff. This gave her work schedule relative predictability so that she could still be available to her family (a husband and two children) without going head-to-head against the people who were in the "hot" part of investment banking at that time. She still had to work very hard, and she still had to travel sometimes for a week at a time, but the ability to predict that was very important in maintaining the different segments of her life.

Eveillard became one of the top retailing investment bankers on Wall Street in the late 1980s and early 1990s, including leading a secondary offering of stock for Staples. One of her most enduring memories was the $2.8 billion sale of Giant Foods to the European corporation Ahold. No one thought Giant was open to an acquisition by another firm, but because she had been following the industry for so long, calling on clients and understanding their needs, Eveillard saw an opportunity to put together the big deal. Its eventual accomplishment represented the culmination of goals she had entertained over her whole career, goals that matched her values and dedication to her work and family.

Integrity

We don't think there has ever been a time when you should take integrity for granted, especially in the face of competition over possible prosperity. On the other hand, the track record of the 1990s seriously called this aspect of business success into question. Integrity is not only a hallmark of enduring success, it supports resiliency. Even though the people we studied have nurtured ambitions for external acclaim of some sort, doing what was right fed their soul. It helped them make the right choices and motivated them to swallow the costs even when external rewards failed to materialize.

Integrity is more than staying true to transactional values like honesty, fairness, and promise-keeping. It is about an *intactness* between what you do and the purposes you believe are most important for you to serve. Entrepreneur and CEO Ken Hakuta summed it up as he looked back on the ups and down of his incredibly exciting career as television host, toy importer, online herbal medicine distributor, and member of the board of several national American art organizations: "Success is something you will confront constantly in business. You will always be interpreting it against something, and that something should be your own goals and purpose." When Hakuta's last business (the Internet herbal company All-Herb) failed, he didn't veer from this philosophy. He kept his eyes out for the next opportunity that would "feel right" to him in terms of contribution.

Bill Oakley reported he felt his greatest success was *Mission Hill*, a cartoon series that was disappointingly nixed by the network after only two episodes. He and Weinstein had pushed the show to what they felt was a new creative edge, and they were proud of it. As Oakley summed up why he had such a strong sense of success about what was on external measures a failure, he pointed with self-mocking satisfaction to the fact that a small but dedicated cult following was still keeping the episodes alive on the Internet. In other words, what he valued as his own creative venture was significant and enduring on a measure that was important to him.

Self-Pacing

Enduring successes work hard, but they depart from the media profile of "never eat, never sleep." They have and are willing to go the extra mile, stay up to 2 A.M. on occasion, not as a lifestyle. **If you scratch beneath the surface of their ambitious schedule, you'll find that they build in repeated moments of rest and renewal.** Winston Churchill and Teddy Roosevelt, two incredibly energetic leaders, were perhaps the most famous "nappers" in history. Ken Blanchard, the one-minute-management guru, has been recommending a daily 10-minute "timeout" for years.

Today the timeouts are not just needed to renew physical energy but social and familial components in your life. One young manager was so unprepared for her personal mix of goals that she literally had to absent herself from the sight of her child in the mornings.

When her eighteen-month-old toddler woke early one day and caught her leaving the house, he clutched her leg and wailed. There she was, literally clawing him off her leg, when she suddenly caught a view of herself in the mirror. She came to the conclusion it was time to negotiate a new job assignment with less travel and more predictability.

There are any number of truisms about the time investment that high ambitions require: Rome wasn't built in a day. Good things come to those who wait. The story of the tortoise and the hare. High achievement and multiple targets take prolonged effort. To turn around a demoralized neighborhood in Los Angeles, Ueberroth not only had to sustain his own commitment over a long period of time, but he had to find a source of what is nicely called "patient capital" to see the renewal through. Obtaining these resources is a taxing process. You have to have stamina.

But it's important not to confuse stamina with walking on water and holding your breath. You get there by pacing yourself (and your investors) for the big picture. That means knowing what the real prize is, how to conserve energy, when to stop, when to rejuvenate. Psychologists Jim Loehr and Tony Schwartz, who've studied the ways in which people use energy, argue that most people have a natural cycle of energy depletion around 90 to 120 minutes.[9]

We saw many different ways in which our high achievers changed their pace each day. Some stopped to pick up their children from school and touch base for half an hour before returning to the final round of daily work. Others exercised at midday. Many were not so much nappers as rappers—they regularly took a turn around the workplace to talk to people on a more social level. The trick was in being able to start and stop these exercises. Some use an alarm clock, others limit the call from a child to five minutes—but they'll always take it to make sure the child knows they'll always be there in an emergency. **As we shall see, one of the primary techniques of pacing is the ability to put one thing down and switch focus not just to the next achievement task, but to another category of the good life that satisfies different emotions.**

Enjoying the Process

Attention to the Happiness category, rightly understood, is critical to this process. When we interviewed Ueberroth, who is notorious for his ability to work all hours, he punctuated our work with several moments of enjoyment. At one point, our interview was interrupted by the delivery of a big cooler. His assistant mischievously brought it into the room. A client had sent over a treasure chest of ice cream. The famously focused and strict Ueberroth surprised us by immediately breaking off his comments and inviting the whole office in to celebrate the gift. Such moments of pleasure enhance the ability to do good work and they don't always have to be quite so spectacular. As we closed our interview, Ueberroth again turned to appreciate his surroundings and noted a beautiful white orchid on his table that another client had sent him the day before to celebrate their business launch. It was a symbol of the achievement, but one could see he also was experiencing a genuine *pleasure* in the flower itself.

By contrast, some of the people we interviewed who were most dissatisfied with their current career profile had adopted the permanent view of Tom Sawyer, that happiness and enjoyment were reserved for the parts of their life that were outside of the grind of work. This approach depended on a very unrewarding stamina: making it through the work till they could cash out at thirty, or through the week so they could chill out on the weekend.

Family-Oriented

Enduring successes do not invest 20 years in their achievement to the critical neglect of their family. On the other hand, many surveys, including the interesting work of Jim Warner, show that a significant portion of high achievers report family problems.[10] **We did not feel ourselves to be in a position to "judge" the relative health of our interviewees' marriages or relationships with family. What we did do was ask them to describe their desires, satisfactions, and techniques for meeting these commitments in their life.** What we found was that all of them cared deeply about managing this process well as a part of their definition of enduring success. Family presented its own set of moving targets, and like other targets they valued, this one needed regular attention.

Fred Sievert, president of the giant New York Life Insurance Company, had one of the more challenging tests. As devoted father of five with a horrendous travel schedule, he felt that the daily household family dynamics were never quite enough to give each of his children individual attention. One day, when he was away on yet another business trip, a friend mentioned that he always took at least one trip a year alone with his child. Sievert picked up the phone and asked his wife to put his eldest on the plane that very day (it was school vacation and he was staying near Washington, D.C.). After that it became an unbreakable ritual. Over the past 19 years, Sievert has made at least one trip a year alone with each of his children. Their sharing of his work and his sharing of their lives has been an enduring feature of his—and their—life.

Concerned

James Bond enters the lair of Dr. No. Danger lurks everywhere, yet even his collar stays starched. Nothing gets to the born winners, right? Wrong.

Some people confuse the focus and expertise of the successful with a state of inhumanly "cool" detachment. **Enduring success is not based on a state that is devoid of anxiety and therefore sensitivity, however much wealth and freedom you may acquire.** People who enjoy this more complex and continuing kind of success are highly sensitive to their environment, and it's not always a happy experience. During our conversations, we paid attention to our interviewees' eye movements. Some of them literally scanned the door every 30 seconds to see what was going on outside, even as they focused on our questions. Their expressions displayed everything from avid curiosity to clear anxiety over what they saw. On a more meaningful scale, we found that acting on their concern for others was a critical and growing aspect of what our high achievers wanted to do with their lives. Many took on second careers after retirement to extend this aspect of their work.

Versatile

In the 1980s, Harvard Professor Howard Gardner revolutionized our understanding of intelligence, arguing that different types of accomplishment require different types of "smarts."[11] Emotional intelligence, for example, allowed people to develop social skills, make alliances, gain support for their ideas, and fulfill their desires to be of help. Without this, the smartest person in the world might as well go and live in a desert as try to become a leader of other people. Logical intelligence was more suited to other types of strategic and scientific problem solving. Physical intelligence was great for warfare and hunting. Why then, he asked, did we try to measure all these necessities of a successful life on a single IQ test?

Enduring successes have the rich palette of multiple intelligences that Gardner identified—emotional, logical, linguistic, spatial, even physical—and in addition, they have the ability to direct their skills and emotions to the right endeavors. (More on this later.) They do not use the same strengths for every situation. They know they cannot be winners every time on all fronts, so they choose to compete in areas that emphasize their strengths. And whether a business or a person, enduring successes invest in the continued development of their skills. Rather than be Johnny-one-notes, they stay mindful of needing to put more time into areas where they are weak or where they anticipate their future context will require new skills.

When you observe the versatility of outstanding leaders, it seems obviously important and uncontroversial—until you have to make the hard choice for yourself and your children of how much time you will invest in pursuing one skill above all others! How many people today start their youngsters on grueling reading or sports schedules out of fear they won't "make it" if they don't put in the maximum learning now? **But versatility, like the other factors cited here, is**

not enough on its own. You can look at multiple intelligences as one part of the richness of high achievement, or you can look at it as an impossible standard of Superman. Without a sense of limitation—what we call "just enough"—the high achievers cannot enjoy their success. The kid who scores perfectly on his SATs may become the closet bulemic because he's not also captain of the track team. The CEO who loses on the golf course throws a tantrum.

Humility

Nothing succeeds like success. High achievers are particularly vulnerable to internalizing this shopworn platitude and assuming that their strongest card is near to invincible. As psychologist John O'Neil notes in *The Paradox of Success*, becoming a success is a lot easier than being a success.[12]

Ancient Greek tragedy even had this pattern nailed down to a formula: The leader's high achievement leads to a certain arrogance stemming from pride (*hubris*), which leads to a tragic error in judgment (*hamartia*, literally missing the mark with an arrow) which ends in a certain downfall (*até*). These lessons are easily forgotten as people experience not only victory from their efforts but ego-stroking rewards for this success. The one-way, Excelsior! emphasis of celebrity success models reinforces this tendency. And yet some of the greatest victories amongst our interviewees were inspired by the insights they gained from a previous failure.

To approach changing targets with a positive view, you have to have a healthy sense of humility about yourself. **By humility, we don't necessarily mean self-effacing modesty, but rather an ability not to be thrown off by the distortions of a big ego.** You have to be able to take a dispassionate view of your strengths that takes into account your own limitations, whether they are imposed by your circumstances or a deeper part of your makeup.

That may seem counterintuitive in a culture that associates success so strongly with self-confidence and the power of positive thinking. Tony Robbins and cohorts may promise "unlimited power," but these paradigms can fail to take into account that a sense of personal limits is at the heart of leaders who truly appreciate the contributions that others make toward their own success, who understand that what worked yesterday may be wrong for today, or simply may not be as easy to exploit.

Jack Groppel has made a career of studying how and why successful people fail. He notes that one of the most common patterns he observed in his research was tripping up on a skill that comes most easily.[13] The more skillful, the bigger the trip. After a series of stunningly difficult moves, an Olympic gymnast loses the gold when she flubs the final dismount—probably the move she had done most frequently and that came most easily at this point in her career. After a hundred successful acquisitions, a CEO fails to check the details and places the company in jeopardy with one last gigantic takeover of an unsuspectedly weak business.

Our enduring successes correct for these dangers through an attitude of humility in the sense we are using it. With their general propensity for pragmatism, their humility cannot rely on a continual *reflection* about their own limits, it has to be a habitual thing. **It can be increased, however, by taking time out to ask who else contributed to the success I'm experiencing.** By feeling gratitude and voicing appreciation. We sometimes had trouble getting a person we admired to agree to be interviewed, not because he or she felt our topic was unimportant, but because they didn't want to be falsely portrayed as sounding their own horn. When asked what was most wrong with success today, the most frequent issue mentioned centered on CEOs who think they did it on their own—people who are only about raw ambition for themselves. Their response was notable, for these interviewees were people who generally cut a pretty wide swathe themselves. Fully aware of how much more could be done, they were not consumed by envy or greed to have it all, but were humble even as they looked back on their accomplishments with satisfaction.

Sharing

One of the most talented people we interviewed was in a slump when we first started our research. "Tracey" was a thirty-something PhD who had left academia for a career in media. After a series of memorable but far from perfect jobs at national magazines and magazine web sites, she found herself in the job from hell. An insecure boss had formed a consulting agreement with someone who knew next to nothing about marketing on the Internet. This person also happened to be the boss's good friend, and the budget for this task was literally 20 times what Tracey had estimated it should cost. The money would come out of Tracey's budget, over her strong objections. As the project moved forward, Tracey found herself in a completely inauthentic environment, starting with her coworkers' ideas of success. To them success was an exercise in egomania. Her words are chillingly familiar to many in large organizations:

> People succeed in corporations because they have this ideal mix of ambition and insensitivity and at the same time some sort of deep-rooted survival instinct that allows them to avoid speaking their mind. I don't know if they're conscious of it, or at what level they're playing politics. Ideally, they don't have a particular mind-set, they just reflect back what the prevailing thought is. Then everyone thinks, gosh they're *good!* I think these people are less ambitious and less creative. They feel whoever is in the position of power deserves to be there, so the only game is to try to figure out what's on their mind and give it back to them The whole idea that one gets hired for his or her perspective is complete baloney. Disagree and your boss feels betrayed. You're out because, whatever, you haven't found a way to flatter them, cajole them. You have to feed them their power.
>
> You can get hired for any number of reasons but you stay and survive and ultimately succeed by being able to present the leaders' opinions back to them in a way they find charming and appealing.

Tracey's time in this firm was completely unproductive. Not surprisingly, the division that had adopted this view went into a financial tailspin and eventually folded. When Tracey had tacitly bucked these rules and spoken up about what she thought would work or not, she found herself repeatedly sandbagged and ridiculed. Pills and sheer orneriness got her through, but barely. Her bitterness was painful, but the sentiment unfortunately rang true for many people's experience with people who have power. **Is success truly reserved for the selfish and those pitiful folks who figure they can eek a little bit out for themselves by going along with it? Why would a company buy into this much selfishness?** A key source of this dysfunctional behavior is a belief in the legitimacy of egoism, the same belief that fed the prevailing ethos of selfish greed in the 1990s beyond any scale recently seen in business.

Sometimes you best understand your values by seeing what they are not. Tracey's impression of her not-successful time at this job hinged on two deeply felt outrages: the lack of integrity to pursue the truth at this firm, and the incredible ethic of selfishness that drove its incompetence. What then, we asked Tracey, would form the basis of a successful organization in your mind? Her answer truly defined the attitude of integrity and sharing that we feel is an essential ideal of enduring success:

> You look for bosses who are the perfect parent, who can say, "I know we said this but then X thing happened, and you're still a good person." What I do consider one little success of my own is that I've always been able to create teams of people who were not bored to tears, who trusted me, who felt they could come to me with any concerns, who could run short, to the point meetings that were relatively entertaining. You know, environments where it wasn't a nightmare to come to work. And they did the best they could given the structure they were given to work in. So I always felt good about that, I did it the best I could given what I had to work with.

Tracey was a fighter. She didn't walk out without a backup plan. Eventually, she was able to negotiate her own severance, at which point she started over. After another stint with another publisher, she felt she'd finally learned enough about the market to give it a try on her own. Today, she is in the first stages of a very exciting new book packaging business, and we wish her well.

When Your Goals Are Not Adding Up, It's Time to Change Your Perspective

As we warned at the start, there is no standardized profile of enduring success. No perfect example of getting it all in perfect proportions. But then again, those examples either promise too much or leave you without resources when the going is tougher than you'd imagined. Now more than ever the world needs people like those profiled in this chapter: individuals who can work hard and well over the long-term without burning out their other lights. Each of our enduring successes has built his or her own library of accomplishments in multiple categories of life. Not all their attention was in equal proportions, but they addressed their many needs regularly over their entire lifetime. What can we learn from them beyond these important qualities of character and worldview outlined in this chapter?

People who build enduring success have many targets, and they are prepared to address each one every day. They have encountered serious conflict amongst their goals, just as Jane has and just as you may be. Although the personality traits and work habits discussed in this chapter were important factors in the successes we observed, it is this last—the ability to focus and switch focus on a variety of emotional and tactical playing fields—that was particularly important. It is also, we feel, understudied as a critical component of any pursuit of success that matters to you and others. As we argued in the last chapter, **the inability to manage this problem is at the heart of the stress so many people feel about their careers today.**

Jane's lack of clarity on how to pursue her various needs was fundamental to her sense of loss and confusion about her career. We asked her to take a step back and think through the satisfactions each of her goals represented. Without ranking them, what was the full picture and what was she trying to fulfill with success? Even a quick screening of her story through this lens was helpful to her. She told us that she had been trying to weight all her many goals equally and only between two categories: emotional happiness and financial achievement.

We suggested that instead of trying to make it all add up in one financial/emotional calculation, she start with a larger but more organized framework of possible emotional needs around success. As Jane held her own needs and accomplishments up to the light, a new sense of possibility began to emerge. Perhaps she could find a multi-part pattern to commit to without feeling she was simply losing out on something essential no matter which career she chose. Perhaps you can, too. But first Jane had to unlearn several assumptions about the nature of high achievement and contribution, starting with the ends these seemed to represent in her mind. She needed a framework for organizing this chaos and diagnosing the salient factors. We began to walk Jane's problem through the complex, kaleidoscope world of the four components of enduring success, and we will walk you through this same process beginning in the next chapter.

Quick Points: The Satisfactions of Just Enough Success

How to identify enduring success:

- Growing toward an ideal of excellence, but without frustration at partial victory.
- Striving toward aspects of life that you regard as necessary and meaningful.
- Contributing something valued by society and people you care about.
- Having an impact beyond your present influence on the lives of others.

(continued)

Personality and style traits shared by people who personify enduring success:

- Dynamic equanimity.
- Realism.
- Resilience.
- Integrity.
- Self-pacing.
- Enjoying the process.
- Family-oriented.
- Concerned.
- Versatile.
- Humility.
- Sharing.

Why enduring success is satisfying:

- Success enhances life, it is not the goal of life.
- You can work with punctuated response and achievement, not over-the-top commitment.
- You can be realistic about your energy, skills, and needs.
- You can bring others into your life with concern.
- You create enjoyment and satisfaction as you go through life.

PART TWO

THE KALEIDOSCOPE STRATEGY

Chapter 4

Your Success Profile

Whatever you cannot understand you cannot possess.
—Goethe

Time and again, as we interviewed people who are by any measure models of enduring success, we found that they naturally honored and expressed many diverse facets of themselves and their lives—beyond their money-making business selves. Instead of creating more conflicting and confusing targets, this action actually *transformed* those targets into pieces of an ever-changing and satisfying life pattern of success. Instead of being an oppressive necessity, their work occupied a positive but not exclusive position in their lives.

Jane also entertained a multifaceted intuition of her ideal life. It was rich with moral and aesthetic possibilities, but the various pieces were so unformed that she could not find any *actionable* focus for work. For her, the good worklife was beginning to look like Tom Sawyer's worldview—something you are obliged to do and not part of the fabric of human expressiveness.

The difference between Jane and our more seasoned high achievers was not just in finding a vocation that engaged their real self, but in the way in which they were able to engage work in the larger picture of their lives. As Jane struggled with her plans, it was as if she was looking into the wrong end of a telescope. She would fix on one action in her mind and then test it against the whole field of her desires. Not surprisingly, no job or activity held up to this severe test. She was searching to immobilize all the moving targets. First, she needed to go deeper into the basic desires driving these dissatisfactions, and then bring them into some kind of order.

The Four Satisfactions of Enduring Success

In the *Nicomachean Ethics,* Aristotle notes that no one can really understand or describe the ultimate embodiment of the Good, but that we are quite capable of identifying "the many desired ends that make up the good life." In line with our own quest for the "Good," we asked what people were seeking when they speak of success. As we studied the almost limitless variety of specific experiences and benchmarks people describe, a larger, more generalized pattern emerged. Whether they are Jane, Tracey, Peter Ueberroth, Clint Eastwood, Rosie Eduardo, or Donald Trump, time and again they are alluding to satisfactions in a core set of four categories that we have labeled Happiness, Achievement, Significance, and Legacy. For example:

- Tracey, the publishing executive who lost her job for speaking up, wanted time to read books and do what she wanted (Happiness), she wanted to build a great business (Achievement), she also wanted to be recognized for creating something valuable for others (Significance). Pushed further, she certainly hopes the books she produces will outlast her company and create a literary inheritance of some sort (Legacy).

- When writer-producer Bill Oakley reflects on the alternative success of *Mission Hill,* he touches on a combination of satisfactions around setting a new standard in creative cartoons (Achievement), his enjoyment of the project despite its hard work (Happiness), pride that a select group of cartoon mavens have valued the few episodes that did air (Significance), and satisfaction that this achievement will remain over time to set new standards against which other cartoons will be measured (Legacy).

- The same set of factors colored Peter Ueberroth's interpretation of what the Los Angeles Olympics accomplished. He took on an incredibly difficult project, fraught with problems, and managed not only to pull it off but to put the games on a better financial footing than ever before (Achievement); the endeavor had great national and international value (Significance); he regularly experienced pleasure in the process despite his legendarily strict temperament (Happiness); and the Legacy of this event remains as a standard for measuring the diplomatic, civic, athletic, and financial success of future games.

- In *Trump: The Art of the Deal*, The Donald writes of his enormous *pleasure* in deal making (Happiness), work which represents problem solving, fame, recognition, money, power (Achievement), family, setting a new architectural standard (Legacy), rebuilding a skating rink for the city of New York, and scoring one for the little guy by tweaking New York's establishment (Significance). Although he is a controversial figure and not everyone would agree with his style, the generic set of "goods" in this portrait are not unlike Oakley's or Ueberroth's.

These same four expressions of satisfaction seem to drive most people's idea of what they seek from success—however well they execute the process. Our four categories organize the baseline set of "desired ends" for success, as it were, and we've tried to pin down the essential differences of each category in a simple set of definitions:

1. *Happiness:* Feelings of pleasure or contentment in and about your life.
2. *Achievement:* Accomplishments that compare favorably against similar goals others have strived for.
3. *Significance:* A positive impact on people you care about.
4. *Legacy:* Establishing your values or accomplishments in ways that help others find future success.

These four categories (as shown in Figure 4.1) form the basic structure of what people are trying to establish about themselves through the pursuit and enjoyment of success. They are not just theoretical goals, but the living out of deeply felt emotional needs.

Take away any one and the resultant success profile seems to have something essential missing. Who would consider themselves a success, for example, if they were unable to feel pleasure? How often do you encounter successful people who don't want to believe that others

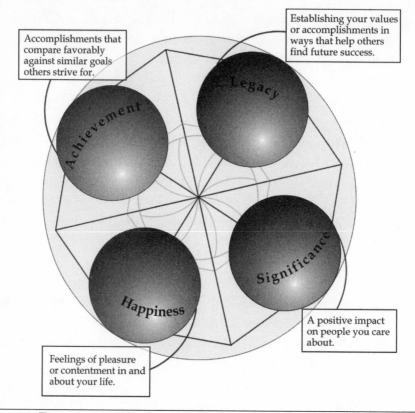

Accomplishments that compare favorably against similar goals others strive for.

Establishing your values or accomplishments in ways that help others find future success.

A positive impact on people you care about.

Feelings of pleasure or contentment in and about your life.

Figure 4.1   The four satisfactions of enduring success.

admire and value them? We're familiar with the idea that most successful people want to be Achievers, but scratch beneath the surface and you'll find that even the most driven contenders, like our friends at the world's greatest corporations and universities, also *want* to be of Significance, experience Happiness, and leave a Legacy in their lives. When they evaluate other Achievers who have not exhibited these traits, they have reservations. Was that really success?

Sorting Your Conflicts

Anyone who takes these four elements seriously quickly becomes aware of how complicated they can be. Moving targets don't always fit neatly in just one of the categories. Because activities in pursuit of these goals are often partially aligned with other forms of satisfaction, most people do not realize how inherently *different* the categories are.

The distinctions between types helps sort the chaos of your conflicting impulses. **Once you understand the basic nature of your aspiration, you can more easily determine what you should go for and what you need to accomplish to capture it in real time.** Not only do you need to know what the components look like, you need to understand the emotional skills that drive their accomplishment. Certain cognitive perspectives are also important, such as time frame and relational orientations. **These skills are the equivalent of success intelligence and are what particularly interested us in our research.**

As a quick memnonic throughout these chapters you might want to think of the four categories as actions:

1. Happiness = Enjoying
2. Achievement = Winning
3. Significance = Counting (to others)
4. Legacy = Extending

Madonna: An Interesting Test of the Model

In 2003, just as the Iraq War was heating up, we saw these conflicts in, of all places, the launching and subsequent withdrawal from release of a video by Madonna that featured images that could be read as antimilitary.

Madonna is a brand, an artist known for making strong statements through her music and performance. She clearly cares about Achievement, and works incredibly long hours despite having enough money to retire very comfortably. She also pursues Significance, creating new musical styles and ideas that others value as expressing something of importance in the culture. In this case, however, it appeared her particular stand was on the wrong side of that last goal, and she took her video off the market. Or did she withdraw the release as a mere publicity stunt? Maybe. But if you believed her words, she was facing a conflict between the target of putting out a new hit song and the target of being valued positively for something larger than the music by those she cared about—her fans. It wasn't just about music hits, it was about her views on her country, her identity as a citizen. These two personas created a conflict between Achievement and Significance, and failure on the latter would seriously jeopardize her continued frustration to establish a real legacy of music leadership. (You might even argue that her pursuit of pleasure—Happiness—is the target that regularly frustrates her chance of hitting the others.)

Though we are not psychologists and can't back up our findings with new evidence of a neurological basis for these drives, we think of these categories as inherent, deep attractions to goals that are driven by fundamental emotional needs. As a little mind test of your own, try leaving one category out of your idea of the good life and see if it holds up to a standard of achieving, enjoying, contributing, transcending the moment. **If you are ready to address these four in all their richness and complexity, you are preparing yourself for a transformation of success—from a disappointing exercise in getting never enough to the fulfillment of some of your deepest human desires.**

As we were sifting through our research, a metaphor surfaced that we felt perfectly crystallized the always-changing complexity of filling these four success categories with activities and accomplishments: the kaleidoscope.

The Kaleidoscope Strategy

Remember the old-fashioned kaleidoscope that you hold up to the light? It is a simple mechanical device with a lens and a long tube, at the bottom of which are four separate chambers in which pieces of colored glass are sandwiched. By turning the end of the tube, or merely letting the force of gravity take over, the glass pieces shift in relation to one another, forming an ever-changing pattern. This picture is formed not just by the pieces themselves, but by mirrors that create a more complex design out of the reflected images of the entire set of "chips." In reality, the pieces are still separate, but the instrument makes it possible to see a unique picture of the whole. Its beauty comes from the variety and the symmetry.

You twist the end of the kaleidoscope until you fix on a pattern you find particularly pleasing . . . and just as you try to show it to others, it shifts out of place. Only you have seen this pattern. Although the patterns you discern are inherently unstable, changed through outside forces or your own movements, the pieces have a *lasting* ability to provide ongoing satisfaction as they take their place within a new arrangement.

Now imagine a slightly different kind of kaleidoscope, an instrument that is your own life vision. This kaleidoscope also has four chambers—Happiness, Achievement, Significance, and Legacy—and you can *add* brilliant glass pieces (goals sought and fulfilled) of your own creation over a lifetime, making your unique pattern richer. The mirrors are the external reflections of these accomplishments, and create their own distortions and enhancements of your activities. At the same time, the overall structure of the tube, your life boundaries, delineates the possibilities and limitations of success. Coherency is gained at the expense of infinite vistas. You cannot accommodate an infinite number of glass pieces in your life, so those you do choose become more valuable and meaningful in the overall pattern. It is yours.

This is the skill we discovered in our research: **People who achieve the qualities of enduring success have constructed a kaleidoscope strategy to structure their success aspirations.** Not only are they continually creating new chips in each of the four categories, they structure their actions in such a way that there is room for every color and pleasing proportionality in the picture as a whole. Whether intuitively or deliberately, they have constructed a framework that allows them to sift through the confusion of moving targets and select those that will bring them more lasting rewards.

When you envision your life as a kaleidoscope, it quickly becomes clear that variety is a virtue. If you just keep trying to add more and more chips of the same color, you will soon create a monochromatic and uninteresting picture of your life. And if you add all of your chips to just one or two chambers, you will create a lopsided pattern that is vulnerable to sudden shifts. On the other hand, a careful eye and a skilled hand can create a multifaceted set of shifting patterns, formed out of many primary and secondary points of brilliance that you may once have passed over in pursuit of the absolute best. **The key is in striking a satisfying relationship between all the pieces.** This is the strategic challenge we address in the rest of the book.

The kaleidoscope strategy is by nature limiting, but ultimately it is freeing. *You* can decisively choose "just enough" pieces—you're not limited to just one, and you can't pick *every* one—from the infinite choices that could make up your pattern of success. It gives you a structure for holding your competing commitments separate and going after each one with energy, knowing that you are creating a pleasing relation among them.

How will you approach your idea of long-term enduring success in a way that gets you to these future goals but energizes you *now and for the long haul?* How will you trace a journey that gives satisfaction on many levels every day, yet creates enough extra energy to help you achieve long-term goals? How will you choose goals that give lasting satisfaction and yet allow you to put them down? You can start right now, by creating your personal success profile.

What's Your Success Profile?

To understand your own beliefs about what real success is, you need to get your bearings: What is it you *really* want when you think of success? When we spoke to our interviewees, we used the four categories of enduring success as a starting point, and found that it stimulated a great deal of new thought.

Jane, for example, began to break the logjam she'd created by seeking the answers in one activity "out there." (In psychological lingo, she was breaking through her pattern of "premature cognitive narrowing," which was creating such a narrow view of the problem that it was causing her to miss alternatives. It was hard for her to see this narrowness because her dreams were just the opposite—drawn from a landscape of infinite choice.) We encouraged her to step back and simply be open to the idea that she might be seeking four *distinct* and noninterchangeable kinds of satisfaction. Could she think of any individual examples where she'd already "scored" on one category?

This new perspective had a remarkable effect. Whereas before she had been channeling everything in one narrow stream, now suddenly she was making new connections between her situation and possible alternatives. She began to accept the idea that church music, for example, should be framed primarily as an exercise in significance, and not a platform for achievement, with all its competitive and financial associations. Making room for this at a satisfactory level, however, would mean recasting the terms of work and not going for the top position there as well. Few heads of companies are also on tap twice a week for choir practice, but many people find great joy in their achievements at every level of a firm. (Later in this book, we'll discuss how to make this actionable.)

Exercise 1: Establish a Baseline

You can use the kaleidoscope framework to order your own reflections and jumpstart your ideas.

Sketch Out Your Framework

First, on a piece of paper, draw a quick sketch of four intersecting circles to represent the four chambers, and label them Achievement, Happiness, Significance, and Legacy.

Then, in each circle, write the following list:

- Work.
- Family.

- Self.
- Community.

This will enable you to do a full inventory of the mix of activities and how they fall in the context of each major domain of your life (see Figure 4.2).

Then quickly jot down whatever comes to mind as some examples of your successes or great satisfactions. This is not a test! You do not have to complete every bullet in every circle—it's just a quick sketch of your beliefs about yourself, not the full picture. Don't spend time worrying whether you should put a particular target next to a particular bullet item—just work with your first impulses. Use a pencil so

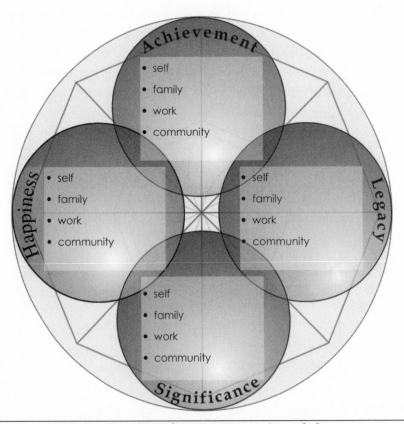

Figure 4.2   Your four successes: A worksheet.

you can change things around later. You can also refer back to Figure 4.2 for the precise definitions of each category.

If you have trouble getting started, think of each circle as capturing a certain kind of *accomplishment* that gives a certain kind of *satisfaction* because it partially answers a certain kind of *need* that you feel is important. For example, you may feel that graduating from college was a major achievement in your life. An education is a benchmark need in your overall career plans and something you will value for your whole life. It represents mastery of new intelligence skills. You had to be competitively successful to get there and get the grades. You felt satisfaction when you succeeded. So you would write college in your Achievement chamber, next to your work bullet.

But what if college represents other things for you? Significance in your family life, for example, because your parents or spouse really valued what you were doing. In this case, you might also put college in your Significance chamber, next to the family bullet.

The point is not to compulsively divide your life into little circles and lists. Rather, it is to provide you with a *baseline* of what has satisfied you and *the basic shape of that satisfaction as indicated by where it falls in your profile of needs and accomplishments.* Depending on your age, you might even want to fill out framework profiles for several periods in your life. Did you want the same things at age forty as you did at twenty? Will you want the same things at sixty? At eighty-five? Note how age changes the overall pattern of chips you placed in each picture.

Key Diagnostics

Now, metaphorically speaking, you can hold your kaleidoscope up to the light. Look at it objectively. What do you see in the overall picture? Chances are, you've already had important accomplishments in the four sectors of success, but probably at disproportionate levels.

Think about the following key diagnostics:

- *How integrated is your profile?* Are some of the domains fairly empty? Others too full? Is each "realm" of your identity—work, family, self, community—a depository of only one satisfaction, or is there a broader basis for success in each of these areas?

- *How varied is your profile?* Where are most of your episodes of success, your greatest satisfactions so far? Where do you see the holes? The obsessions? Are the chambers and realms enlarging or repeating the same thing over and over?

- *What have you learned about what you actually do?* Where is your time going? How does it speak to what you really want from success?

Simply by identifying where your activities are located on the framework, and asking yourself why, you gain immediate insight into what you are seeking and getting from your efforts to be successful in work and life. In the following chapters, we'll walk you through ways to think about enlarging but not maximizing your range of possible actions within each of the four chambers, and we'll continue to re-fine the skills for getting there. *Just Enough* is about the dynamics of complex choice, and first you have to have a firm idea of what it is you are choosing.

Exercise 2: What Is Your Ideal Picture?

You'll probably notice some thin spots in the profile. Perhaps you have been working too hard to make a life, or you've been having too much fun to get your career started. Like Jane, your work activities may have pushed certain other categories out to the margins of your life, or even completely out of the picture. What if you could redis-tribute time and energies so as to have chips in each chamber without having to stretch the universe to accommodate a 48-hour day?

Sketch Out Your Framework

To channel your efforts effectively and creatively toward what you really seek from success for your work, for your life, for your family, and for your community, it's critical to test your profile against your idealized view of yourself. **What do you want your profile of accomplishments in each of the four categories to look like tomorrow, next month, over a lifetime?**

To begin, draw a new set of intersecting circles, label them in the same way, and add the bullet lists.

Then choose at least one example in each category of something you would have to accomplish to feel that your efforts in life were both successful and worth it. Some people have very specific ideal goals: to reach the moon, to reinvent the operating platform on PCs. Your ideals might be less developed. You might feel that the only achievement that would feel like a real *success* is one in which you were allowed to exercise your own judgment and stretch further than you'd ever thought possible.

The challenge aspects of achievement are very high in this statement. Sharpen the picture by asking:

- What is the most positive challenge you hope to master.
- What is the ideal achievement most like it that you'd like to see in your life?

For Willy Loman, in Arthur Miller's play *Death of a Salesman*, the ideal achievement was to be honored and respected by all the other salesmen on the train from New Haven to Boston, to be "well-liked." But this dream had no further content: He couldn't really fill in the precise challenges of sales or marriage, which made him both pathetic and tragic at the same time. On this basis, he could never achieve his dreams. You have to be concrete.

For a jumpstart, try envisioning what your life would be like with some of the circles permanently empty. You'll probably find yourself quickly filling things in.

Key Diagnostics

Now hold your ideal kaleidoscope up to the light and compare it to the first picture of where you seem to be now:

- Are you *really* willing to give up happiness for the sake of achievement, or does your ideal suggest you are you searching for a mix of the two in some proportion?

- Can you foresee a time when it would be unacceptable if nothing of your values and accomplishments were to last beyond your own presence, not even in the hearts of those you care about?

- Would you consider it a success to walk away with lots of money but no record of delivered value for others?

Exercise 3: An Organizational Success Profile

As the leader of an organization, you can also create a kaleidoscope profile for your company or your work unit to understand the nature of what you are really trying to achieve in a successful business. This is a terrific exercise to conduct in private or to discuss as a team. Many companies have difficulty describing a vision that is both broad enough to encompass the many stakeholders they are committed to and specific enough to generate real energy and commitment from employees to succeed at their goals. Choosing volume over tone, they seize on a vision of grandiosity—We will paintball the world!—and then try to motivate success from their employees with a single idea: Win!

No wonder employees go in undesired directions, suffer stress, become deceived into thinking they are above the rules, get burned out. They have no shared grounding for their pursuit of success. One manager in such a position confidently described to us why success was no problem to him: "It's simple," he said. "Just focus on winning." We explained the four chambers and asked him to fill out his profile of his company's values. Its idea of an important achievement? Winning! What made it significant? Winning! What made him most happy about his company? Winning! What would be his legacy? That he won!

One senior executive in our class at Harvard noted that while all the CEOs in the room wanted the four categories for themselves, in hiring and promoting they would probably favor the person who was most fixated on Achievement. Many agreed—but then noted they were *not* exercising good leadership in doing so. We believe that organizations have a responsibility to attend to all four categories of success, to have a well-thought-out profile in each chamber, and to structure their activities so that everyone in the company finds their job a significant part of their platform for building enduring success. Leaders carry the special responsibility as keepers of the categories— they will determine the mix that fills each component of an organization's vision of ultimate success.

Kaleidoscope Approaches to the Organization's Strategic Objectives

Each of the success categories is easily extended to order the activities and strategic objectives of a firm. Here is one short-list of approaches:

- In what broad areas will we find a satisfying area in which to compete (Achievement)?
- Whom does the organization care for and thus seek to deliver things of value to that group (Significance)?
- What pleasures and contentments are built into the way people work, compete, participate in community (Happiness)?
- What platform for future success (financial, technological, national success) will the company want to create (Legacy)?

Leaders who can make clear why they chose to complete the chambers as they did, and in what way those choices express their organization's unique core, will have a vision that is organized around a fuller set of "desired ends." Communicating this picture is a powerful exercise in what Stephen Carter has seen as one of the central duties of the leader: **Telling people where you're going, why they are doing it, and why it is worthwhile to put in all that effort.** You can simply promise a bonus *or* you can ignite the deeper dignity and desires of the people in your organization. The kaleido-scope framework will help you, as a leader, frame the answers in a way that appeals to all four basic desires driving employees' success aspirations.

Leaders who not only have a vision about all four categories but who can live out specific examples that are consistent create a power-ful platform for leadership. They build a good foundation for strategic clarity, organize the accomplishment of resources, and shape what others will value and hold the company to accomplishing. The stan-dard of "winning" will not clarify all these important functions.

Tactical Benefits

There are also important tactical benefits in this exercise. The suc-cess profile is at heart a critical overlay to the arrangement of time and energy—both of which are pragmatic tools for success. **Work teams that can explore the economic or social logic they share around the four chambers can begin to develop a much tighter sense of shared values. This creates not only trust but quick re-sponses when alternatives are there to be taken advantage of—or not.** Such discussions also help companies draw important distinc-tions about where and why certain activities that are critical to an individual's idea of the good life should *not* be sought in corporate activities—and then make sure there is space for employees to pur-sue these things privately. Nothing is more cynical than the com-pany that stresses volunteer community work as one criteria for advancement and then never leaves time for individuals to do any-thing more than get themselves listed on a board.

Discerning the Domains of Success

Many people use the domains of life—family, work, community, leisure—as their main sorting mechanism for success. If you view the picture of your entire set of activities through the lens of the four cat-egories, you will probably find that certain domains fall into certain

categories more easily: work into Achievement, family into Significance, leisure into Happiness, and your reputation or your financial
portfolio into Legacy. Like the emphasis in the Young Presidents'
Organization on Self, Family, and Work, each of these domains provides a basic opportunity for balancing out your four categories of
need in the face of pressures to achieve.

On the other hand, any one activity whose primary boundaries
seemed ringed by a specific success category could be enormously en-
riched through the inclusion of all four components. For example,
consider tennis. For many people (except those on the U.S. Open cir-
cuit or the neighbors you don't particularly want to play with), tennis
falls squarely into the Happiness category. It represents a moment of
enjoyment, Tom Sawyer's idea of play. But what makes for a truly satisfying game of tennis? This list usually includes *improvement:* mastering new skills and competing against an external measure of
competency—the Achievement component. Tennis is also more fun
if you play the game in way that gives value to the other people playing—Significance. It's a social activity, and to make it successful requires a certain degree of empathy and caring about the welfare of the
group. If you always throw a fit when you miss a shot, or fail to get to
the court on time because this is *your time,* your tennis will ultimately
be less of an enduring success (if only because it will get harder and
harder to find partners willing to meet you at the court!).

Where does Legacy fit into a leisure activity even if you're not a
world-class player holding some record? Drawing on our definition of
Legacy, to create something that will build others' success, you
might ask yourself what you could do to create a legacy around your
love of tennis that will outlast your game. Take a look at most community courts and you'll find volunteers ensuring the facilities are
kept up, organizing the youth programs so the next generation of
tennis players grows to fruition. You don't have to see Legacy as a
passive result of your brilliancy at tennis, but by ensuring that your
love of the game continues for others you'll find tennis a more enduring experience in your life. Watch out, however, if your child's
tennis skills become *your* achievement!

As we compared successes among people of different age groups, talents, and opportunities, we continually observed the development and fulfillment of the four categories of success. No one of our enduring successes stayed stuck in one box; but conversely, we saw many high achievers in business and education who were ruining their lives by feeling that the only path to success was to dedicate themselves to one category, whether or not the rest followed. In a way they were cheating themselves, their families, and society. Thus, the single most critical skill for enduring success is the ability to switch your attention from one category of desire to another in a way that leads to new chips in another component.

The Ability to Switch and Link

We are such an intense and yet freewheeling, shoot-from-the-hip culture that deliberate change of attention almost seems counterintuitive to successful behavior. If Happiness, Achievement, Significance, and Legacy are to be the minimal set of categories of success that lead to lasting sense of accomplishment and a good life, and if these components need to be operative in every domain of your life—family, work, friendship, community—why don't people who pursue success behave like deer caught in the headlights, overwhelmed by the sheer brilliance of their own ambitions? If success is about realizing the extraordinary, how do you handle four conflicting goals? You cannot maximize two things, never mind four. What, then, helps people finesse high achievement within these parameters?

In later chapters, we will strongly argue against the idea that these goals can be separated into 10- or 20-year segments in your life. Some people like the formula "learn, earn, and return"—hoping to give something back after they've achieved enough. Others like the idea of half-time or end-game as a way of expressing their change of focus from achievement to giving. **While the sentiment of sharing and contribution is critical to enduring success, you need to anticipate and practice it at every stage in your life.** Legacies can be left by high school students. Even the hardest-working twenty-something needs to rest and recuperate. And no business can truly achieve lasting greatness without delivering something of positive value to others.

Success requires the equivalent of Darwin's multilevel selection theory: You have to select well to survive, but simple sequencing of your focus won't do it. What will get you there is a reasoned sense of enough, a rational facility that seems to be underappreciated or even actively resisted in today's world of the infinite more. In the next chapters, we address the art of choosing and switching among the components of success, starting with the key assumptions that will get in your way, and moving on to a deeper understanding of the factors driving each of the four categories. Knowing how these work will help you clarify your goals in a way that is more likely to gain you the emotional satisfactions you seek from success, and make the contributions that others depend on.

Going Deeper—Sharing Your Profile with Others

We can't overemphasize how important it is just to take a hard look at your actual success profile and the activities that fill each category. You can't subcontract the four chambers in your life: You have to experience them to gain satisfaction, to really feel you're doing enough.

A recent anecdote about President Bush's newly appointed campaign finance head brought home the power of hands-on involvement in the categories. Mercer Reynolds is used to thinking big about raising money for Bush, having taken in over $600 million in the last campaign. Let's assume that he sees his fund-raising clearly as an Achievement, but also an act of Significance—that it is his way of serving his country. He could think he'd fulfilled his Significance goals in the dollars raised. Instead, he was out ringing a bell in a Salvation Army Santa Suit at Christmas, spending hours to raise a few dollars in front of a grocery store. When asked why he did it, he told a colleague, "It felt satisfying."[1]

If you want to deepen the inquiry into your aspirations even further, try discussing your profile with your spouse, a close friend, or your child. What does your family think? How do they fill out their own profile? Many parents pass on practical tips for success to their kids but never have a real discussion of the meaning and values behind their own personal moments of victory—or their children's. Several wealthy people told us they'd consider their life a success if their kids were happy. We were fairly sure their kids had a larger vision of their future than that and if they didn't, wouldn't their parents be sad!

The wealthy young "trustafarians" we've met who are able to buy toys and prestige but who *can't* find an Achievement that is theirs and good enough usually find little satisfaction in their lives. We interviewed one fourth-generation scion who, after thinking about the four chambers, noted that he'd unconsciously challenged himself all his life in certain areas of the arts and philanthropy precisely because it allowed him to make his own mark in some area of competitive achievement. (In fact, he had shown great leadership in these fields.) His family's wealth had set the financial bar so high that almost no one could achieve it today—either you found an alternative or you simply felt empty in this category of achieving an *important* win. You could envy or pity his situation. We admired his ability to use his talents and opportunities for such good purposes that he deeply cared about. But in the end he had to find his own proportioned profile of Achievement, Happiness, Significance, and Legacy—just the way everyone else does.

Rules for Strict Accounting

Be careful. One of the great temptations is to confuse a satisfaction with the ingredients that led to that satisfaction. You may, for example, recall the pleasure you got from your first bonus and assume that money from a job well done is a core satisfaction. But unless you identify your underlying emotional needs and how you think they are fulfilled by money (or not), these external rewards are like a sword—they can cut both ways, for good or ill. You may find that at some point in your career, your greatest satisfaction will come from an activity that brings less rather than more money. You may feel great about winning, but some satisfactions—like being there for others—are not gained by dominance and mastery.

Many people's success goals are simply hopes—a form of wishful thinking for a way to ward off things that are out of your control. Their search for satisfaction stays stuck on the drive for control, which may put them at odds with the full spectrum of what they conventionally think of as success. Money buys health care and is important. But what is enough money? How many wealthy families have ever been able to ward off a terminal disease? The answer is not necessarily to reject outward symbols of success like money, or your need to satisfy practical matters of financial need, but to find more precise measures of what these goals actually deliver. **Ask yourself where your expectations about money and power fit into the four chambers, and how having money might satisfy or be irrelevant to the satisfaction of deeper, more specific desires.**

It's an easy confusion. Our preliminary survey of 90 executives revealed that their most frequent measures of success—after "making a difference in the world"—were money (coded as "financial success"), happiness, family, business health, and status in the community. For many, these achievements are supposed to fulfill a baseline of goals, but they do not fully articulate the underlying *desires* these goals are supposed to fulfill. Left unexamined, it's only a small step from such goals to measuring your success solely by how much money is made. If you never know what you really seek and why, you'll never be able to appreciate what you get. Nothing will be enough.

When we probed the generalized success goals in depth in our interviews, we discovered that typical success measures served very different purposes for business people. As results-oriented creatures with a bias for action, they were not prone to reflection on the deeper meaning that their end results carried for them. (In fact, it was a proof of the value of this model that as we walked them through the four categories and pressed them to explore how they had achieved in each one, a number of people had so many new insights into their sense of self and purpose that they asked for a second interview.) One person sees money as the logical symbol of achievement. Another views money as the means to pleasure or freedom from having to do what someone else tells you. Some think of money as a general talisman against *anything* bad. Money can stand for many ends, taking you all around the four circles of success. Starting as the result of Achievement, it can morph into being a resource within your Significance category—a means to doing things valued by others, like giving to charity. But what satisfaction does *that* give? And how about the Legacy of financial resources you create with your money? And the Happiness from that Porsche? Once you see the place of money in all your categories, financial goals can be tailored to experience just enough.

Know Your Success Profile

What are each of the four satisfactions about for *you?* What category do your successes best fall into? What did they mean at the time and what do they mean to you now?

Say you reach the position of president of the community soccer league. Are you enjoying this as a way of connecting with the interests of others, which brings a deeply satisfying sense of belonging, or for having special power by reasons of being regarded as the leading "good person" in the community? Or because you just love organizing things your way and were miserable watching the whole thing get botched up in the past? Depending on what you seek and take satisfaction from in an event, the same activity falls into different circles. If it gives you multiple satisfactions, the chips in your kaleidoscope have an even richer pattern of their own.

It's important to alert yourself to your own satisfactions—not only to see the pattern that is larger than the many small events that catch you up each day, but in order to make your specific commitments positive and feeling essentially right. What follows this step is deep, authentic confidence, not the phony optimism and image of self-esteem that can be bottled in a fashion ad or positive-thinking course. When people lose touch with the actual feelings they are satisfying in an event, the "dark shadows" take over: their reasons for seeking success become unknown, mysterious, out of control. You work at a crazy pace for three days running, and at the end simultaneously feel miserable and exhilarated. Your very next activity could either compound the exhilaration or prolong your bondage to misery.

Remember: The key point of conducting this initial inventory is to surface a menu of underlying satisfactions you attach to success, as seen in the examination of your actual experience so far. This will create a general picture of your overall "portfolio" of satisfactions as it has worked in real time. This is a comprehensive picture, but it's not quite complete. Right now, it's only an indicator of the general landscape of targets you're aiming at and have hit. The underlying foundations of your pattern—essentially, your self-definition—are what help carry you through the complexities that every life choice presents. We will look at these in the next chapter.

Quick Points: Your Success Profile

Understanding these four categories, and creating a balance between them, invites enduring success:

- *Happiness:* Feelings of pleasure or contentment in and about your life.
- *Achievement:* Accomplishments that compare favorably against similar goals others have strived for.
- *Significance:* A positive impact on people you care about.
- *Legacy:* Establishing your values or accomplishments in ways that help others find future success.

Success is *not* satisfying when:

- Achievement is equated with work.
- Significance is only for family and community.

(continued)

- Happiness is confined to leisure and a selfish pleasure.
- Legacy is defined as the things that remain when we are gone simply because they were big enough to last.

Key points of the kaleidoscope strategy:

- Knowing the possibilities and limitations of each success category frees you to choose your targets.
- Structuring your success aspirations helps create satisfying relationships between all four success categories.
- Variety is a virtue.

Chapter 5

Who Are You? And
Why Are You Doing That?

I, who for the time have staked my all on being a psychologist,
am mortified if others know much more psychology than I. But I
am contented to wallow in the grossest ignorance of Greek. . . .
So our self-feeling in this world depends entirely on what we
back ourselves to be and do.

—William James

It seems so simple. When we tell people about the landscape of
moving targets, and share our conclusions that there are really four
basic components most people want from success, they tend to
react in a gratifyingly engaged way. They want to understand what
these categories are, and with great excitement they draw connections about how their own lives fall into each category. The strategy of the kaleidoscope seems to be equally accessible: The idea of
ordering the fragments of your dreams and accomplishments in a
unified framework with a visible pattern begins to provide more
occasions for pleasure and self-correction. These insights alone
can be extremely influential, especially when you discuss them
with those you care about. We've held many fascinating discussions with executives and spouses and friends, simply trading our
version of our patterns, discussing what Achievement means and
doesn't mean to us, and talking about how important happiness is
and where we find it.

Yet, it is possible to go much further with these frameworks, and
we believe that the inspiring goal of making enduring choices in a
world of moving targets requires us to do so. At this point, however,

the salient factors begin to pile up and the picture begins to become more complex. If you try to take it all in as one thought, or run through it at the rapid-fire pace we sometimes require of people in our executive programs, the concepts begin to impinge on each other. People raised on the model of books that offer "seven simple steps" or "one big concept" impatiently ask us why we can't just make it simpler. Why so many factors?

The Case for Complexity—And for Taking It a Step at a Time

Our answer is that nothing in our research indicated that people had simple expectations from what they regarded as real success. Moreover, their inability to understand the full dynamics of complex choice in relation to success goals is what keeps them from achieving the kind of lasting and more balanced success we saw in the people profiled in this book. **Although it might be seductive to adopt a simpler motivational framework to secure an easy early sense of victory, we are more interested in success for the long run, consistent with our complex self, social values, and ideas of the good life.** In warfare, you can motivate intense soldiery by appealing to fear and fight. This has been the standard emotional formula of most success books: Pump up the passion, get out there and fight! But what about the next step? Fear and fight do not build a lasting peace, and at their extreme they can even cause an army to rout, leaving it open to enemy attack. Does worry over market forces help you understand how to motivate creative solutions?

People *are* complicated. Success doesn't run in a straight line from effort to happiness. Once you have your baseline profile, as outlined in the last chapter, you have a good starting place for understanding where your satisfactions lie. The next step is to look more deeply into how this process works given the complexity of your human self. **As you make leaps and linkages between the success categories in order to create the ever-changing vision you see in** the kaleidoscope, the components of your self-definition determine whether these actions will be not only sufficiently challenging and satisfying, but doable.

Drawing on Your Self-Definitions for Success

As Jane discovered, the fuller your self-identity, the more complex this process becomes. We were profoundly impressed with those interviewees who had set their success course not only by the dictum "to thine own self be true," but to thine own self in its many splendid forms. This idea is not new. Socrates, for example, received a similar dictum from the Delphi Oracle: Know Thyself. On the other hand, any serious intention to draw on the self to make the right choices about success raises its own dilemmas. Many people know it's not really success unless it feels right to you, but success places the self in a permanent state of change and transformation. Which self is the baseline to which you will remain true? If, like Jane, you've already done a good job cultivating your capabilities in several areas, then you know the feeling of having presented yourself with more options than you may actually desire. How to get clarity? How to know the real self that needs to be expressed in your success?

To prepare yourself for this quest, you have to be open to a multitime, multidimensional understanding of the self. Noted psychiatrist Leston Havens has studied the problem of self-knowledge throughout his career in connection with a field called *empathetic therapy*. He points out that self-examination often involves the employment of the present to build conceptions of the future.[1] Just so, success straddles multiple conceptions of time and one's self.[2] Jonathan Lear, a philosopher and psychoanalyst, helpfully suggests that the mysteries of knowing your authentic self are somewhat less murky if you think of the self as that self which is evaluating the question, "Is this who I really am?"[3]

In this chapter, we identify the basic components of self-definition and show how the interplay between these components and the four satisfactions can give you a working framework to apply to success. This framework can also help you understand the source of failures, which often can be traced to a disconnect between your ambitions and your core. When you can identify the components of your own self-definition, you have a set of tools that helps you

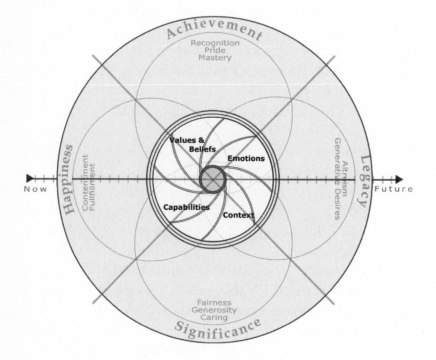

- The capabilities that set you apart from others.

- The values and beliefs that determine how you see the world.

- Your unique context with all of its complex interactions.

- Your various emotions that cause you to respond to people and events.

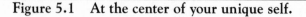

Figure 5.1   At the center of your unique self.

organize your goals around your deepest ambitions and enables you to pursue them in a way that actually gets you there. Their interdependent functioning can always come to your aid when you seek to express your vision of what is good and excellent, emotionally pleasurable, morally satisfying, and capable of achievement.

We conceive of these components as though they were the aperture at the very heart of the kaleidoscope (see Figure 5.1).

To begin, ask yourself:

- What are your values and beliefs?
- What are your emotional needs?
- What are your capabilities—your signature skills and available resources?
- What is your particular context in which you are trying to operate?

Self-Definition 1: What Are Your Values and Beliefs?

What does it profit a person, asks the *Bible*, to gain the world and lose one's soul? No achievement will feel meaningful and satisfying unless it resonates with your own values and beliefs.

Your *values* shape your definition of importance. Your *beliefs* are your sense of how the world should work when it works right. They shape and explain why you attach value to certain moral stands and preferences about desired ends. This rather free mixture of values and beliefs is self-reinforcing. When your values are buttressed by a strong belief system, they offer more strength in the face of daily temptations to go for the sucker solution.

To get a sense of the values and beliefs that drive your idea of real success, you must have a set of values that speak loudly in your actions. This starts with the examined life. Your values diagnosis, whether it is profoundly esoteric or common sense, must include some critical perspectives.

Purpose

The first perspective is *purpose*. Many people with sound values about honesty and trustworthiness sometimes find themselves feeling success places them in an uneasy moral position, and yet they do not quite understand why. Frequently, the source is an underdeveloped sense of purpose. For example, in *Habits of the Heart* Robert Bellah noted that many people today have a conception of the good life that is so oriented on securing personal freedom that their idea of success has been emptied of other people and nonmaterial values.[4] They get the longer vacation with the new promotion but time on the job still feels flat. Without a sense of purpose that reflects your deepest normative values about what *should* be done and in what way, success becomes a mere means to a lifestyle end, a way to get money. Ask yourself: What is the purpose behind what I'm doing? What purpose will link me to my ideal of excellence? Of a good person? Of a good society? Am I likely to fulfill these conceptions with my standards of success? What is the right purpose for my corporation? Unless you address these questions in full, you are unprepared for the complex appetites you may have around success, and unprepared for leadership.

A sense of right purpose is one of the most powerful sources of energy and commitment to be found. Purpose motivated the stoneworker at a cathedral whose work held an uplifting sanctity because he understood he was about the task of glorifying God, while his coworkers drudged along in the belief they were merely "breaking rocks." This perspective is critical to realizing satisfactions in your success, and it plays a concrete role in enhancing performance. Authors Jim Loehr and Tony Schwartz note the many enabling functions of purpose in the organization of energy, including focus, direction, passion, and perseverance.[5] Jim Collins argues in *Good to Great* that having a strong sense of purpose fuels what he calls the "buildup-breakthrough flywheel" that drives good companies to great status. He also notes that core values and purpose remain stable, preserved by enduring great companies even as they embark on market changes.[6]

Importance

To connect values and purpose more fully, ask: What is most important about what you are doing for yourself? What is most important about what you are doing for others? These questions help clarify your general norms about right and wrong, and what you think the consequences of such activity are in terms of accomplishment of valued concrete goals.

Some may wonder if we have it backwards. Do your beliefs lead to your success values, or does your success create and reinforce certain beliefs? It's an important question—we all can slip into self-justifying values frameworks. Try testing this possibility with a reality check: How important would *others* say your work is? Our concern here is that you identify the *expectational power* that the interplay of your values and beliefs creates around the pursuit and experience of success. If I keep 99 cents of every dollar my company makes and feel that I am being generous, what expectations go along with this worldview? Will I expect to (1) be considered a financial genius and treated with respect and acceptance, (2) be disturbed about being criticized and mistrusted and not treated with the respect that money should buy me, or (3) be ashamed and unable to look myself in the mirror? The answer sharpens my knowledge of my deeper moral beliefs and worldview. If, for example, you apply the above belief system to all four categories of success, it becomes clear how this exercise can help you identify the source of certain problems. Imagine the Significance profile of the person who holds this worldview!

Once again we issue a warning to avoid the *maximization syndrome* when you articulate your values and beliefs or try to put concrete goals around your sense of purpose. Servicing any single purpose or value to an extreme necessarily leads to the neglect of the others. **You have to recognize that you have many internal and external sources of belief about purpose and calibrate your goals to the whole.** We used the concept of *important enough* to help shape your activities with consistency to your values without going overboard on the idealism to the point you find every job not noble enough to present real success (one of Jane's problems).

Values and Your Sense of Enough

Max Weber noted that there is an ethics of ideals and an ethics of action. You need both as the basis of integrity. **What is important enough to be worth it?** What benefits do you seek, what potential harms are you preventing? Do you believe it's important to "make a difference" in whatever you do? Then how much achievement is important enough to satisfy for today? What do you expect to occur from this "making a difference"? Understanding this can help you calibrate the level and direction you have to reach to feel committed and "right" about success. The proportions will vary from activity to activity. **Your tennis, for example, may be valued, but it may also not be important enough to qualify as a value. Recognizing these calibrations of importance are key to parsing your time and energies around your core.**

It can also surface inconsistencies. Say you are ambivalent about how you value money. You think it's very important in your life, but you don't think money is everything. How do you determine what is *enough* money? Unless you can fine tune your answer with an understanding that you may want several things from money that can't be bought, you will be unable to calibrate your achievement goals. You will, like Jane, be stalled in the pursuit of other aspects of success that have nothing to do with money. How much money is enough is a very difficult question, one that tends to keep changing. Probing your expectations can aid in uncovering these deeper beliefs. **When you find the place where money allows you to do or get something you feel is "important enough" in one success category or another, you will be able to set limits on your financial needs.**

Try discussing your expectations with others. Perhaps you expect that money will provide you a means to numerous desired ends, such as buying pleasurable things, gaining social acceptance, securing power against others' control, giving support to others? Does this provide with you a broad parameter of minimum and maximum expectations? Can you anticipate how your spending habits fit into these purposes? How much is enough to fulfill each purpose? What do you need to achieve in order to have enough not only to help someone now, but to grow your resources so as to help in the future? Besides examining the degree to which money actually provides these things, you can look at your past, talk to a wealthy mentor, explore the question with a person you know and respect who lives below the level you aspire to.

It's very important to make sure your profile of the core values and purposes around money is complete, and the four categories can help guide your examination. Consider this anecdote tweaking Western materialism that we've heard attributed to many sources. We heard the following version from a group of Brazilians we were interviewing. Early in the morning, a man takes a walk down the beach and sees a fisherman by the shore. He watches him catch a fish, put it in his basket, fold up his gear, and walk away. Running after him, the man says, "Wait a minute! What are you doing?"

"I'm going home."

"You're *leaving!??*"

"I caught the fish."

"But it's early. You could fish quite a bit longer."

"Why would I do that?"

"Well, if you caught two fish you could sell the other one in the market."

"Why would I do that?"

"Well, then you'd get some money."

"Why would I do that?"

"Well you could save the money and buy a boat."

"Why would I do that?"

"Well you could go out in your boat and catch whole barrels of fish and take them back to sell in the market."

"Why would I do that?"

"Well, you'd get a lot of money for that. Someday you'd be rich and you could retire and just sit in a hammock all day."

"What do you think I'm about to go do?"

Lovely as this story is, our fisherman's values of "just enough for my needs today" doesn't pass the standards of enduring success.

But neither does the man's who is questioning him. **Both are caught in very narrow expectational principles.** The fisherman's level of enough achievement gives him no extra money to put into activities of Significance: earning enough to also help others out, having enough for tomorrow so if he can't fish his family isn't in trouble. On the other hand, the man's logic of achievement is equally constrained: he, too, has no thought for the needs of the world in connection with money, and he can't even envision a scenario where he would reach a state of enough money for now so as to go experience contentment in a hammock *today*.

What will be enough for your own needs in all four categories?

Values and Your Context for Success

When people feel their achievements have not been "enough" to create the sense of success they seek, they are often caught in an inconsistency between their norms and their expectations about the way the world works that seems to imply it takes something very different to succeed than what they would like to bring to the game. If you entertain a fundamental sense of contradiction between your values and the context in which you are seeking success, you will never find enough to satisfy you.

Conversely, if your belief about the way the world works has a logic that is consistent with success, then a strong connection to your core values reinforces not only your determination to stay the course, but your sense of satisfaction when you win.

Gene Kohn offered a poignant example in the days after 9/11. Kohn is cofounder of the noted architectural firm Kohn, Pederson, Fox (KPF) located in New York City and London. He and his two partners founded the firm on July 4, 1976 on the conviction that most of the stark steel and glass skyscrapers of the period were not only aesthetically sterile, they failed in their relationship to the public sector, the street scale, the pedestrians, and other buildings, between people on the streets and the office space that occupied the city. Their first major project was the green and glass semi-circular building at 333 Wacker in Chicago, a building that has become a beloved landmark in the city. We first interviewed Gene about six months before the terrorist attacks on the World Trade Center. We were drawn to his ideas of success because they were so heavily influenced by attention to all four components we were studying. Kohn carries an expectation that success is, at a minimum, about success for his firm and for those who work or live in KPF buildings and for himself. Attending to each, and especially to the client, forms the foundation of these successes. There is, after all, a self and other orientation behind success that is not capable of reduction to some final judgment about whether leaders are acting out of self-interest or self-denial.

At the time of the tragic events at the World Trade Center towers, KPF was already deeply involved in a project to construct what would be the tallest building in the world, the Shanghai Financial Center. They were, however, still more than a year away from starting construction. Financing for this landmark structure was initially by a consortium of Japanese bankers and investors and more recently joined by Chinese investors. The complexity of this project presented enormous risks and challenges at every level. Design had to conform to a far stricter standard of safety than in the United States, due to Chinese building codes and the conditions of the site itself, which was located in a tidal area that frequently experienced earthquakes and very high winds (the most serious condition for the design of the tall structure). Kohn was especially proud that his client, Mr. Mori, had indicated that KPF had been chosen for the project because of the quality of the design, experience, and values its partners shared.

On 9/11 in 2001, KPF also had projects underway in the area around the World Trade Center. These were immediately put on hold as many clients left the area to relocate into empty office buildings outside the cordons. Some clients had already suffered their own financial setbacks. The market meltdown that had begun a year earlier in March was now fully underway, hastened by 9/11, with Enron's disclosures about to hit the press. KPF's financial situation, like many institutions, could not be taken lightly in response to a declining economy.

Then there was the emotionally wrenching public questioning of the very prudence of having such tall buildings. Were mega-skyscrapers nothing less than a modern form of hubris, an invitation to disaster? Kohn wrote several articles and gave numerous speeches, passionately defending the value of tall buildings. Not only are they a unique symbol of deep civic aspirations, they are a space solution to density in overpopulated areas that could possibly reduce rather than increase dependency on the automobile, reduce energy consumption, and maintain greenspace. While the WTC collapse revealed concerns with the codes and design for tall buildings, this didn't mean he felt all tall buildings were flouting public safety. The question was important enough, however, that KPF reviewed a number of their tall buildings in design, including the Shanghai World Financial Center. Comparing European and Asia codes to the U.S., they realized how well SWFC would perform in a similar crisis.

Meanwhile his staff, like so many others located in New York City, was suffering from the trauma of 9/11. There were daily emotional fires to put out with clients, staff, the press, and the public. In the midst of this situation, a personnel problem was brought to Kohn and his partners' attention. It is too confidential to be discussed in detail here, but involved an extremely talented person in a senior position who they discovered had at times been treating some employees with extreme disrespect in front of their peers. By chance, the situation came to Kohn's attention just as we happened to be interviewing. Despite all the other issues on Kohn's plate at that time, he immediately responded. The partners called a special meeting and it was evident that this person could no longer be an employee of the firm. A settlement and immediate departure were worked out.

Kohn's ability to focus on this uncomfortable problem at a time when the company and the nation were overwhelmed with other important issues rested strongly on his values and beliefs. He believes that the way people treat each other in the firm, no matter what their status, and those outside the firm is a critical measure of a firm's value and a demonstration of leadership. Kohn believes that professionally KPF must stand for quality of design, of execution of its work, quality of client relations and service, but equally important, that within the firm great respect is shown for all employees and to all its consultants and vendors. As you walk around KPF, this expectation is almost palpable in the way people speak to one another, and in the appreciation factor that pops up in attitude, aesthetics, and even the pace of the day. To Kohn, this is the way the world should work when it works at its best.

Recall Rabbi Hillel's famous prayer: **"If I am not for myself, then who will be? If I am only for myself, what am I? If not now, when?"** As the prayer implies, having deep values and beliefs does not erase the eternal tensions between self and other-oriented purposes by posing an either/or choice. The philosopher Robert Nozick pointed out that each of the lines in the Hillel prayer have their strengths and weaknesses. The trick is to be able to combine them over time.[7]

That requires finding a moral middle ground where your values and beliefs can be pragmatically applied, not to reduce your integrity but to expand your aspirations toward higher purposes that you will find important and enduring. Unlike the "absolute best," this is a concept that many philosophers would find abhorrent to their standards of absolute clarity and consistency. It also flies in the face of economic philosophy such as utility theory, which assumes the possibility of assigning a fixed ideal value to the future combination of all goods and experiences and making a comparison by discounting to the present based on the appropriate discount rate. Beyond the computational impossibility, we think it important to have an adaptive calibration to guide your calibrations of what price you will pay to get there.

Three middle-ground ethical questions follow. Together they sketch the moral minimum and the realistic possible that we feel represents the range of enough so as to keep decisions and actions connected to your core values and beliefs. They are drawn from consultation with a number of top corporations on the process of maintaining high ethical standards within an organization in ways that are responsive to public concerns:

1. What is legal? (Valuing compliance with the law.)
2. What is unacceptable? (Going beyond the letter of the law to comply with the spirit of what is ethical.)
3. What is desirable? (Taking ideals of purpose and excellence into account.)

The first two address the *process* of living up to your values and beliefs. The last takes you to the concept of *purpose*. Determining these parameters in advance ensures that the success you seek is true to your core. Sharing these values can help you, your family, and your organization hone its ambitions to workable, ethical choices, no matter how grand the scale.

Self-Definition 2: What Are Your Emotional Needs?

Nothing is more complicated than our emotional makeup. We have all these emotions, driven by deep-seated needs and deep-seated attractions to things that fulfill these needs: the need for security, pleasure, acquiring, continuance of the species, bonding. Whatever motivational theory we choose—Maslow or Lawrence-Nohria—there is a built-in complexity. We're told success is all about focus and passion, right? But it's more complicated than that. Passion is the volume control. We have to be careful not to let it erode our ability to make reasoned, emotionally appropriate choices as we pursue the different components of success. Indeed, it turns out that each of the categories of satisfaction specify a *particular* emotional stance that is not interchangeable.

Emotion versus Reason

Typically, people place emotion and reason in opposition, from which we might conclude that tactical success and emotional appetites could never be complementary. Indeed, many of our appetites for love, power, esteem, aesthetic pleasure seem if anything to *threaten* what our reason says is necessary for success. We can't put our nose to the grindstone *and* spend the day sniffing the flowers. At best, we can give play to our emotions when we go to enjoy the *rewards of success.* But this underdeveloped view of the role of emotions can be traced back to an underdeveloped view of success as being about one thing only: achievement and its reward. As we have seen, no one really is this constrained in their dreaming.

George Ainslie, in his brilliant book, *Breakdown of Will,* summarizes the various schools of thought that attribute mistaken decision making to the triumph of emotion over reason, and notes that this theoretical assumption goes as far back as Plato.[8] We take a different tack: emotions are not only inescapable, they are critical to the willful pursuit and experience of success. Success is not just about getting what you want tactically, but about satisfying your emotional needs. The problem is, for most people success creates a paradoxical agony between grandiose searches for perfect control and the need to explore the unknown. The trick, then, is in knowing how to use your core emotions wisely and with a reasoned sense of *enough.*

Even during our interviews, our participants' views of success showed great emotional variation. Our high achievers were not consumed by one big drive. They had an ongoing ability to keep their diverse emotions on the front burner without being sidetracked from accomplishing important things. They seemed to have gotten what they wanted on a regular basis while avoiding self-defeating temptations (for the most part). In the eternal contest between passion and reason, their emotional intelligence had directed success into a constructive balance between the two rather than self-defeating reliance on one alone.

Their stories of the challenges and rewards they have encountered revealed a very consistent pattern: The fuller their experience of success without regrets and without a deep sense of loss, the fuller the daily emotional menu from which they were feeding their reasoned pursuit of success goals. We concluded that they had two finely developed emotional skills:

1. The ability to draw on a broad mix of emotions.
2. The ability to direct specific emotions to the appropriate category of success.

This process was an interesting mix of intuitive response, reasoning about cause and consequences, and being able to control emotional appetite with a sense of enough.

Emotions and Achievement

Achievement is driven by emotions that drive learning, such as curiosity, discovery, and mastery. High achievers tend to feel a "draw" to certain unsolved problems, seeing an opportunity to master the puzzle that most interests them. **A person's curiosity level is strongly a function of how closely a problem touches on certain intrinsic "appetites" or affinities they felt all their lives.** For one person, it's an attraction to understanding and mastering numerical puzzles such as a balance sheet; for another, it's the social scene; for another, it's the way a mechanical system works. The need for security through dominance also comes in: Achievement feels important partially because of your intrinsic sense of interest and affection or draw to a particular problem and partially to the degree that *others* have regarded these problems as important: the conquering of disease, provision of food, acquisition of property, mastery of technological or even intellectual skills.

Hence the competitive condition we placed on our definition of Achievement as a success category: simply achieving for the sake of completing a problem is not enough for enduring success. It must refer to a playing field in which others strive as well. If you only choose to "win" in areas that are not particularly important to others, you may be engaging in a form of self-handicapping to protect yourself from failing on a more competitive playing field. As author Julie Norem points out in *The Positive Power of Negative Thinking*, people devise enormously creative ways of justifying their self-imposed restrictions on worldly achievement. They may believe that by limiting their participation in externally recognized achievement they seek a higher good, or simply that setting the bar lower is the only way not to be disappointed. In all such cases you handicap not only your performance but the satisfaction you receive from success[9] (see Figure 5.2).

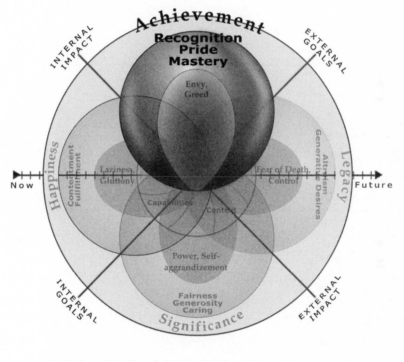

- Balancing the future and the present.

- Receiving recognition in competition with others.

- Mastering future challenges.

- Avoiding insatiable envy and greed.

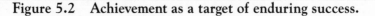

Figure 5.2 Achievement as a target of enduring success.

Emotions and Happiness

Happiness has a somewhat blurry boundary. It is both one of our four categories of success and an emotional driver in the core self-definitions. Happiness is itself an emotional state; but we are also using it here in its second sense, as a judgment about the state of one's life, a sense of satisfaction that is both emotional and reasoned (see Figure 5.3).

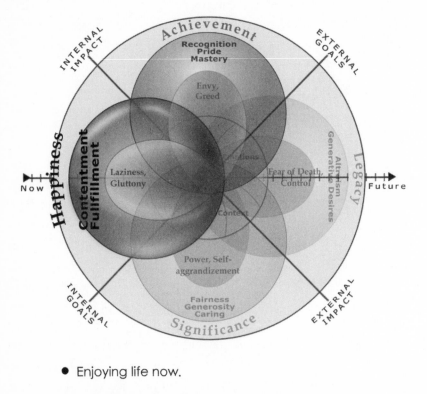

- Enjoying life now.

- Feeling good about yourself and your life.

- Finding contentment and fullfullment in your daily activities.

- Avoiding a search for continuous feelings of laziness and gluttony.

Figure 5.3   Happiness as a target for enduring success.

Optimism, which is usually associated with happiness, is actually a somewhat unreliable indicator. Though successful people seem to be more optimistic, several important studies have shown that some of the allegedly gloomiest countries, such as Denmark, rank very high in life satisfaction, while some of the jolliest, such as Italy, do not. So too, Norem's book has shown that strategic pessimism can be as motivationally successful for some personalities as the power of positive thinking is to most. A critical difference, however, is which state of mind better prepares you for leadership. While we haven't tested this empirically, in our observation, no matter which type is more likely to make it to the top, the optimistic leader creates a more willing followership.

Research on happiness, ranging from work on "flow" to recent studies of life satisfaction from happiness expert Martin Seligman,[10] have helped expand and refine our understanding of the emotions and states people describe as happiness. As an indicator of success, happiness is driven by a variety of emotions ranging from contentment (passive) to ecstasy (active). While we may not understand definitively how much is baseline genetics and how much is environment, the pragmatic value of these emotions is clear and capable of rational understanding. Contentment, pleasure, aesthetic delight serve as a source of rest and renewal, a need for time-out. Studies of flow and energy use indicate that this cyclical dispersion of energy is critical to long-term performance.

There are also more active emotions that qualify as happiness: delight, silliness, sensuality, ecstasy. These satisfactions are expressions of letting go, opening up to the surprise of a joke, the newness of a physical sensation, the surrender of intense pleasure. They are a way of not being in control all the time. Indeed, since time immemorial the most reliable dramatic jokes come from the physical letting go of control of our basic bodily functions. Walk on the stage and fart, piss, or burp and you're guaranteed a laugh. Farce is not the only outcome. Creativity expert Theresa Amabile has shown that letting go of control is an essential ingredient of creative outbursts.[11] In her research, people reported their most creative moments most frequently occurred when they thought they were doing something else that involved movement and relaxation: taking a walk, enjoying a joke, or like Thales' eureka moment, taking a bath.

Success can seem to demand tighter and tighter control over such emotional release, but we noticed our interviewees constantly taking timeouts for a joke, a sensual pleasure in food, even a nap. This observation carries an important guideline: **If you think, like many people today, that success is about delaying happiness while you achieve, and that the final point of success should be to put aside all effort and lead a happy life, you are unlikely to achieve real success or happiness.**

All scientific research shows that happiness has a fading quality: the first taste of the hot fudge sundae is terrific, but if you ate four of them, you would find little pleasure. You have to renew happiness on a regular basis, not look for some state of unending pleasure. So too, some of our interviewees who had delayed all sense of doing things for their own happiness, found themselves baffled when their retirement golf games were being transformed by their own emotions into yet more occasions for competition and achievement. They simply hadn't learned how to enjoy themselves, nor did they realize that they would need continued doses of real achievement no matter how old or financially secure they were.

Emotions and Significance

If happiness is an essentially self-generated and self-pleasing experience (you can't make someone else happy if they're not cooperative), Significance is an interesting mix of other and self-oriented emotions, such as empathy, caring, and contribution. These are all connecting emotions to a social environment, but you still exercise choice over whom you care about, what you choose to contribute to. The emotions that drive Significance fulfill deep needs for belonging and bonding, and like the other emotions, can be supported by reason. Doing unto others, for example, is partly an exercise in empathy and partly an exercise in reasoned creation of community (see Figure 5.4).

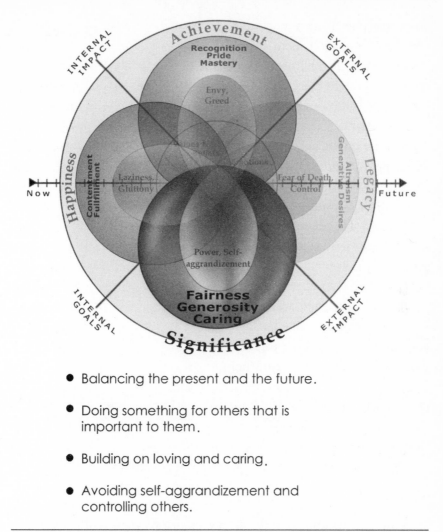

- Balancing the present and the future.

- Doing something for others that is important to them.

- Building on loving and caring.

- Avoiding self-aggrandizement and controlling others.

Figure 5.4   Significance as a target for enduring success.

In our interviews, people varied enormously in how strongly their activities of Significance were motivated by reason or emotion. Some "gave back" simply because it was the "right thing to do." Others had a more felt ethic of caring. Again, the achievers who could change emotional hats from the self-regarding, ego-asserting emotions driving Achievement to the self-suppressing empathetic emotions of Significance, were leaders whose own people trusted them to understand

and care. This in turn created deep loyalty beyond the self-interested rewards of an employment contract.

At Johnson & Johnson, the Tylenol crisis demonstrated management's consistent adherence to the caring values of their Credo that put public safety and customer health above all else. This message created a trust in the company's ability to do the right that not only assured the public and formed the foundation of its remarkable comeback; even more so, it paved the way for deep trust from employees themselves that the company really meant to live up to its committed way of doing business. This was a commitment they personally valued. When Tylenol was being reintroduced, J&J scheduled a phone-in for customers to get a dollar coupon. All that weekend employees stayed by the company's phones at headquarters to deal with the volume of calls they were receiving. They came with their children. They didn't get paid overtime. This is an indicator of Significance working both ways. Like most emotional states, it's contagious.

Emotions and Legacy

Legacy is also supported by positive emotions. Among these are the desire for generativity—extending your accomplishments to the next generation—commemoration, and nurturing. Passive legacies are less emotion-driven, but may still be emotionally satisfying—the interplay between self-definitions and the categories is not one-way. Say you drive yourself to athletic heights and set a record. That record forms its own legacy, but the emotions were really about actively driving your Achievement. If you are lucky enough to meet someone inspired by your legacy, your emotional investment in generativity and others' success will surely increase. Active forms of legacy require more emotional investment: in order to put your resources into creating a Legacy you have to really feel impassioned about the continuance of something you value (this is the emotion of generativity) for the sake of others in the future with whom you identify. That's a specific kind of satisfaction that cannot be fully replicated in Achievement or Significance alone (see Figure 5.5).

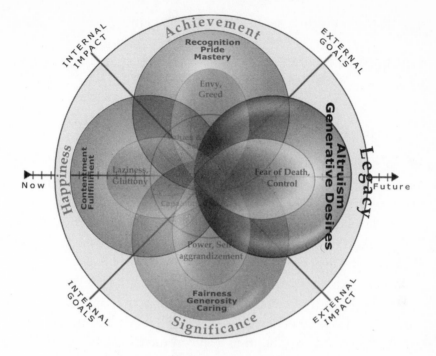

- It is about the future and will truly never be fully known by those who create it.

- Establishing your values or accomplishments in ways that help others find future success.

- Fulfills generative desires and altruistic tendencies.

- Must avoid need to control others and the fear of death.

Figure 5.5   Legacy as a target for enduring success.

Enduring success requires a reasoned control over these emotions. You cannot have them all at once. You have to put one down in order to have another. This may sound contradictory: Can you really subject emotion to reason? Can you make choices about suppressing one emotion for the sake of other needs without being repressed? We think so, but only if you give all of them regular play.

The high achievers we studied had developed this kind of emotional intelligence both by knowing themselves, caring about others, knowing what best fit certain goals, and exercising a reasoned sense of enough.

Measuring Your Emotional Mix

When you think about your emotional makeup, ask yourself: Am I switching categories frequently enough to fulfill my own rich sense of success, or am I trying to squeeze all my emotional needs into one accomplishment or one category? Am I trying to get Happiness from competition? A sense of Significance from mastery? A sense of dominance from Legacy?

Such misdirection will only cheat your efforts. How often do you find a hard-hitting executive trying to apply the same competitive instincts to his or her charitable work? Sure they may win the title of raising the most money, but that won't ensure the donations are actually going to the right place. Indeed, the game of philanthropy has become such a celebrity achievement in its own right that it risks becoming totally dependent on motivating ego rather than caring for its real success. Should it succeed in this ego celebration, it may get more attention but its larger mission of helping and caring for others will surely fail.

Ignore the directional patterns that successful use of the emotions requires and you may frustrate your own pursuit of success in practical and emotional terms. Beware: You will regularly be challenged by the public to put your efforts into one category alone. The drug maker Novartis, for example, innovatively tried to strike a good balance between caring contribution and competitive mastery by pledging it would make certain drugs available in third-world countries at cost—on the condition that their proprietary patents on some of their other drugs were protected in those countries, along with their pricing. When India failed to comply, Novartis threatened to withhold some of its at-cost drugs—and was widely painted in the press as hypocritical. Once again we see a lesson here in the need for leaders to better understand the dynamics of enduring success and be able to articulate this message to the public and their own employees. It's a real challenge, but the framework can help structure this difficult balancing exercise.

Applying Enough to Emotions

There is an even darker warning: **Each of the emotional clusters that positively drive success have their evil twins.** Achievement, for example, can be very effectively driven by greed and envy. Happiness by gluttony and escapism. Significance by the desire for recognition and dominance. Legacy by a need for absolute control and the fear that leads to a denial of death.

In each case, however, the end result will not fulfill the expectations of each success category in terms that endure. Legacy that is about control can't let go enough to let others build on the legacy and succeed themselves. Significance driven by the need for recognition is essentially self-absorbed and unjust. It takes advantage of those in need for your own sake. Happiness that seeks eternal escape or satiety of your appetites is an *unhappy* state. Remember Midas? Achievement that is driven by greed fails to satisfy because there is always something more out there you don't have or didn't do (see Figure 5.6).

Note the repetition of *enough* in these observations. You not only have to direct your emotional core properly, you have to exercise a reasoned sense of enough as to the extent you give play to any emotional impulse. What is enough caring? What is enough mastery? You can only answer this with reason, supplemented by your appreciative skills as you experience each of these emotions.

We realized that our interviewees had become the object of our interest precisely because they were exhibiting such a rich emotional experience of success. They were enjoying themselves. They were feeling fulfilled in making important contributions to others. They were driven to find ways of helping the next generation succeed. They enjoyed the competition without becoming addicted.

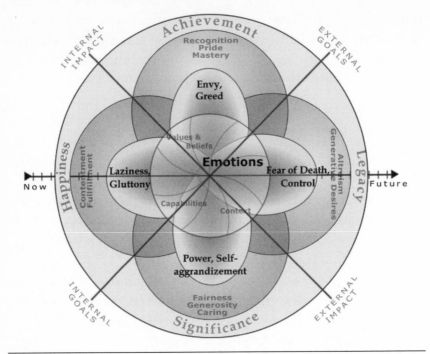

Figure 5.6   Mapping the success territory: Avoiding negative emotions.

Enough helps you make the distinction between the good and bad emotional drivers. Many of our interviewees had been drawn to the Jungian concept of "the shadow," a hidden layer of motivation that is felt to be far stronger and less positive than we might like. The shadow asserts its force and, if unattended, causes us to seek that which does not give us happiness, and yet, according to Jung, it is an inevitable part of our psyche. **The hardest part is that it is almost impossible to see its face. You can, however, detect the footprints it leaves behind.**

Shadow motivations addict you. All the evil twin emotions of success have a strong element of addiction: Never enough money. Never enough love. Gluttony and escapism are not good emotional drivers of success because you never want to stop having fun. They are the emotions of substance addiction and out-of-control consumerism. Greed is another addictive emotion: it has no limits and observably entraps people with its eternal promise of something more—led by the observation that someone else has it. The demon that can drive people to create horribly controlling legacies is a sour addiction to life to the point of denying your own death. Fear, like anger, is an addictive emotion that is very hard to turn off. Many people today launch their success out of their fears of failure or abandonment: I might not have enough money, enough pleasure, enough giving. Ask yourself:

- Am I doing this for negative or positive reasons?
- Am I driven by the positive emotions or their evil twins?
- Have I been unable to find enough satisfaction out of an addiction or perhaps because I'm directing my emotional needs to the wrong category?
- How broad a range of emotions am I allowing myself to express in each category?
- What fears are preventing me from taking emotional risks?
- Am I seeking an absolute fulfillment of this need (absolute control, absolute happiness) or is what I have enough to experience a specific kind of satisfaction?

Enough is your weapon of choice: It helps turns the positive emotions into incentives and drivers of success. Revisit the ones you care about often and make sure they are part of your strategy. Do you have enough control already? How much do you really need? What will you get from more? More range of satisfaction or more bondage to one category? When have you done enough in achievement to justify a time out? Just enough will keep you keenly open to the emotional possibilities of success—and help you experience the full spectrum.

Success can throw you off emotionally. Social expectations such as today's emphasis on celebrity can create an over dependence on values that ultimately feel false, and yet they will become *your* self-definitions the more you operate from these assumptions.

Self-Definition 3: What Are Your Capabilities?

If you could choose to do anything you felt was important, how would you decide which to go after? High achievers bring a third self-defining characteristic to this question: an inventory of their capabilities. It sounds obvious, but how often do you meet a person frustrated in their success goals but without any real idea of what is, as we say, "stretchable but reachable"? Instead they are lost in a day-dream of unrealistic expectations, fanned by celebrity glamour. In today's world of maximization and reinvention, it's easy to fall for the idea that you can stretch your capabilities to infinite capacity. You can leverage your energy if you just eat right. You can work smarter if you just adopt a new learning paradigm. Self-Improvement is a particularly American phenomenon, and the territory of success resonates with this value.

When A. G. Lafley was elected president of Procter & Gamble (P&G) in March 2000, he inherited a dog's job. The company had lost $85 billion in market capitalization since the beginning of that year. Everyone was expecting either a spectacular defeat or a miraculous recovery. Lafley took a more sober view. The first thing he did was conduct an inventory of P&G's products to winnow its focus back to four core businesses. These were the areas where the company's core capabilities were strong, and they had opportunities for growth in the marketplace. He didn't try to save everything or beat out Wal-Mart's record in one year. He began rebuilding in incremental steps, piece by piece.

When Jane tried to resolve her anxieties over success, she kept casting her choices in extremes: How to get herself to the right state of mind and in the right job so that all her desires could be met by one career?

Many of today's self-improvement models are exhausting. They require perfect execution and maximum efficiency. The problem is, we can't escape the fact that capabilities are finite. **You can exceed your own sense of what you can do on occasion, but don't count on it.** You have to pick a goal where you have enough capability to reasonably succeed. Jane was very capable, very talented. But to financially support the lifestyle and values about friends and urban culture that she had, she would have had to be a concert musician—not a church organist. On the other hand, if she could get to the point of feeling that volunteer work in the church was still an important part of an overall picture, just enough for Significance and still leaving room for Achievement as a software manager—she would have seen a pattern of reachable goals that matched her capabilities.

Why do we adopt definitions of success for ourselves that start with the idea that we have to be superhuman or super-lucky to make them work? That we have to pump ourselves up with success steroids or be born with a silver spoon in order to make it? It starts from the philosophy of *never enough*. Some organizations structure their entire culture on this idea, tying up their own creativity and coordination in a knot of fear and anxiety. Others, like the people on the set of a Clint Eastwood production, get high on who they are. *Enduring success* is not necessarily about maximizing the efficiency of your capabilities, but making sure you discipline your success goals to reality. Done correctly, you will also grow your capabilities over time. But not if you burn yourself out.

Your Signature Skills

There's no magic formula here. People stretch their perceived capabilities all the time while others bring too little to the table. **The first ingredient, however, is acceptance and appreciation. You already have talents.** Are you choosing contexts and goals that allow them to flourish? Acknowledge what they are and you can develop them further. We found that everyone's idea of *real* success had a strong element of self-expression in it. Meaningful achievements were those that drew on the special gifts of each. Some call this their "signature skill," a capability that defines who they really feel they are. We saw it as the core talents that are found in what most attracts your curiosity and affection. For some people, it is the logic of numbers. Put them to a task that requires quick numbers skill and they don't tire at the effort. Others have a skill with people, or interpreting information, or with their hands. The point is, these signature skills are what mark your place on earth. If enduring success is that which makes a mark that lasts for more than 15 minutes of fame, you have to bring your signature skills to the process early.

Sometimes these skills are easily apparent in play. A great teacher we know reported she used to play school in her garage, setting up blackboards and chalk and assigning herself and her friends math problems and writing tasks. Another person who became a human resources manager was always the school cheerleader, the one who would put on the mascot uniform and be there for the team. In an earlier book, Laura reported on the remarkable accomplishments of a real estate developer. His mother had been so poor that he'd been put in an orphanage, attended by dedicated nuns who were themselves leading lives of harsh poverty. There wasn't enough heat, wasn't enough food, and this boy began working odd jobs at age ten. He remembered that as he walked along the streets of Chicago, he was always drawn to the construction sites. He'd stop and watch. "I don't know," he said. "I just always liked seeing things being built." His signature skill was engineering—structuring large building projects. He put himself through high school and college, and finally got a civil engineering degree. Eventually, he oversaw several landmark projects—333 Wacker and the Oakbrook shopping mall in Chicago, and parts of Copley Place in Boston.

When we interviewed him, he'd had enough of this super-demanding career and had "retired" to enjoy his family. He was still an entrepreneur, though—and had expanded his interests to start a successful enterprise in audiotapes of business books. He was sharing this business with his daughter and her husband, starting the next generation of success. Laura met him and his wife one evening for dinner at the University Club in Chicago, a place this man had once never dreamed he'd be asked to join. As they walked through the entryway, he began pointing out its architectural details, eagerly naming the architects and artists. His signature skills were still giving him satisfaction in the categories of success. He'd developed an ability not just to put them to good use for achievement, but to inform his activities of happiness and legacy as well.

Anticipation

Anticipation is the next important skill. What capabilities is your vision likely to require? Are you honestly recognizing the limits in which you can work? Conversely, does your work test you enough? To strike this balance, you have to anticipate a good match between your capabilities, your values, and your context. George Lodge, a revered professor of business and government at Harvard Business School, ran on the Republican ticket against Ted Kennedy for Senator in 1962 in the highly Democratic state of Massachusetts. It was a heroic struggle, and they both made the cover of *Time* magazine in the process. Even his father, ambassador Henry Cabot Lodge, advised him not to run against Ted Kennedy. For over a year, he worked every hour of the day on the campaign, and told his staff that if he didn't drop on the last day, they hadn't worked him hard enough. For all that, he lost the election.

Lodge told us this that despite his loss, this episode had been one of his most enduring successes. "Winning had nothing to do with it," said Lodge. "I cared about the problems (civil rights, unemployment) and I felt they were being handled poorly. Something in me said 'you cannot *not* do it.' And I had 5,000 people working with me who were also showing by their dedication to the election that this was important."

For Lodge the seeming naturalness of his choice was not about never struggling. Indeed, he believes life is always about "paddling along in an environment that is only partially in your control." But the struggle itself—whether at his beloved clarinet or in building new alliances between businesses and developing countries, is not unpleasant because it is about giving in to your affinities, that is, your values and signature skills. Whether you know where you're headed or not. The senate campaign had lasting satisfaction in that it had expressed his values about community and pushed his talents far beyond what he thought he could do. It helped him learn how to channel his resources. But he also had to recognize his own limitations and work within these parameters. Before the campaign, he was tested for his ideal sleep pattern, and the coordinators adjusted the schedule accordingly whenever possible.

Lodge's reflections highlighted the interesting richness that the recognition of limitations can provide, provided what you do "give into" pulls you into a struggle that you feel is worth fighting for. Said Lodge, "When it comes to the clarinet, I've had to say, 'Face it, you'll never be a Mozart, and yet I keep practicing.' It's enough that I get such satisfaction in this struggle. That's really no different than the great CEOs who can't keep away from getting into the mess of a problem and trying to solve it without pretensions. Just oriented toward saving the enterprise." He cited Charles Luce, former rescuer of Con Edison, once known as "the company you love to hate," as one such CEO, and contrasted it to the never satisfied—never enough ethos of many achievers today.

Investing and Using Capabilities

Anticipation of needed capabilities is as important as appreciating what you already have at hand. In today's fast-paced world, you need both skills. You don't have to restrict anticipation to a passive assessment of what is realistic, you can anticipate more actively to see when you must *build capabilities* to achieve your success goal. **The self-definitions, like the goals of success, have to be viewed on an extended time frame rather than as a snapshot of fixed resources.** Enduring success is as much or more about investment in the right things, about building capability, than about a set of rewards. Witness the immature or greedy managements that depleted all their company's resources through excessive bonuses and perks. No doubt they felt they were building their power base for success. In most cases, they were wrong.

Fred Sievert, now president of New York Life, always had a particular talent for numbers. When he first took the job of chief financial officer of the largest business unit at New York Life, he built on this skill by adding to his capabilities. An outsider from the Midwest, he dug into parts of the business that weren't technically his responsibility. At meetings, he would share this knowledge. Soon he was being asked for his advice and input on a larger scope of responsibilities. Soon after joining New York Life, he worked the numbers on their disability products and found it just didn't add up. Under any realistic scenario, increasing disability claims would jeopardize the rest of the business in the coming years. Fred couldn't ignore this strategic issue, and his ability to put together a rock-solid argument by the numbers themselves helped him get his message across. But any decision to drop disability would radically disaffect the salespeople in the field, who were making a good living from selling these policies. Most were agents who could choose to represent a number of insurance companies to their clients. Would dropping disability cut New York Life off from its lifeline? Many argued it wasn't worth the risk.

Fred's second signature skill is his strong identification with the people in sales. He travels often to the field, meeting with agents and sales managers, discussing their issues, motivating performance. When the disability issue came up, he was well aware of how difficult this would be. Using a combination of irrefutable logic by the numbers and ongoing follow-up with the field, they were able to drop this product line and not disenfranchise the agents. Sievert, who has a surprising mix of modesty and confidence, home values and worldly experience, told us that one of his most significant occasions of success was in bringing the disability question to a successful conclusion without alienating the agency field force. He did what he believed was right, and this event confirmed the capabilities and values that he had long regarded as his special strengths.

Direction

The third skill in using your capability is direction. Are you directing the right capability to the right category of activity? Most of us have many skills, but an episode of success is likely to kill the others off unless you switch directions frequently. Ever met a high achiever who tried the same approach to *everything?* Are you trying to have a successful moment with your child by acting like a problem-solving CEO? Do you adopt a mommy approach to a competitive situation at work?

We can't tell you the exact skill you need for every episode in your work and life. What we can advise you is to make sure you expand your expertise to apply your skills to different categories throughout your life, and not wait until you think you might need them. Among our interviewees, those who seemed closest to a sense of knowing what was enough in success and yet continued to grow, were those who had developed a versatility in their own personality. Again it's a virtuous spiral: To be satisfying, success must be an expression of your signature skills, who you *are.* Who you are is shaped and extended by what you do. If you structure all your fun around winning as a competitor, and all your moments with those you love around winning as a competitor, and seek to establish the biggest legacy anyone ever established, your competitive skills will be incredible. But will it establish your significance with your family? Will your legacy be valued by anyone as much as yourself? What will your kaleidoscope look like?

Applying Enough to Capabilities

Success is both an individual and social activity. This requires a certain mutability about whom you present yourself as being. A friend rises in social position after having a success. "How he's changed!" we remark, as if the real person was being disguised and the new persona is a fake. There is inevitably a sense of strangeness about your own growth. For people with a high need for expressiveness, these aspects of success become a serious problem. Jane wasn't sure which person she should be out of all the successful talents and capabilities she had. Software engineer? Church musician? What element of disguise is acceptable, no, *successful,* social adaptation?

As a biological resource for social assimilation, mimicry is a tried and true way to develop your capabilities of success, but you have to know how to draw a line well before imitation becomes self-betrayal. Otherwise you may win a success that's not really for you.

Two of our interviewees who were the same age discussed the usefulness of watching and imitating whoever has power in a room. One thought it an exercise in humility, a sign of realizing that there was an institutional history at a good firm that was far more experienced than you. Keep quiet and learn. This had served him well and he counseled new recruits to do the same if they wanted to be a success. The second was Tracey, who appeared in an earlier chapter. She worked for an extremely insecure and inexperienced boss in a suck-up corporate culture. You may recall that when she stood out by voicing her concerns about the marketing projections, she was ostracized and eventually left the firm. It was a bitter experience, but also telling. Her division did indeed fail, while Tracey moved on to a more successful firm.

Ask each of these interviewees when imitation is smart and when it begins to work against the values and self-expression that they both feel are necessary to success, and they have very different answers based on their self-definitions. Our first interviewee was a team player deep in his blood, it wasn't just a value it was a *skill*. He was politically savvy and convinced his company always took the noble high road. Our second interviewee was a born cynic and a straight shooter, a tire-kicker and individualist whose strengths were if anything in lampooning the status quo. In a way, each of them had drawn on their signature skills to get to their right point in the process of building capabilities through imitation given their contexts.

What degree of self-expression of your signature skills is a must for satisfying success and what adaptations are enough for effective membership in a group? These questions test the very nature of the real self. There is a classic debate in psychology over the authenticity of mimicry: Is a good actor talented at mimicry because he or she has an underdeveloped identity or is mimicry an expression of the self that is born to be a mimic? Only you can find the right answer to this question. The interplay of our core definitions can help you find it. Capabilities are one expression of the self, values another, and emotions yet a third perspective. To test for whether your success is really being true to yourself (the only basis for it to be enduring), it's important to conduct regular exercises in the examined life on these three facets:

1. What you believe is right (values).
2. What you feel curious and interested about and find yourself solving (signature capabilities).
3. What you are emotionally attracted to because it satisfies (emotions).

You Can't Succeed Alone

Capabilities not only have to be diverse, they have to come from sources more diverse than yourself. Even if you are one of the most capable and talented people on earth, success at a scale you regard as enough is rarely achieved on your own. Our high achievers realized this early. Even those who had enormous self-confidence harnessed ego in the service of this knowledge. Values of caring and sharing as well as shared purpose obviously supported their ability to build the capability of a well-working team. Have you done enough for others to deserve their help as a resource for your goals?

On the other hand, the skills that create great teamwork are not necessarily the same as those which lead to success on personal achievement goals. Again the only solution our interviewees found that worked over the long term was to alternate, not collapse these problems. No one who is indecisive or self-doubting about their own skills can persuade others to follow their lead. No one who is so taken with self-confidence that they fail to listen with empathy and attentiveness can lead for long.

While you need to make sure you have the capabilities for what it takes before leaving your day job, it's also important to leave room for growth through failure. Ironically, many people are caught by surprise and fail in the areas they know are their most capable—the pro golfer misses a tap-in in the last round of the championship; CEOs with a stellar record stay with their winning strategy for one last big one before they retire and blow the final score. Being open and alert to failure, using failure as a positive insight to capacity, gets you the kind of resilience that is often noted in highly successful people. Life feels out of joint in such moments, but these are the occasions for building your strengths.

Elmer Johnson, former executive vice president of General Motors, retired president of Aspen Institute, and currently partner at the law firm Jenner & Block, spoke frankly about this process: "At pivotal moments in my career, I was always visited with a deep sense of my own inadequacies in the face of critical challenges. I felt I was inadequate to the job. I feel this [open questioning of capability] is necessary before a leader acts." In *Letter from Birmingham Jail,* Martin Luther King Jr. made reference to the same kind of humble self-questioning in terms of penitential confession and prayers for purity before engaging in any nonviolent civil dissent.

We knew someone rather like Jane who told us a moving story of his own journey 20 years earlier to find the right path to success in his life, and how an inventory of capabilities helped him make his choice. After a full career as a tough Wall Street financier in a family firm, his life changed course. A difficult bankruptcy that was out of his control wiped out the family security. A religious man, he happened into a chapel and got down on his knees. A nun sitting nearby got up to leave and thrust a note in his hand. It was a passage from Isaiah, "Fear not, for I am with you." He decided to attend divinity school and go into the ministry. Upon graduation, he was called in to have a discussion with his bishop. To his surprise, the bishop told him, "It would be a trap if you went into the ministry." He was advised to pray for a way to really use his gifts and skills.

At first he was angry. Why did they think he wouldn't make a good minister? Then he took an inventory. He began to envision a different calling, "I know how to straddle the two worlds. I know how to work with heads of investment firms. I know the power structure." He joined a church-financed nonprofit business to provide housing for the elderly. As its president, he raised over $8 billion in financing for housing and carved out an extremely satisfying second career helping develop independent assisted living units under the sponsorship of his denomination.

Self-Definition 4: What Context
Are You Operating In?

This man's realignment of his career was successful because of his ability to express his signature skills and values in a suitable context. He also learned a hard lesson about success: context changes. Externals may define your context, but your context is also a critically self-defining factor of success. The landscape of your dreams has to be mined for the workable context in light of the other three self-definitions. Is there enough opportunity to present a reasonable chance at success for someone with your capabilities, values? What context gets your emotional juices flowing in a constructive direction?

As we saw with so many of the CEOs of the 1990s who later did the perp walk, if you don't have limits you will over-reach. If you don't have openings, you'll never succeed. Is your context not only reachable but a close enough fit to your own values and skills so as to give you the success you value? Success in some contexts demands a headline life. Before you know it, you're expected to provide the next buzz. Manuel Arsenio discovered this after making several great market calls. One good call as a short seller and you become an instant success. Now you have to *be* the image, not just prescient but unnaturally prescient. Call it the Ivan Boesky syndrome. One day you've located a promising market opportunity to do something differently, and the next day you're a success and having to keep up an image of preternatural foresight. Therein lies the downward path from making it to faking it.

It's easy for anyone to get off track. You carefully build a platform for success and suddenly discover it's obsolete for the future context of the marketplace. You identify with certain career ambitions, but in your situation you do not have the financial resources to get the training to go this far. Do not give up just because you can't go for the max! The trick is to place yourself in a context where, even if this is not your ultimate goal, it is enough to keep the momentum going. That makes it easier to finesse changing jobs, getting more education later, or rebalancing your life down the road.

Success is not just about matching your particular situation to job goals. You have to take your context into account, but also see it as being like your skills, something over which you have some control. It is important to keep your self-definitions actively engaged in whatever you choose to do. If you've never done anything but work, it's very difficult to suddenly be placed in the context of being a full-time parent. Conversely, many full-time parents who thought they'd return to work when the children were grown find themselves in a panic when the possibility of a job becomes real. For 20 or 30 years they'd confined themselves to a context where they never had to answer to another adult besides their spouse, and couldn't face the anxiety of doing so at this stage in their life.

When Missy Carter downsized her paying job to support her husband's increased responsibility (he eventually became chairman of State Street Corporation), she continued to find contexts for her writing skills, editing the community newspaper on the military base where she and husband Marsh were first stationed, writing position statements for nonprofits, and even a book that is in draft. She uses her unique situation as a template for her work in career development, work/family issues, and stress management.

A Change in Context Is the Perfect Moment for Insight into the Self

Nancy was an extremely talented human resources manager at a large insurance firm. Some of her deep attraction to human resources came from having experienced early childhood trauma: an alcoholic mother, and the death of her father at a young age. She was highly attuned to the needs of others. Yet she was determined to be a success in a wider arena. For years, she had struggled with her own sense of having to defer to others, not sound her own horn. She worked to make everyone else feel a success, telling them they were great. She would give credit to other people on a team to the point of not being rewarded for her work. She would apologize before expressing an opinion, dotting her contributions at meetings with phrases like, "Maybe I'm wrong here, but I think . . ." In an attempt not to be arrogant she'd even say "I'm not sure I'd be good at that."

Nancy's hesitation was deep but also not the whole story. She was also extremely perceptive and deeply confident of her skills, as long as she wasn't sharing this perception with others. Over the years, a close friend coached her: "You're trying to get people to express your inner feelings and say, 'Oh no, you're really great, you can do that.' But all you're really doing is making people think you're not capable."

When she left for a new job, she asked a new question of herself, "How do I want to be?" Her answer came to her as the truth: "I want to be confident, to honestly reflect what I know." She stopped saying things that implied she didn't know the answers. She learned the technical parts, building her skills at persuasion and assertion. She learned how to stop apologizing. And she was promoted, until at last she headed her division. Outwardly she was a confident, capable success, a person who cared about people in organizations and had the chance to do something in this area every day. She was learning: invest in your own currency, not the currency of others. "You can't imitate someone else's success."

Finally, she decided it was time to change contexts. It was a difficult decision, because she valued loyalty and she had valued many aspects of her company. Nancy started her own human resources consulting firm. It wasn't a total break from her previous context, but was critically more satisfying. She was able to take this risk by saving money from her previous jobs and building up contacts.

Nancy reported a few months later that for the first time she felt in control and unapologetic at work. She felt honest as she advised others not to disguise their competency out of some need to be given permission to succeed. "I used to feel as if I blended into the walls of corporate America, as if I were turning gray," she said. "Now I have color back in my work life. My passions and talents feel integrated."

It wasn't perfect, but it was enough. As she freed her ability to bring her real self to the job, her creativity also soared. The last we heard from her she had become head of a professional association in her industry and was devising creative new programs not only through her business but for other colleagues as well.

Critical attention to context requires critical openness to change. If your core values or your signature skills are not thriving and growing in your work, it could be you—or it could be your context. Like Nancy, you probably have learned how to gain some measure of success in spite of these problems. Ask yourself what is enough, not just for today but for next year and for your life. Will this context take you there? If not, don't feel you have to make the break tomorrow—your resources may not let you do that. But *do* start building toward that goal now, or your context will enjoy more success than you give yourself.

As we reviewed the particular talents of high achievers to secure a sense of enduring success, we noted their uncompromising ability to takes risks and change contexts if things weren't likely to keep growing. They didn't waste themselves on longing for a context that was clearly contradictory to their skills. Even more striking, they actively exerted control of the contexts in which they would ultimately be pursuing success. This decisiveness was rewarding to the point of irony. Earlier in his career, Fred Sievert was senior vice president (or #2) of a small Midwestern firm. He successfully demutualized the company and sold it to a large foreign enterprise, only to realize that the new parent firm was going to let the business languish, no matter how hard he might try to save it. In his mind, he had to change contexts. When an offer came to be chief financial officer of the largest business unit at New York Life, it seemed far from perfect. His family loved their community, loved their church, and the position itself was a step down in scope of responsibility. But Fred saw the opportunity to grow, in a context that would stretch his skills, and a firm whose values he felt sympathetic with. With the family's blessing, he took the leap. Recently, he had occasion to be in his old hometown, and out of curiosity he sought out the headquarters building where he once was senior vice president managing over 500 people. No sign of the old business anywhere. At last he found it—in the basement. Four employees were there maintaining records and not even a sign on the door. Funny how luck comes to those who are prepared to find it.

The Context of Enough

What is the context you are engaged in? Is it enough for you be challenged and grow? Do you have enough capability to make it in that situation? What is practically possible for *you* versus the one who can jump the highest and be the fastest? Some things are not possible, others can be created. The test of what is enough for you and why on the four dimensions of success can help you tell the difference.

Are you able to experience moments of happiness and release at work or are you always having to push yourself to achieve? Is there a feeling of work being worthwhile enough to justify the effort? Does your family share this feeling? Contrary to the one-stop blasts of glory that typify many depictions of success, our four components of success suggest it takes many different targets to get to a state of enough. Is your context suitably flexible for you to make these transitions? Many people do not realize that they will achieve more in each component of success when they occupy a "middle ground of glory" than always striving out at the margins. Ever felt like an outsider in your own home after being away for week? Ever been the only woman /black/engineer/writer/white/Hispanic/marketer/whatever in your office? Even if you can succeed to get things done in such contexts, it is like being an army of one.

Being in the midst fulfills a deep need for belonging and also allows you to acquire additional help. To get there you need to be

in a context that is open enough for you to belong. However, be prepared for the other side. Social belonging can create its own tight fences around the value of loyalty, jealously preventing you from doing other things on penalty of ostracism. The welcoming work context can turn into a nightmare if everyone regards your effort to experience all four categories of satisfaction in multiple realms of your life as organizational betrayal. **One of the greatest responsibilities of great organizations, especially today, is to create the context in which all employees can achieve the four components of enduring success in a way that positively aligns with their self-definitions.**

Many organizations are actively working on improving their cultural contexts in terms of inclusiveness and flexibility. They do it for many reasons: moral belief, practical anticipation of changing workforce demographics, a sudden new awareness by a CEO whose own daughter or son-in-law is encountering baffling sexism at work. Our belief is that these measures, applied with consistency and openness to diversity, will not only develop enormous potential for productivity in people whose talents have been wasted in the past, it will create the kind of platform in which everyone can succeed in ways that draw on the core definitions that make success not only likely, but important.

Synergies within the Framework

Synergy is one of the most overused words in business management. As you consider the core self-definitions in relation to the four categories of success, it becomes clear that ideally you want to create a feedback pattern between the core definitions and the domains of satisfaction: If you bring your signature skills and the right emotional mix to an activity that conforms to your values and make full use of your context, you create more power to achieve your goal in any of the categories. If the context truly stretches you, the rewards from this accomplishment, whether material or nonmaterial, will grow your core further, adding to your skills, increasing your emotional capacity, and building new resources and capabilities. That in turn increases your chances of success in the next endeavor.

We witnessed the struggle of one interviewee to assess this challenge as he pondered whether or not to retire. He had always made heroic efforts to spend time with his family, but if he accepted a new promotion, he knew he would be required to travel overseas more than before. His last child was reaching high school age, and he wasn't sure his capacity to travel would be as keen as before, knowing he was leaving his last chance at parenting behind. When another interviewee faced this same situation, she too felt a sense that she hadn't had enough time to be a parent during her career, and this was her last chance. Would weighing their capabilities help them decide which direction to take in their careers? Would other capabilities, such as a drop in financial resources if they did retire, make a difference to them?

Despite our emphasis on the importance of each self-definition, the answer was not to be found completely in the question "Who am I?" or "What do I do best?" Rather, they had to look back to the four success components and reexamine the distribution they'd already established in each of the compartments. Both found the family area "thin" in terms of their own happiness (they hadn't had time to enjoy the process that much) but the actual provision of things and moments their family valued was very high (Significance). Knowing this allowed them to resolve to develop their capacity for appreciating the experience of happiness with family in the here and now but also continue to take on new challenges at work. This simple awareness resulted in several small adjustments of their schedule that allowed them to participate more fully in their child's activities that counted most to the child. He really didn't want them to give up their careers for him, just be there more predictably.

By contrast, consider the CEO of a major corporation who had just retired. He was attending a retreat and was thinking hard about his values and his life. He said he'd worked all his life for his company, had received many fine rewards, but somehow it was always about the company, not about his real self. "Now" he said, "it's time for me." Unlike many, he knew he was searching for more than happiness at the golf tee. We were intrigued. Who did he feel "me" really was? What did he plan to do that was higher in significance and happiness? "I don't know," he replied bleakly. "That's why I'm here."

Alignment and Calibration between
Self-Definitions and the Four Categories

As we warned at the outset of this chapter and this illustration confirms, this is a multifaceted, complicated process. You have to take it in pieces, keeping in mind the larger picture you are creating.

The key to this complexity is alignment and calibration: When you align your values with the employment of your signature skills in a context that reinforces these same strengths, you create a powerful and emotionally engaging force for achievement, significance, happiness, and legacy. When your internal choice of success goals aligns with the group in which you operate, the rewards are even higher (see Figure 5.7).

Professor Howard Gardner's comparison of satisfaction and energy in the professions of journalism and medicine makes a strong case for the benefits of this type of pattern.[12] He and his researchers found that in journalism institutional and individual professionals share a belief in what are the critical skills, values, and contexts for success. Because these are relatively well aligned with the public's expectations of the press in terms of rewards and allocation of resources, they have a powerfully reinforcing effect. Professionals perform well under these circumstances; they feel authentic, good about their work, take hard stands, are notorious for their dedication. They respond quickly when someone's behavior defies these ethical norms, as with the James Blair case at the *New York Times*. And they voluntarily pass on the wisdom and capabilities of the profession as mentors to the next generation of professionals. Despite our cynicism over the new celebrity factor that has crept in, we feel few fields have this strong a Legacy mechanism.

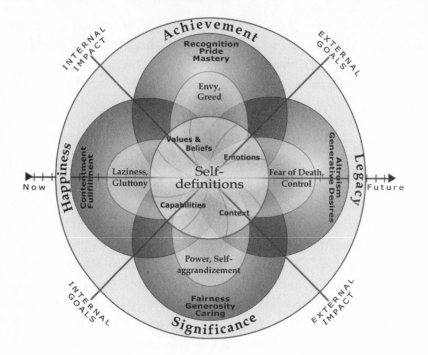

- Observing the opposites.

- Mapping your emotions.

- Avoiding the dark side.

- Getting the right success for you.

Figure 5.7   Mapping the success territory: Finding success consistent with your sense of self.

By contrast, medicine is in a misalignment between values, capabilities, and context that has left doctors *and* patients emotionally drained. The economic context is emphasizing management and efficiency, while the individuals see healing as the salient screen for determining which skills and values to bring to the table, invest in, and reward. Even the public is misaligned, honoring doctors for their healing but feeling that a rich doctor is inauthentic. The demoralizing and dysfunctional fallout from these misalignments has rendered the state of health care one of the most critical social problems today. Our expectations and tactical allocations of resources to the problem fight against each other and don't add up to success.

The Never-Ending Quest

In *The Power of Myth*, Joseph Campbell points out an archetypical pattern of heroic endeavor: the hero leaves home, literally or metaphorically, and makes a journey into an unfamiliar context. The quest to realize his or her larger nature involves at some point what Campbell calls a "Supreme Ordeal" that transforms the hero.[13] This dragon-slaying moment defines legendary heroism, but in our framework, it is not just one episode that defines your enduring success. Odysseus never tired of recounting his considerable exploits at Troy, but it was his many adventures afterward that won him enduring fame. In enduring success, the process of accomplishment and reward continues to unfold. The self-definitions change and grow as your accomplishments accumulate.

The patterns of success operate in multiple formats—in a yard sale, a course you take at school, a business project, and for a lifetime. Organizations find the significance of their success tested in transactions with the marketplace, votes of trust from investors, expressions of welcome from a community, in the commitment of their own employees. None of these rewards occurs without the critical elements of values, skills, understanding of the context, and an emotional bang. A company can pay the highest salaries, but if it doesn't bring out a sense of worth in employees, they will not stay committed.

Some heroes rest on their laurels, leaving the enduring aspects of their success for others to savor. For those who seek enduring success over their own lifetime, the quest for meaning and satisfaction never end, the need for mastery over new problems in the universe remains. They entertain the belief that a life which is not giving something every day is a life of the abandoned or, to borrow a phrase from Sophocles' *Antigone,* of a leader who "would be king over a desert." To keep the success process from jamming, stuck on its own good fortune or moments of discouragement, those who are most likely to succeed and those who are still finding their first real sense of success need to stay in close touch with the wondrous complexity of their core self.

Quick Points: Who Are You? And Why Are You Doing That?

Enduring success is complex because you are complex:

- Your present and potential capabilities.
- The values you hold dear.
- The emotions you experience.
- The unique environment in which you operate—family, work group, community—and the time in which you live.

The categories of success satisfy emotional needs that are both positive and negative:

- Achievement.
  - o Gives us recognition, pride, and mastery.
  - o But also can be driven by envy and greed.
- Significance.
  - o Fills our desire to be generous, fair, and caring.
  - o But can be driven by the lust for power and self-aggrandizement.
- Happiness.
  - o Makes us contented and renewed.
  - o But in excess can lead to laziness and gluttony.

- Legacy.
  - o Can be created out of a sense of altruism and our highest generative desires.
  - o But it can also grow out of fear of death and a desire for permanent control.

Enduring success requires:

- Recognizing that these forms of success compete and have different emotional drivers.
- Recognizing the complexity of our emotional makeup.
- Avoiding the insatiable emotions that represent the dark side.
- Defining successes for you.

Chapter 6

Complex Patterns in Real Life

I fear the popular notion of success stands in direct opposition in all points to the real and wholesome success. One adores public opinion, the other, private opinion; one, fame, the other, desert; one, feats, the other, humility; one, lucre, the other, love; one, monopoly, and the other, hospitality of mind.

—Ralph Waldo Emerson, "Success,"
Society and Solitude, 1870

In this age of endless opportunity and nosebleed travel through the targets of success, it's important to have some preliminary idea of what really drives the feeling of *just enough* for you to enable you to get more satisfaction from your activities and make room for a wider variety of satisfactions.

Look again at your baseline profile. What are the deepest "attractions" in your makeup that lead to a sense of satisfaction in all four areas of success? Why are these events so fulfilling? What skills, in what context, actually helped you realize these goals to a satisfactory accomplishment and reward?

Then there is the emotional element, which Jane commented on: Success is not just a logical getting of what you want. What you want is determined by your values and emotions. Is the profile of emotional satisfactions as rich as you'd like it to be?

We would like to share in this chapter a selection of fascinating examples of the interplay between the self-definitions and the four components of success to show how subtle and yet powerful the kaleidoscope framework can be. Each of these examples is a real experience, drawn from our research. We have chosen them to explore four critical lessons to keep in mind as you think about the components in your own kaleidoscope over time:

1. The four categories, though broad, have distinctive attributes that distinguish why an event seems a success or not—from a small episode to the sale of a business.
2. The self-definitions must drive the specific goals in each category, or success will drive you to places you don't want to go.
3. When you test for all these factors, you may detect a misalignment or blank spot in your overall picture. That will explain a key source of your dissatisfaction about the success of a particular situation or strategy.
4. When the factors are well aligned success feels "right," even if it doesn't make the *Guinness Book of World Records*.

If enduring success is about multiple conflicting goals, with important values and emotional drivers, and realistic constraints and opportunities in the form of resources and context, then *the ultimate moments of enduring success would be those in which the person acted in conformance with the most complete set of these factors.* We interviewed people with widely differing styles, skills, emotional makeup, and contexts. Some were scaling up, others scaling back. What was critical for each was the ability to create coherency between the core elements of their self-definition so as to bring all of them to bear on the choices and goals they pursued. This had pragmatic and emotional benefits.

The first example is a case story of a legendary moment of corporate greatness in the history of the Levi Strauss & Co. The second is a small episode about a yard sale. Both provide examples of the possibilities and dynamics of the framework of enduring success.

The Blackstone Plant at Levi Strauss & Co.

In the late 1950s, Levi Strauss & Co. (LS&Co.) faced a production challenge. Consumer demand for its products, especially its blue jeans and working pants, was exploding. Fueled by a combination of patriotic nostalgia for this affordable and iconographic piece of clothing, and reinforced by Chairman Walter Haas's brilliant understanding of the post-World War II baby boom market, the company needed more manufacturing capacity.

Given the real estate crunch in California and competition with the military for manufacturing labor costs, LS&Co. could no longer afford to rely only on its West Coast manufacturing sites. Like many other firms during this period, it decided to locate some of its manufacturing in the South. Two members of the Haas family, descendants of founder Levi Strauss's family, headed the firm at the time. Walter Haas Jr. had taken over the position of chairman from his father, Walter Sr., while his brother Peter was in charge of operations. It went without saying that this company, which had always stressed diversity and opportunity, would never open a segregated plant.

Peter Haas had joined the family firm reluctantly, only to throw himself into the production and financing side of the business. He loved nothing more than a perfectly scheduled production line: It was critical to him that any plant, however distant from California, meet LS&Co.'s standards. They waited until they could find the right context: a site where all the white males were already well employed, so that a new plant would be able to draw in African American and women workers without friction in the local job market. It needed to be a one-plant town to give them leverage to do it their way.

They finally found such a site in Blackstone, Virginia, and began to seek the permits to acquire an existing plant. One day one of Peter Haas's top managers took him aside. "You're not going to like this. The local officials in Blackstone are balking at our plan. They want to know where the separate lavatory facilities are. We haven't been able to get them to move on this stuff."

Haas was so worked up about it that he immediately flew to Virginia, rented a car, and personally drove himself, alone, to Blackstone. (This was a few years before the passage of the Civil Rights Act of 1964. Racial tensions were high at this time throughout the South over the issue of desegregation and outsider interference. Blackstone was a notoriously "rough" town near a military base.)

Haas met with the local officials, arguing his point, sticking to the plan. A quiet man without a bit of preachiness, he nonetheless was not going to give in. He eventually prevailed. LS&Co. opened the site, the first desegregated facility in that state, and within a few years, the town of Blackstone was celebrating its chief employer. This plant was one of many the company would open in the South during that decade, and its success at running an integrated facility would set the tone. If it worked at Blackstone, other new LS&Co. plants would believe it could be done. These new facilities were critical to LS&Co.'s phenomenal growth during the early 1960s, and they established its continued leadership in social responsibility for the next three decades. Within a few years, the company was a leader in the corporate coalition for so-called "minority" economic development.

What Made This Episode a Success

What made this episode a moment of enduring success in the history of Levi Strauss & Co. was the complex integration of its genuine *values* about social responsibility *and* marketplace success, its *capabilities* to use its manufacturing skills and its investment resources to set up successful new operations. It was also critical to be able to pick the right *context* for its success. As for *emotions*, Haas's emotional commitment at the time was very clear, not only to himself but to the employees who worked with him.

When LS&Co.'s current management team, under the direction of Chairman Robert Haas and CEO Phillip Marineau, reviewed this episode as one they felt embodied the values and drivers that had made the company great, they concluded that four seminal factors were in place. In their own words: Empathy (Walking in Others' Shoes), Originality (Being Authentic and Innovative), Integrity (Doing the Right Thing), and Courage (Standing Up for What We Believe). These were adopted for their values statement, with a commitment to use these values for social good and marketplace success.

The success of the Blackstone plant could not have happened at that time, however, if Peter Haas had not had such a gut-level emotional drive to make sure the plant opened without bending to segregationist practices. His emotional energy was shared by his financial officer, who first told him of the problem, and by the culture of the firm, which is the sign of an organization's values, beliefs, and emotional commitment. When Laura spoke with Peter Haas about this event, so long ago, he was very modest about it. Yet his emotional and values commitment was still vivid. He said he felt it was "just wrong" to give in to segregation. "I never hesitated to straighten this out right away. I just went down there to get it done. I never really thought about the safety issue . . . I guess I was pretty stupid!"

Pushing harder, she asked him what had been the most meaningful aspects of his career. Haas thought a long while before answering: "The thing that made me most proud was that as far as I know, I never caused a person to lose a day of work because I hadn't scheduled the cloth deliveries properly! That gave me great satisfaction."

Values and Beliefs, Skills and Resources, Emotions—all brought to the right Context—these drove Haas and the company's enduring success. You further may have suggested that you choose your fights. We are saying you have to choose your accomplishments too. Realism is critical to satisfaction.

Jonathan's Yard Sale

The interplay of the core drivers and four categories of enduring success are not just for historic deeds, the moments of greatness that we typically celebrate in success advice. This framework is a fractal pattern; it is important to operate from this perspective even in the everyday events of one's life. Staying open to the multiple targets, knowing what helps you get there—this kind of success intelligence is about creating a constructive sense of "enough" on an ongoing, cumulative basis. Take the simple story of Jonathan Fernandez's yard sale.

Jonathan Fernandez is a successful young producer and screenwriter who has achieved a higher degree of financial and professional rewards than most writers will ever experience. He had joined us at a café overlooking the Pacific Ocean in Santa Monica, California and was discussing his experience with success so far. Jonathan has already "made it" on many measures. After deliberately putting aside a career as president of a video line for Roger Corman; he became a producer in his own right, and executive producer of a major movie, *Breakdown*, that had been a box office hit. Still, his core drivers were telling him he had to try to make his mark as a screenwriter.

Success as a Hollywood screenwriter is a multipart process. Each step is fraught with risk, luck, and anxiety. Will you attract an agent who will accept you? Can you really complete a script? Will the agent actually give you the attention you need? Will a producer or actor pick up your work? Will an investor provide the backing? Will the production actually be wrapped up or go into financial meltdown? Will it retain the artistic goals you'd hoped for? Will a network buy it? Will they carry it in a good slot? Will the audience like it? Will it last?

Jonathan had scored on many of these benchmarks. He was represented by a top agency (ICM); he had seen several of his scripts produced already and had sold a pilot to Fox Network. A president of the *Harvard Lampoon* in college, he now saw writing as serious business. Six months earlier, we'd talked about his dreams, and since then he had notched up even more hits. Just recently he joined the writers at Star Trek Enterprises. Still, he hadn't yet crossed the threshold that would say to him, "You're definitely on your way." *That* would be an Emmy or his own smash hit—and he knows that will take time and luck to get there.

Film is a notably cruel industry. When I asked Jonathan what kept him going, he suddenly burst into laughter. A smile of absolute pure delight came over his face, a face that is always impish even at its most serene.

"I have to tell you this story. It's so ridiculous. I don't know where it fits into your success boxes, but it has something to do with all this."

Jonathan had held a yard sale the day before. Having just bought his first house (a four-bedroom home in the Hollywood hills area), he was moving out of his apartment and getting married. Over the years as a producer, he'd been given a number of terrific freebies—leather jackets, caps, sports equipment—the typical bachelor furnishings, and most of them had gone into a closet. Rather than throw them all out, he decided to have a sale. (This is Santa Monica, which is not exactly downscale.) He put all his stuff out on a table and within a few minutes he'd set up a game for himself. He decided that if anyone looked the least bit interested, he was going to find a way to see that they left with it.

Jon was madly selling things all morning, having a wonderful time. About two hours into the sale, his writing partner walked over, shaking his head. He couldn't see it. As a former lawyer, he thought the whole thing was a stupid waste of time. But Jonathan said, "I was having a blast. I loved guessing what made each person tick, what they wanted, and seeing if I could make the sale."

After about four hours, he'd taken in almost $700. He remembered one fellow who came with his kids and offered to buy the table itself. Jonathan took one look at the family and decided from that point on, everything would go for a dollar. Then someone tried to argue him down to fifty cents for a baseball hat. He'd had enough. "I could either spend the rest of the day trying to win the game of selling everything at a dollar or I could go walk on the beach with my fiancee. I shut it down. I boxed up the rest and gave it to charity."

What Made This Episode a Success

Jonathan began this story with the observation that he didn't know which of our success categories his experience fit into, just that it *felt* like an incredible success, one he'd remember for a long time. If you can understand the reasons behind his experience, you have the essential pieces of what makes an episode in life feel really worth it even when you entertain larger ambitions for the future. You have a new understanding of what goes into the definition of *enough:*

- Enough requires filling all four components through lightning switches of attention and meaning.
- To truly be satisfied, you tie these activities to the core drivers of what you consider important and satisfying.
- The episode "fits" in your larger success picture by providing a missing piece.

Jonathan's lasting satisfaction from the yard sale came from accomplishing something in all four categories, which required lightning switches of attention. It worked because his actions were tied to the core drivers: his skills, a good context for them, and self-awareness to focus on what he considered important and satisfying. The sale sparked his competitive business nature. It was an Achievement to empty his apartment this way and to see if he could figure out people's thinking and how to get the objects sold at an acceptable price. Figuring their price point, however, required knowing what they valued and giving it them (Significance). He scripted the event in a way that touched his funny bone and made him extremely happy. The overall purpose, however, was made more meaningful in that it had significance to others, like the family that bought the table, or the teenager who strutted away with a new leather jacket. There was also Legacy here: The objects themselves, instead of disappearing, would continue to give others some of the value he had seen in them. By ensuring they would continue to be used, he'd created a legacy rather than a wasted resource for the dump pile.

Still. It was only a yard sale, after all. Why was this particular event so satisfying, so filled with the elements of enough? The four components of success were not only in alignment in this event; they were closely connected to the core drivers that shaped Jonathan's personal ideas of enough. They reflected his skills in selling and in reading human nature; they made good use of the context at hand, exploiting the situation so that it was transformed from hassle into meaningful and entertaining event. Jonathan is drawn to the particular context where art and business meet. He once convinced his reluctant younger sister to work in a gallery for two years before going to art school so that she would never be bamboozled by those in the business side of her work. The experience was further intensified by his recent dedication to his writing. Emotionally, he was hungry for a *little* commercial victory while he labored at his more distant goals. The sale also expressed his values (beyond his respect for any event that contains humor). He believed it would be a waste simply to throw out the things in his closet. Making them available to people who would actually want and need them would give him a sense of contribution. And the sheer humor of holding a yard sale in Santa Monica and haggling over the junk gave him great and immediate pleasure.

As he indicated, Jonathan had made decisions about the yard sale that fulfilled each of the four satisfactions of success intuitively. As he commented, he wasn't really sure why it was so satisfying. He knew when he had just enough, and when to shut it down to walk on the beach.

Sarah's Story

When we saw how Sarah, a woman with career decisions quite similar to Jane's, made a fascinating and creative career transition, it helped clarify for us the complex pieces of the kaleidoscope. Her story demonstrates how staying within the main categories can discipline a radical job change without losing your best skills.

Sarah had been a buyer in a large retail chain for 14 years. Blond, petite, and gutsy, she had started as a sales clerk right out of junior college, and had quickly moved from junior manager to assistant buyer, to buyer. She'd toughed her way to her current position, diplomatically resisting her boss's crazy schemes to fool customers or squeeze suppliers. "I'll never work in a job where I compromise my values," she'd tell herself.

Now, at age thirty-four, Sarah was experiencing a new ambivalence about her ambitions. A new owner had introduced a draconian performance plan that placed every person's job in jeopardy.

Looking around her, Sarah saw a herd of disempowered employees, whose morale ranged from scared to selfish. She began to feel as if every negotiation was a make or break deal for her. When she was home with her son she couldn't concentrate on his stories of the latest soccer score. She bitterly recalled the words of her first boss, who had once said, "You know, anyone can do a job in good times, it's those who can do it in bad times who are the leaders." Sarah had always been inspired by these words, but now she was feeling as if no matter how hard she tried, there was no real chance of success in this environment.

It didn't take an irreversible wakeup call in the form of an ulcer or a delinquent child to turn her around. It was her husband, Dan, who gave her permission to ask herself what she really loved about retail and about the family. "Why not think it through, Sarah, and go for what you really want?" Sarah began an inventory of her satisfactions: she loved the mechanics of buying and selling in retail; the reliance on her own taste and feel for the customer; the pride at outselling the competition. When customers told stories of how a purchase made their day, or admired the goods she'd ordered for her department, Sarah felt important, and she liked knowing that people felt better off for having bought her items. Until recently, her expertise at this job had also made it possible to do the work and still have room for daily interaction with her son. What she most missed, however, was the exposure to elementary education, which she had majored in at community college.

Sarah and her husband decided that instead of making a planned addition on their house, she should take out a loan and start her own children's toy store. She knew that many parents at her son's school were dismayed by the big discount houses. They hated much of the merchandise and they hated the way their kids became little buying monsters at the sight of so many well-advertised items. Sarah rented a small space in a street corner shopping area not far from an upscale neighborhood. Part of the reason the space was cheap was that it needed work. With lots of paint and careful selection of toys that emphasized craftsmanship and exploratory, hands-on play, she was able to attract a strong customer base. Her store became a magnet for children *and* parents, and it gave her great pleasure to see their shopping experience be a positive family episode rather than an occasion for warfare. The store made money. Her first two success categories were spilling nicely into each other: by being seen to deliver value to her customer (Significance), she was able to accomplish Achievement as well. By careful anticipation of the competitive realities (Achievement), she had the cash flow to keep the inventory fresh and appealing to the parents.

But these satisfactions weren't fed from the same source. The decisions she made about profits and costs came from careful review of the competitive success of the store. The appeal to customers was a result of her empathetic ability to get into their mind-set, to observe their needs and what they valued from the shopping experience. The benchmarks for her Achievement were her own accomplishments measured against certain other stores—she wanted to be the best toy store in town and she had to master a number of financial problems to make this happen. The benchmarks for Significance were her customer's actual experience, which required a keen sensitivity akin to empathy. These skills were a far cry from the desires that fueled her competitive strengths.

As time went on, however, Sarah became concerned about the amount of stress she was under. Originally, she'd been able to see more of her son after school. But as the success of the store grew, she was spending more time visiting wholesalers, negotiating an expansion of the space, responding to the needs of a growing customer base. She was working such long hours that she'd forgotten how to stop and actually enjoy the shop she'd worked so hard to create. Nor was her family happy. Either she had to hire another assistant or give up on this venture's promise for happiness. The choice was not automatic. Sarah took a hard look at the balance sheet and realized she was going to give up some of the personal financial rewards that were associated with her Achievement up to this point to pay for the extra employee. She did so, and found herself once again shifting between the three chambers with relative harmony.

The satisfaction Sarah received from this success was so great that about two years later, her achievements led her to venture into the Legacy chamber. Through her store's success, Sarah had become a local authority on children's activities. When the library approached her to get involved in an after-school reading program, she turned her energies to making this commitment a Legacy of her store. She used the store's wide reputation to sponsor and advertise the library project. This linkage, which lasted years, came back to the store's interests in the form of new customers. Sarah's values on learning and fun, which had built her financial success, were now becoming a Legacy, a model on which others were building new kinds of learning experiences.

Enough

Our code word for the process by which Sarah and the other interviewees achieved lasting satisfaction and ongoing success is *enough*. To break out of the iron cage of success stress, you cannot simply go for extreme simplicity or extreme wealth. You have to know what is *just enough* to set limits. This allows you a reachable win from which to assess your capabilities and have new contexts for your next goal. This incremental growth in accomplishments keeps success on track, close to your core definitions. Rather than go for broke, you can determine how to take the next step, identify what you need to accomplish to get to a sense of enough in each of the four categories, across every realm that is important to your values—family, work, self-expression, your place in your community. None of the people we interviewed, no matter how satisfied or successful, did it perfectly. Mistakes and corrections go with the territory, but each demonstrated critical aspects of how to get the overall success approach in dynamic balance.

Were Jane to rebalance her own profile within the parameters of this framework, she would no doubt see a "practical possible" in her seemingly bleak situation. It probably wouldn't be a career in church music, but she would find a job context where she could continue to volunteer at her church, build the choir, and see this as an activity in her Significance category. It might even prepare her to continue an avenue of Achievement for herself were she to put her career on hold or half-time when she has children. We think she'd find she was making better use of her own capabilities and values were she to consider this course.

What's Enough for You?

As you read the next two profiles of two very high-powered achievers, you may be asking yourself what you have in common with these situations. Go back to your baseline profile and self-definitions, and consider these questions: What are the deepest attractions in your makeup that lead to a sense of satisfaction in all four areas of success? What attracted you to or gave you reservations about their stories? Does your mix look richer or thinner than that of the people profiled here? What did their self-definitions have to do with the choices they made? What signature skills, in what context, actually helped you realize the goals you've achieved so far?

Then consider that emotional mix that Jane referred to: Is the profile of emotional satisfactions in these stories something you would associate with success? Notice that each has its own share of ups and downs. How do you explain their overall sense of having won a positive, no regrets success?

Finally, this is a good place to begin to begin applying the concept of enough with more frequency. What in their stories tested this concept? Did they have to deal with it at all?

Katharine Graham's Journey

Katharine Graham fired a lot of bullets at her own dreams until she got to know herself and her own capabilities a little better. Her story did not begin at all well.[1]

When Phil Graham, legendary editor-in-chief of the *Washington Post*, decided to make a bid for the ownership of the whole Washington Post Company, Katharine Graham found herself in the unwelcome situation of having to oppose the husband who had cruelly walked out on her. Already broken and bitter, she now faced the loss of her family's beloved publishing company, knowing that her own father (now deceased) had given Phil the major part of the company's stock and considerable financial backing throughout his tenure. Ms. Graham was despondent. She didn't want to lose the family company but she also didn't have someone who could plausibly oppose Phil Graham. Meanwhile the *Post's* financial situation was desperate.

Two friends, *New York Times* correspondent Scotty Reston and Washington bureau chief Luvie Pearson, helped her hang on. Reston offered to begin training her son Donny to take over, which gave her a new hope that her "father's paper" could continue to be a Graham legacy. Pearson, a lifelong friend, put Graham in touch with her own core drivers, scolding Graham for being so unaware of her own talents after years of being put down by the men in her family. Writes Graham: "That was the first time that anyone had mentioned the idea of my running the company, or that I had even contemplated it in passing. The whole notion struck me as stunning and ridiculous, wrongheaded but sweet, coming as it did from my good, loyal friend who was trying valiantly to buck me up but who obviously didn't understand what running the business was all about and what it would take."[2]

The rest, as they say, is history. Katharine Graham became a publishing legend. Despite immediate crises like the printers' strike and the Nixon administration's attempts to obstruct the *Washington Post's* coverage of Watergate, Graham's leadership broke new ground on editorial, journalistic, and gender issues for over 30 years. In her autobiography, she paints a portrait of a woman never totally sure of herself and yet completely certain of her publishing judgment. It's unlike our Jane, who knew her skills but had no idea which context would suit her ideas of success, Graham knew how to assess the context in which she found herself from the standpoint of success in its four categories. The passage quoted is a significant inflection point in that process: though outwardly resisting Luvie Pearson's advice, Graham was indirectly working through her own core self-definitions of success and testing whether the drivers of the paper's success could be wedded to hers.

Time and again, Graham's instincts for understanding what resources were needed for success and how to acquire them when she was not fully equipped supported her, building her capabilities, expressing her values, engaging her emotions. Was she satisfied in all the categories and all the domains of her life? Hardly. Her autobiography is poignantly frank about the emptiness of her marital life, the put-downs from both parents, and her alleged shyness at social events. Nonetheless, she managed to notch up repeated episodes of enduring success. In the domain of work, she frequently hit on all four categories: Achievement, Significance, Happiness, and Legacy.

Graham did not escape having to make hard choices in order to be effective, any more than Jane can escape her hard choices. We can't promise you a perfectly happy life—in fact, we're quite convinced very few people actually want this. But we hope we have shown you how to approach your choices around Happiness, Achievement, Significance, and Legacy in a way that makes it more likely you'll achieve success—success that not only makes your mark in the world, but is worthwhile to you.

Marshall Carter: Crisis as a True Guide to Your Values

We would like to end this chapter by revisiting the concept of understanding your values that we started in the last chapter. Why? Because we have found that those who pursue the promptings of their deepest convictions, who believe that what they are doing is right, usually exceed even their own high expectations. This can place, them, however, in positions that seem to *inhibit* their chances of success. As one CEO noted, if monetary recognition is your highest value, then you probably have to ditch loyalty to one organization in favor of moving around to increase your title and enhance your compensation. On the other hand, if you define success as developing your leadership and expanding your scope of responsibility, then a longer term commitment is beneficial. You can't have it both ways. What's your time frame? Is it enduring?

Marshall Carter, recently retired chairman of State Street Bank, learned the power of core values at an early stage when he acted almost purely on instinct in the heat of battle in Vietnam. The leader of an infantry unit, his company was caught in an ambush from two directions. As they backed off, a wounded soldier was left behind. Carter had to get the platoon out of the area at once. But he wasn't going to leave the wounded man. He looked around and realized no one was able to move forward without being in great danger. "Well, no one else is going to do it. It's my job." Carter raced forward and carried the man out under heavy fire. How he dodged the bullets is something he himself can't answer. The soldier was, as he expected, dead. It didn't matter. Said Carter, "I didn't even have to think about it. You just don't leave your men behind."

As he reflected further, he acknowledged there was a practical logic to this: A commander depended on the trust of his platoon, and a basic ingredient of trust was that you'd take care of your own. But for Carter the episode ran deeper. It simply was what his values told him to do.

This incident earned Carter the Navy Cross, the military's second highest honor. He doesn't tell the story to brag, but to mine it for what it told him about success and the obligations of leadership. One lesson was the deep, driving force of doing what is right. Carter is a deeply conscientious person. He has frequently subjected his own success to the deeper scrutiny of his idea of ultimate purpose. When he realized, for example, that his compensation as chairman of State Street was going to become "truly significant" in terms of his stock options, he and his wife immediately set in motion a plan for sizable personal charitable contributions far beyond the typical 1.6 percent that is the national average. The same values orientation was given play at almost a gut instinct level in episodes he regarded as typifying successful management in his eyes.

For this kind of values consistency, sometimes you have to be willing to display a surface inconsistency. Carter compares two instances of takeover opportunities during the early days of his chairmanship at State Street. The first was in the Midwest. A failing bank was in play for acquisition. If State Street moved quickly, they had an opportunity to forestall a competitor's chance at growth, which would probably further the competitor's decline. The second target was in Boston, again a bank whose balance sheet and customer base made it a likely target for takeover by someone in the near future. For State Street, this acquisition would expand the customer base and allow for significant economies of scale through downsizing. Some of the administrative jobs in the acquired company could easily be taken over by current State Street personnel. He knew that whatever he did, both of these companies were going to be taken over by someone.

Carter decided to make the first acquisition, but not the second. Why, we asked, when both presented a competitive advantage to you? His answer was purely on values—his own and that of the corporation. "We couldn't do that. Not in Boston." Why? "That's not who we are in Boston. We can't be cannibals feeding off our own community." This was from a chairman whose nine-and-a-half-year tenure saw a 16 percent compounded growth rate of operating earnings, including an eightfold growth in revenues outside the United States. Carter brought these same values of community welfare and effectiveness to his first official task after retirement. At the request of the Massachusetts governor, he led the state investigation of security at Logan airport after September 11. Carter's team brought this important and sensitive report in on schedule, despite the incredibly short time frame (six weeks).

We heard about the Carter family's community giving again recently, when they pledged $5 million in seed money to the Boston Medical Center for a program to consolidate its 12 inner city cancer care locations. Their interest in inner city problems is absolutely genuine, an important part of their beliefs, and they also know how to turn these values into success. In this case, as Carter will tell you with rapid-fire statistics should you happen to ask, the $5 million was donated strategically to challenge the wealthy community that is outside the medical center's fund-raising screen to donate the

$100 million necessary to address appallingly neglected inner city medical problems.

When Carter was interviewed on the radio, they kept asking him what was his interest in the inner city? He finally replied in frustration, "Because for the last 10 years I'm one of those guys you're always talking about making an obscene CEO salary. I wanted to give something back." The remark established its own legacy and was widely repeated as a challenge to the public.

Living from Your Real Values

We can't all live our charitable impulses to the monetary degree that the Carters have, but if a life of achievement, prosperity, and contribution that is true to your values appeals to you, enough gives you a framework to find *your level* in each of the categories. Missy Carter found that level in scaling back her career but growing her charitable skills. Marsh put a cap on how much wealth he'd seek for himself and his family, and stayed in touch with his former sources of enough. On his sixtieth birthday, at his request, his two children and Missy threw a party that featured family casserole favorites that he liked when meals were a lot simpler in the Carter household.

Many of the businesspeople we spoke to had also retained a closeness to the simpler things they really valued. They worried about the short-term spin that today's celebration of quick fortunes was imposing on traditional values about profit. It wasn't that they didn't think profit was an important value in business. They simply felt other values were trumping real profit and undermining the prospect of enduring success. It wasn't honest. Pleasing the analysts with short-term victories was their number one complaint.

This is the second important reason to reexamine your self-definition in connection with real, enduring success: sometimes the values and emotions you are bringing to bear on success are *wrong*. They won't get you to the performance heights you seek, never mind provide a means to an enduring sense of satisfaction and worth. If your core values are truly selfish, then an examination of your expectational assumptions may cause you to reconsider.

A far more frequent problem for many people was feeling that somehow they simply weren't "close enough" to their real values in the choices they were making for the sake of success. In some cases, they hadn't considered the role of enough in calibrating and appreciating their values. In other cases, they simply hadn't thought about it enough. Values don't always sit on the surface. Sometimes you have to extrapolate. Joe, a top executive who had made enough money to retire very comfortably, told us that the highest moment of his career was playing a round of golf with a PGA winner and being able to hold his own. Did that mean that golf was his highest value? Digging deeper, it was the sense of going beyond what was expected, making a mark in the presence of someone whose excellence he valued that really made that moment so enduring. It was the proximity to someone else who seemed to *embody* this excellence that had cemented the moment in Joe's mind.

Knowing that Joe was in the medical supply business, we asked him if any particular values had been important to him there that resembled that moment on the golf course, he laughed. Of course, he said, he'd been exaggerating. In fact he had had this same deep satisfaction (if not glee) on many occasions. One in particular was the time he met the family of a child whose life had been transformed by his product. Joe's value in healing, building, creating, were critical to his idea of success. Don't stop with the cheap thrills. What are your deeper satisfactions? What is the achievement you could make that would be most important to you? And when would it be enough?

Helping Jane Make a Decision

Given the range of choices today, and the pace in which we all live, intuition is inadequate to the task of sorting and pursuing the right success for you. The framework we are exploring in this book will help direct your goals and how you get there today, but the process of real and enduring success is a lifelong journey.

The point is to get started in the right direction. As we reviewed the incredible power of this framework in helping provide meaning and direction for people who value success, we were brought back to

Jane and her frustration over not being able to accomplish all she wanted. Unless Jane began to live out the full spectrum of success *now*, she was in danger of never fully launching any of her dreams, swamped by her own talents and confusion.

At the time, we suggested she take one small step beyond her baseline profile. We asked, "What if you stopped trying to see the church organist position in your Achievement category, but committed to its being the largest chip in Significance? Would this align with what you most value in the profession of music?" She looked at the emotional definers in Significance: caring, having a valued impact on those whom you care about. Yes, that was a fairly obvious fit. "Now," we said, "look at the drivers of Achievement: competitive dominance over something, winning, curiosity." How did that match up? Not so well. These were not the satisfactions Jane was looking for out of her music and service. She'd always believed she could avoid the harshness of these values by choosing a less competitive field, but she began to see that these factors did not necessarily equate with ruthlessness. The curiosity and fun of winning as a manager solving a problem were actually quite exhilarating to her. She began to change her expectations about both activities in a way that was allowing her to make a choice.

You Need to Do This

Howard received a letter from a former student, now a seasoned entrepreneur reaching the age at which many have retired. John Van Slyke, president of Alta Research, was writing about his deepening sense of satisfaction as he grew older. He reported he had a more refined sense of direction and focus than in the past, which was giving him renewed energy. Given the boom-bust events of the late 1990s and the discouragement young people were feeling about the job market, he now felt an urgency to use his own business experience to help the next generation become effective leaders. In this regard, he had a message that captured a core belief that he felt drove his own approach to the world: "One can count on very little except uncertainty." He'd first had this dictum impressed on him by his light weapons instructor during Navy training: "Listen up. Take nothing for granted. The enemy could be anywhere. He has weapons. He has live ammunition. His objective is to kill you. To say alive, you must keep these facts in mind. You must always think ahead, and you must act, and give orders accordingly. You must know yourself, and you must be a master of the weapon you carry. If you do not do these things, you will be killed. Worse yet, your men will be killed. It's that f—g simple. Any questions?"

For many of us trying to navigate today's landscape of moving and unpredictable targets, doing what it takes for success can feel much like war. Moving targets can—and often do—provoke fear and exhaustion. As you think about your own moving targets around success and try to choose goals you would want to have in your kaleidoscope of accomplishments some day, you may see bullets everywhere. Some of them will be fired by your own inability to take your dream in hand. But when we are prepared for them, we can see them in another way: as opportunities for decisive action.

Quick Points: Complex Patterns in Real Life

To define enough for yourself, you must understand your ambitions and your limits—and therefore your choices—in every domain:

- *Achievement:* On which dimensions do you intend to succeed? To whom do you wish to be compared?
- *Significance:* Who matters to you? Limitless ambitions will make your caring ineffective.
- *Happiness:* What makes you happy that is in the realm of the possible? Setting unrealizable goals will lead only to frustration.
- *Legacy:* What of your accomplishments and values will others carry on? What should you enjoy now?

PART THREE

JUST ENOUGH

Chapter 7

Making Successful Choices

Thirty-five years ago, Chip Taylor wrote a little song. Now work means going to the mailbox to collect the checks.
—Andy Langer, "The Songwriter," *Esquire*, July 2003

When Jane reviewed the profile of her success components, she liked the picture much better just for understanding more about why each part of her life was important. The struggle she was feeling was authentic to her self-definition: She couldn't simply throw out the pieces, but at least she felt more in command as she ordered the opportunities ahead of her. Suddenly her whole body sagged, and she said wistfully, "If I could just get into an early-stage software firm, maybe I wouldn't *have* to make these choices!"

Change is difficult, especially in the face of conflicting choice. Our framework had given Jane new sources of power over her situation, but a critical piece was still missing. She would never be able to escape her indecision until she could apply the fundamental concept of *just enough*. By this term we don't mean settling for the minimum. Just enough is actually a vehicle for actively making choices that get you more, not less, through achieving satisfaction on more dimensions in life. It is a key adjustment in applying the kaleidoscope strategy.

Inside the Kaleidoscope Framework

Comparing the framework of enduring success to a kaleidoscope suggests a fundamental shift in thinking. Success is no longer one big target that automatically confers many commensurate (mutually supportive or complementary) rewards in its wake, but rather an ongoing process of reaching many different (incommensurate) goals. The satisfaction of completing a deal does not predict whether you will have a satisfying time at home that night. It does not even predict whether your own employees will feel the effort was as important as you did. To them it may appear disturbingly ruthless and predatory in light of other expectations. Success is more complicated than simply "knowing the one thing you really want and going after it," and so are the choices around it.

Success is about the process of filling the chambers we call Happiness, Achievement, Significance, and Legacy and making a judgment about the pattern you've created. Every time you complete a goal, you've placed a new chip in one of the chambers of the kaleidoscope we call a good life. It is possible to enrich the pattern of each episode in your life, even at the smallest fractal, through the creation of chips in all four chambers. This is what Jonathan's yard sale accomplished. It is what happened when Levi Strauss & Co. created values for the entity itself and its owners, for its employees, for its customers, and society as a whole. To call this win-win, however, can be misleading: **Each piece of what appears to be a "four-chip" accomplishment lies in a separate chamber of attention, drawing on different kinds of emotional energy and rational calculations of the distribution of costs and benefits.**

How Kaleidoscopes Work and How Your Success Works

We chose the kaleidoscope metaphor because it expressed life's complexity in a way we have not seen in other models. Here as a reminder are three important things to remember about the inner workings of kaleidoscopes, and by extension your picture of enduring success:

1. *Variety and separation are critical:* Although the four chambers of a kaleidoscope are framed by a casing so as to form a whole picture, the essential function of a kaleidoscope's chambers is to

separate the chips. This is what gives them a place in the picture while making room for other chips, for movement, and for a multifaceted design.

2. *The key feature of a kaleidoscope's design is movement:* Unlike a painting, a kaleidoscope's special feature is that it presents a constantly shifting pattern. The four chambers allow this movement by keeping their boundaries intact, but the chips are constantly shifting in relation to each other either because the viewer has shifted the dial or gravity has imposed a new force on the pattern.

   This movement is much like the changes in goals and desires that we observed in every person's evaluation of success: what you want is colored by the whole, and the value of certain things changes over time. You can make desirable choices for now that get you a success with a large "empty spot" ten years later. Just enough is about making sure you are experiencing all four satisfactions on a regular basis, in present time, and anticipating that what is enough for tomorrow will require adjustments and costs to this immediate gratification in order to satisfy future needs. You can concentrate solely on reaching a future state of perfection and a final score, or you can experience pleasure in the journey itself.

3. *The only way you can enjoy a kaleidoscope is to hold it up to the light:* Our framework is a way of holding your own accomplishments up to the light and seeing which chamber they've fallen into, how varied your pattern is, and what combinations you'd like to add during the next phase of your journey. So far, we've implied a great deal of choice around this process and the necessity of knowing who you are, what you want and why. Merely holding the kaleidoscope up and examining the four chambers of success in your life will help you better understand what it is you are seeking and what it is you most liked about what you've done so far, or where you need to do more work or less work.

   Success is as much about the process of building the kaleidoscope as enjoying it: You don't spend all your time looking through the glass, but visiting it at regular intervals helps you balance the colors and realign your efforts when one is particularly low.

Kaleidoscpe Strategies and the Choices of Success

But what about the process of choice itself? Can you improve the pattern in terms of its ability to give satisfaction and enduring value? Or are the colors of the chips you create today bound to turn dull and dissatisfying over time? What can you do to make sure you shift the dials with skill and intention rather than simply leaving the pattern to chance? How can you think about multifaceted satisfaction in a coherent frame if the chambers are separate?

We've offered many examples where people have entertained conflicting desires: between what they want for achievement and what they need for happiness; between what they want for now and what they want for ten years from now; between what they want as individuals and what the organization to which they pledge loyalty needs; between what seems purely "authentic" motivation and what seems expedient for the sake of success.

We have also seen problems of calibration: What is enough for the future may demand the suspension of experiencing satisfaction in present time. Simply relying on your current emotional response cannot get you there. Nor can sheer rational calculation. There are plenty of distracting targets out there to throw you off course.

To work the process of success well, you have to handle not only the question of what is a good life, but the age-old challenge of choice between competing desires. How will you evaluate what is the right mix between striving for near and obvious rewards and delaying such gratifications in favor of pursuing other goals? What will make room between your success chambers so as to allow movement and the addition of new chips? Do you throw out your kaleidoscope every seven years in a process of total reinvention (and your spouse and your career and your stockholders and your other commitments as well)? Or can you manage the process with greater deliberation and lasting reward?

Managing the moving targets of desire around success is a complex process of dealing with what we technically called "incommensurate choice," that is, one thing you want *competes* with something else you want and cannot be measured on a single scale. In layman's terms, it means there are no trade-offs. You can't substitute learning for food; they serve very different functions for the human being.

There is a vast body of knowledge about incommensurate choice, ranging from ancient philosophy to psychology and economics to new studies in the philosophy of the mind.[1] These debates about the nature and source of motivation raise important questions about just how much you can control your choices to achieve what you really believe you should do. All of them, however much they are based in empirical studies of motivation, choice, or even life satisfaction, fall far short of providing *the* definitive explanation. Do we fail to avoid self-defeating choices because of cognitive failure, emotional flaws, or some combination of the two? How deliberately can we readjust these tendencies? Should we employ rational rewards and bargaining or irrational, emotional attractions?

We refer to relevant findings on preference and decision making as we consider the ways in which people handle the choices around the categories of success, and we have tried to strike a sensible middle in this debate, based on our own research. Our research was for the most part anecdotal, and not empirically tested. If someone said they felt satisfied or short-changed, we took their word for it and dug into how they saw their reality. Our hope, however, is that the framework and approach we offer here through the concept of enough will generate continued research in this area.

Finding Insight Points

The touchstones we employed to explore preference and motivation are what we call *insight points*. Our research focused on opportunities for rational and emotional self-examination, where the choices of success become either extremely stressful because of conflict or extremely "right" because of their simultaneous inherent satisfaction and ability to create "switching" between categories of success. This is the kaleidoscope moment, as it were, and we believe it can lead to more deliberate and accurate aim as you choose your success targets.

As we noted before, the ability to secure one's goals with intense focus (emotional and cognitive) and lightning-fast switching was the single most striking "success intelligence" that we observed in people who seemed to be able to achieve much and still be well-rounded, pace themselves, and give to others. None of them had perfect control over their emotions, none were perfectly consistent. We've taken what they've reported about success when they did it well and when they slipped up, and created a template of critical junctures of choice that people typically encounter. These are the insight points at which the enduring success framework becomes most useful and defining *enough* becomes critical.

Consider the time David used the four categories to think about cutting back on his workload. David owned his own business and loved being an entrepreneurial success. He had wealth, family, religious meaning in his life, and a very big headache. It got worse when his teenage daughter ran away from her summer camp. And yet he couldn't quite give up the pieces of his business. When he spoke with us, he'd already made some deliberate choices to increase the "Happiness" chips in his kaleidoscope. He'd bought a plane and was taking flying lessons. His family was furious at first. They saw no value in the activity, and did not realize he wasn't doing it for value but for sheer pleasure, something he needed badly.

"Why not sell part of your business?" we asked. David admitted he too had come to this conclusion "for the sake of his happiness," but couldn't quite execute the decision. We suggested he rethink the chambers he was putting this momentous decision into. Why not think about it as building Legacy instead of Happiness? Could selling part of his firm create a Legacy of his Achievement on which someone else could build?

He brightened; the gears were working again. Our suggestion had sorted the choice he faced in a way that felt right because the changed category of success expressed the meaning that gave him the most satisfaction. He suddenly became positive. A former employee who was looking to run a company would be the perfect CEO for the spin-off. He could help him get started and know the business would keep its essential values and character. Already he was more decisive. If he could arrange this, he felt it would be enough to satisfy his need to cut back on Achievement at work and make room for enriching his time with family, his abilities as a spouse and parent, and his skills at flying. This didn't mean *giving up* his business—he didn't accept the classic idea of "half time"—but merely downsizing in a way that made his business enough for his several needs. No hang-ups on price. No hang-ups on time frame. It suddenly felt right.

What screen will you apply to direct your search for the right mix of strengths to bring to success? You may see yourself as a future leader improving the world (we hope so). To realize this vision, how will you direct your many emotions and talents to the right success categories and in the right proportions? What will you willingly sacrifice in the process? How much improvement should you put into your product to bring it up to its quality standards? Can you ever fully know? As we've seen, if your success is to be more than just a search for happiness or what makes your company the most profit, you have to stay anchored to your core definitions. And your core definitions need to be directed by a fully developed understanding of enough.

What Is Enough?

Conventional understandings of *enough* don't capture its full potential to transform ideals about the good life into the pragmatically possible. People tend to use this word to indicate a state of *dissatisfaction,* as in "I've had it! That's *enough.*" Or as code for mediocrity and passivity, as in, "If I'm just happy every day, that's enough." In the case of how much quality is enough for your product, some take enough to mean just enough to satisfy the minimum that the market will accept. One of our interviewees who had maintained her family and her career in a very high-powered industry expressed strong reservations about the title of this book. She said, "I certainly don't want people to think that I tried to get away with just enough work to get by! I worked very hard."

We mean something else by *enough*, closer to its root definition: occurring in sufficient quality or quality to satisfy demands or needs. This use of the word has fallen out of common usage. *Enough* is indeed a place marker of limitation, but limitation need hardly be a negative aspect of success. Enough sets both upper and lower limits. Defining *enough* is the only way we know to access a sense of *greater* satisfaction and make room for all the moving targets you seek or inevitably encounter in the pursuit of success and the good life.

We spotted this use of *enough* in a recent interview with someone we greatly admire, the legendary British author and television commentator Clive James. For the past 35 years, James has had an incredibly rich life as a critic, a novelist, a poet, a memoirist, a performing artist, and now the impresario of a tango salon in his own apartment to fulfill his latest passion. Comments James about his life: "I'm trying to open up new opportunities, which is probably crazy at my age. But there are other things I can do yet. I'm thinking of writing a musical with Pete [Atkin], a tango musical. That could be my ultimate calling. That could be the one where God reaches down from heaven with a lightning bolt and says, enough."[2]

Entrepreneurs are frequently characterized as driven by restless dissatisfaction, but the creative James seems to be describing a sense of restless *satisfaction* in his comment on *enough*. Though superficially leaving the judgment of his *enough* to God, he obviously appreciates the combination of satisfaction and creative seeking that has made him such a humane talent. *Enough* contrasts sharply with assumptions of celebrity success that enslave you to impossible, contradictory standards demanding limitless skill and limitless rewards in order to be satisfied.

Getting to Enough through Relational Choices

The concept of enough usually triggers calculations of quantity: How *much* is enough? Just enough seems even more quantitative, suggesting some tipping point of satisfaction beyond which it would be foolish to go. When David, in our previous example, was thinking about his flying and his business, he found his family was placing very different evaluations on his flying than he was. How should he determine what would be enough piloting in his life? How much money would he put into it? More importantly, how much time and emotional investment?

To answer the quantitative question posed by *enough,* you first have to conduct several other calculations on important dimensions of satisfaction. In this chapter and the next, we discuss the most influential factors in this process: the calculus of relationships and the calculus of time.

Whom do you most want to satisfy in seeking success? How much do other people come into your success picture? Are you cultivating these goals or frustrating them in your assumptions about what it takes to "make it"? Should David take his family's objections seriously? If he doesn't, can he really be of Significance to them? On the other hand, if he *does* give up his dream, his Happiness component would be empty—as it had been for a long time. He posed the question as either/or, but were he to conceive of an additional activity either of Happiness or of Significance to him, he would have two viable solutions. He could take up flying, but would need to invest more in doing something else with his family. Alternatively, he could give up flying on the condition that he actively seek another kind of leisure pleasure with similar satisfactions. But in either case, to engage successfully in the two activities, he would have to place a limit on how much time he spends at leisure or in significance activities. **He would have to determine what was enough in relation to what he felt and what his family felt. Recognizing the empty spaces in his kaleidoscope helped hold him to the task emotionally and rationally.**

Some people—and some corporations—see all relationships as secondary consequences of self-interested behavior. If I succeed, my family should be happy. If my company makes a profit, everybody should be better off. If I am a star, my parents will be proud. Probe these assumptions and they usually take you into all four chambers of success expectation. The company president who aims for the highest earnings per share expects not only a reward for winning but respect from others, which will indicate the social worth of what they did (Significance), a decline in their competitors' share of market and a place in the corporate halls of fame (Achievement), legacy status in the form of guru book summarizing the their special secret of success (Legacy), and lots of Happiness. Not finding this nirvana in high achievement? Could be that your decisions are failing to take the other categories' orientations into account sufficiently (see Figure 7.1).

To summarize:

- *Achievement:* Your goals get set in comparison with others, but the impact of your engagement with the external world is

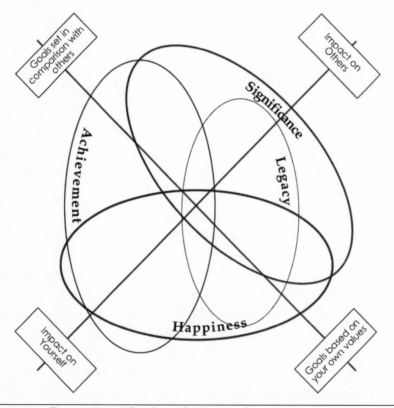

Figure 7.1   Goals and impact of success categories.

largely internal. Even though your actions affect others, it is *your* achievement.

- *Significance:* The impact of your actions is external. You set such goals to be consistent with your values but oriented toward the impact on others.

- *Happiness:* You ultimately decide what makes you happy and you experience its impact.

- *Legacy:* Based on your values and accomplishments, others carry forward your work. For the truly great legacies, your impact is unknown and unknowable in present time.

As the success model shows visually with the axis of Self and Others, each of the chambers has a different relational orientation. For brevity, we will refer to these orientations using the shorthand of in-in, or in-out, and so on.

Achievement Is In-Out

Achievement is essentially an in-out orientation even though it staunchly favors yourself in the competitive arena. You want to win for yourself, but the goal you set is not completely self-referential if achievement is to realize satisfaction. It's one thing to say, "As long as I'm breathing, that's enough achievement for me," and quite another to experience achieving against an external standard that others have also set for themselves.

When Marie Curie discovered the uses of radiation, she was clearly out to save lives (and even gave her own to the cause), but she was fully aware of the competitive meaning of her work and relished the satisfaction of mastering this problem ahead of other scientists. Had she fully oriented her choices simply in a self-denying way (which is how she is often depicted by those who want simple answers), she would probably have spent more time in the present nursing the sick than studying in the lab. To get to her larger goals, she had to delay some of the service aspects of her ambition and secure the funds, compete for attention, and heed the inner-oriented instincts that *attracted her* to the problem of radiation and X-ray diagnosis.

None of this was selfishness, as we generally use the word, but it was about the I. Enough is indicated by satisfaction: you have to choose achievements that really reflect your inner I. Time and again, our interviewees expressed the deepest satisfaction about those achievements in their life that expressed their signature skills or revealed something special about their own attractions and abilities. Fred Sievert loves numbers and being out with the sales field. Eugene Kohn loves the communications aspects of architecture perhaps even more than design itself. Sarah, our toy store founder, loves relational skills, being an anchor in the neighborhood, and she uses these skills to achieve a profit. Her profit, however, was limited by these standards: She set out to make enough to prosper but not so much as to lose touch with the very families whose reading and playtime she was so interested in influencing. She benchmarked her goals in calibration with her own four needs and the success of her store on the same standard. When she found, for example, that some neighborhood kids couldn't afford to buy books there, she didn't lower the prices—she got involved in starting a local library program that funded a summer reading camp, and then used the store to help advertise it.

To reach a satisfying level of competitive goal-setting, you do well to check who you are referencing against. Is being rich being Bill Gates or someone with $\frac{1}{1,000}$ of his money—only $65 million? Is it someone you admire as a person or simply someone whose wealth and lifestyle you envy? So many people spend time with people they don't like when they see them up close, but they believe imitating them will help them get ahead. It's a recipe for disaster. Many celebrity organizations in the 1990s were depicted as "nice" places to work, but when viewed up close their leaders were rotten to the core. Which would you choose? To get out of Enron on your own choice or after it went bankrupt? What would you rather do? Earn a few thousand dollars more while despising your bosses or building your core skills by learning from a supervisor you really admire?

Significance Is Out-In

The relational orientations of Significance are the mirror opposite of Achievement. The significance category still relies on a combination of internal and other-oriented perspectives, but in reverse: the impact is on others, to give rather than receive, but your internal preferences set the arena for action: You have to make some choice about whom you will serve, and it is best made in terms of corresponding to people you actually care about through deeds that have value to them. Indeed, people who never feel any impulse to give back rarely show much capacity for love and affection. In their scheme, people are to conquer not serve.

Your capacity for caring can be emotionally driven (and we think caring, like all the other emotional drivers of success, has to have an authentic emotional and values base), or simply a rational calculation of what it takes to belong, achieve, or get people to voluntarily give you their money and loyalty instead of giving it to someone else. This sounds very other-biased, and it is, but there is still a strong element of the self in order to have the Significance of your deeds be important not just to others, but to *you*. You have to choose to whom you will provide things or actions of value. To pick on Bill Gates again, if he gave all his money away without any thought to his own attractions or to effective use of his talents, he'd be able to make only about $10 difference in each person's life. Instead he's made strategic choices about the causes and people *he* cares about, such as the treatment for AIDS in Africa. His significance there will depend on how *others* value the contribution.

Legacy Is Out-Out

Gates has also focused on Legacy in his giving, donating economic and technological resources to building technological infrastructure that he hopes will help developing countries acquire the capabilities to compete economically on their own. If you are totally cynical, as some are about this controversial richest man in the world, you could see this impulse entirely in self-aggrandizing, competitively beneficial terms for Gates, in which case his efforts to establish wireless and computer capabilities in Africa would have the relational hallmarks of Achievement. But let's take him at his word and believe that he is trying to use what he has achieved, and what he values, to create a legacy that will ensure others' success. In reality, he can't control that outcome and needs to be prepared for this condition of legacy. These people may become his competitors down the road, but for a true legacy, he has to employ an out-out orientation.

It's easy to get thrown off these days. One woman moaned, "I'm so sick of the Legacy question. Every other day someone at the company seems to be asking me, 'What's the Legacy you want to leave here?' They judge your success potential by your answer." Her company is mouthing Legacy, but it may really be asking about Achievement goals: what level, what kind does she have in her sights? Are they big enough for a winner, big enough to be remembered and passively create a Legacy? The confusion was bothering her, as well it might.

To make good choices about the Legacies you create, your perspective should be less self-oriented than that. Legacy is essentially out-out, for and about the success of others, but with accomplishments somehow anchored to your achievements, and to your core values and beliefs about what is important enough to merit continuation. When Legacy is cast in grandiose, self-advancing terms, it rubs you and others the wrong way. It's not about how you will be remembered but about how some part of you that is important can be made to continue *so as to help others build their success.* You shape Legacy by starting with your core values and an understanding of the context and capabilities it took to achieve, but from this internal baseline you cast your perspective externally to envision how these things can be replicated in order to serve what others will need for future success. When we suggested this meaning for Legacy, our interviewee responded with relief: "*That's* something I really believe in, taking others along with you in your success." We know she's onto success that will endure.

What you can enjoy now about Legacy is the special satisfaction in acting on your own needs for generativity, in knowing that you are creating the conditions for the next generation. Those who try to turn Legacy into a completely I-Other activity usually find it backfires. The person who tries to eclipse his or her own Legacy with Happiness from this activity, or who places tight control on its use by others, finds they've actually killed it. Who cares about the purple-striped building with your name on it dedicated to research on a once-prevalent and now eradicated disease? It's nice that you enjoyed Granny's antimacassar, but to structure your giving around who promises to keep it preserved in the same place in the house that you did is hardly about helping others thrive. One woman who headed a hospital unit thought about this definition and nodded in understanding: "My Legacy will never be a building, even though in a hospital you appreciate these donations. It will be more about what my patients take away from here: their good health and a way to deal with chronic illness. I hope I can pass this learning on some day. That would be a great Legacy for me."

When Howard's mother became house-bound, she took the time to pull out all her old photographs. Some of these marked interesting moments in the social history of a small Utah town, but had absolutely no meaning to her children. She instinctively began to apply the four measures of success to her task. She set herself a goal of disposing of all the pictures in a way that provided real value to others, a way she could enjoy the cleanout process, and that would perhaps leave a Legacy of the history of her family's role for others to emulate. She called her friends and family and invited them to drop in at their convenience and pick out the pictures they wanted. Some cared about the town history, others were relishing the family photos. And she thoroughly enjoyed these visits. Legacy-Significance-Happiness in a series of acts around one episode. Was there Achievement? Absolutely. Illness had seriously diminished her physical capabilities: it was time to reassess her achievement goals in light of the changes in her "core." Setting a task that still required effort, pride, and mastery of a problem was all part of her solution. As for competition, Howard rather delightedly noted that she did seem to feel a certain pride in having found a better solution to her old picture problem than most of her friends! She also donated to a university the records of a women's literary club that had met for over 80 years. She realized that she would never know how they would be used in the future, but they might be of great help to a future scholar.

Legacy means being able to let go, but you can anticipate and control the conditions under which you do this. The only way that Legacy will last is for it to be broad enough to be picked up and changed by others in the future. That means you have to have some relational sympathy with the outside world, and an openness to giving away things you most value: money, your old raccoon coat from college, or treasured Brittney Spears albums, whatever.

One of the saddest stories we heard was about a wealthy woman who had never thought about others. When her lawyer suggested she write a will, they soon found that there was no one she cared about. They went through an inventory of her day, her week, her life, and not a single other-oriented thought ever entered her head. Finally, her lawyer suggested she give her money to something *he* valued, say an educational institution. Even then she was unable to pick the one of his choice, and finally settled on a gift to a major university whose reputation she admired. The gift went to a good cause, but was it a success for her? Did it fulfill the conditions of Legacy? It was what you'd call a passive Legacy: it occurred without active thought and without active satisfaction. How much richer her life and her gift would have been had she organized her choices with some orientation on other people.

Happiness Is In-In

Happiness is just the opposite. It is totally inward. No one can force you to be happy, it is an experience of your own. Similarly, judging your life to be happy is not something someone else's judgment can really effect. No matter how many people may envy your good fortune, if you're not happy, it doesn't feel like good fortune.

Similarly, you can't experience someone else's happiness unless you totally suppress your own individuality and morph into their psyche. Parents sometimes try to do this with the best of intentions, saying their children's happiness is enough happiness for them, but that's rarely true. It's about their *own* happiness, packaged in what appears to be a less selfish form. Just ask the children. A recent study of "advantaged" families earning more than $100,000 a year revealed a frightening parenting practice that we would call *cruel permissiveness,*—what used to be called "spoiling." Harvard psychologist Dan Kindlon found that parents of the Millennials (children born between 1980 and 2000) were extremely prone to knowingly indulging every form of hedonism in their kids, but the kids were actually unhappier than their poorer cohorts whose situation required them to experience hardship and achievement. Drug use, eating disorders, and alcoholism were all significantly higher for the coddled. When asked how parents could pursue an approach that led to so much unhappiness in their children, they invariably replied, "We just want them to be happy."[3] Some overvalued the possibility of material goods to confer happiness, others were simply trying to filter out anything unpleasant from their child's life. But all of them were seeking something that (1) they could not achieve for another person and (2) may really have been about their own Happiness needs.

One point of clarification: **Some motivators, such as the drive for respect and acceptance (or the response to fear and anger) can look like one of the categories in terms of the language we use, but they are really different.** Nancy, the woman in human resources whom we met in Chapter 5, struggled with how open she should be about being gay. She said, "I have to wrestle constantly between being who I am and getting things done that I think are important. Often I will wait until people realize the value of what I'm doing and then let them know about my partner. I want them to know that I'm a really wholesome, loving, caring person. It kills me to think that people would think otherwise." When we asked her if this message of being a loving person was important to her, she said, "Yes. It has great significance for me. It has very deep meaning for me." This was an important insight point into her values and their role in her Achievement and Happiness, but it is not the same as the Significance chamber of accomplishment that marks one of the categories of success.

Getting the Right Mix

There is a difference between the in-out orientations that drive successful accomplishment in each of the categories and the servicing of your core values. But we have little distinction in the terms we use: significance, importance, satisfaction—these can apply to your inner core or the way in which you adjust your efforts in each category. **That's why it's important to stop and take a deliberate look not just at how "important" or "meaningful" something feels, but whether you have oriented your goals and intended impact on the right relational mix to get real satisfaction.**

If you feel pride in your volunteer work, for example, that may be a sign of your own mastery of a problem more than a good measure of whether you've really delivered the value you hope for. Many nonprofits fall into this trap, measuring their Significance by activities that are about their internal well-being—how much money was raised, how many phone calls were made—rather than the external impacts of their work. The latter is far harder and more expensive to do, but essential in measuring Significance.

Measures in general should complement these relational orientations, but for most people success in each chamber is a function of intrinsic and extrinsic rewards. Achievement that feels right and expresses your signature skills has its own reward, but the reinforcement power of a bonus or recognition is also an important part of the experience of success. There is a social logic to the rewards of success. You need to calibrate the contract of internal and external rewards carefully so that it doesn't compete with the basic orientations of each satisfaction. If you look for external acclaim for your children but tell them that all you want is their happiness, good luck. It doesn't compute.

Enough Is about Getting More without Wanting It All

Significance, for example, feels *more* satisfying when there is some reciprocity in the form of gratitude or recognition of the value you provided from those you care about.[4] It is this internalized sense of satisfaction that ultimately causes you to put one more chip in the chamber, so to speak, but that sense of satisfaction is not about "pride" or "recognition" per se (these are better suited for Achievement), but about confirmation that others felt you really provided value. If you did all your charitable work for the reward, it would really be about your own ego, and probably wouldn't be as responsive to the needs of others you are trying to serve. On the other hand, if no one ever said thanks, or had the impulse to give something back in return, you would have good cause to wonder whether you were really spending your time on something of value to others. The movie *Pay It Forward* illustrated this in a very poignant way.

Peter was an environmentalist who spent years picking up trash along a river. No one ever said thanks (he sort of believed the fish were thanking him), and every day the trash reappeared. One day it occurred to him that he should be leveraging this act of Significance into something *others* valued, too. He began to share his stories of the riverfront in the newspaper, and he joined several environmental groups, turning their attention to this problem. **Leaders are people who expand the four categories of success not only in their own life, but in the lives of others.**

So too, the rewards of Achievement may be a combination of internal satisfactions about mastering a problem; but if no external rewards are offered, it feels less a success (your standard, remember, comes from winning at what others strive for). We asked a person with the most intrinsically driven values we could find whether rewards were important in order to feel an Achievement was successful.

He was a writer/ producer whose own father spent many years providing legal counsel to prison inmates to the point of nearly bankrupting the family. He replied emphatically: "Absolutely. To the winner go the spoils. If there ain't no spoils, there ain't no winner!" Impact, in other words, was on the self, but supported by the fact that others competed for what you were striving for.

Another interviewee, Jill, considered this issue in thinking about a career change. A Harvard MBA grad, Jill was about to cut back her hours to spend more time with her two year old. She left investment banking to become a manager at an airline company. The pay was very different. She was struggling with her own thoughts on this decision. Would the status in the new job be enough to reflect her own Achievement ambitions? Would the money be enough? Would she be neglecting her sense of obligation to prove that African American women could make it as top managers in the most competitive arenas—a gift she felt she owed to other women?

As we listened to Jill work this problem through and explain why she felt basically good about the choice she'd made, we observed her shifting through the relational orientations around Achievement and Significance with an edifying deftness. She'd chosen a new target for Achievement, one that was lesser in terms of challenge, time, and stress, to meet her own sense of just what she wanted to master in business *and* parenting. Always competitive, her first instincts had been to try to stay in her old job. If she couldn't make that salary and compete at that level, maybe she should just drop out of work completely. Achievement had to be challenging, not just a thing to do. Would the position with the airline do this? In thinking about what would *satisfy her* in the new job, she began to compare her goals with a more generalized framework of external standards: What had other people been paid in similar jobs? Would she be in the eightieth percentile of that group? Clearly, it was ridiculous to apply an investment banking standard to a traditional managerial post in a distressed industry. She would have to readjust to the group to whom she was comparing herself on Achievement measures (not just money, but accomplishments in her job) if this job were ever to be enough.

She began to look at the basics of Achievement, which she knew were about more than money: What would be the challenge for her own growth as a manager? What would be the problems she was attracted to and would want to master? Would that be enough?

Then she looked at the rest of this "chamber" in her personal kaleidoscope. When she thought about how her young daughter's needs were occupying a larger part of her overall picture, she knew she could honestly answer yes. Parenting itself required mastery of new skills, and the airline job would be just enough. Then she thought of her upcoming fifth reunion at Harvard Business School: Everyone would be asking the same questions: How much are you making? What's your job status? She and her husband Dennis vowed they were not going to fall into using that standard to measure their recalibration of Achievement and success. Instead, they were going to switch the questions on their classmates and get into a more meaningful conversation on how their sense of what was important was changing, and how they could look at careers as an important but not exclusive source of getting what they really valued in life.

Choice, change. Jill was always going to feel a little wince factor when she compared her accomplishments to the most extreme achievements of her business school peers. But when she looked for the internal sources of Achievement satisfaction, there was plenty to fill in her kaleidoscope. Calibrating those goals in a realistic framework of what others in a similar position could expect was a great help to her. We generalized it into a benchmark insight point: **Can your desires in any category be satisfied with the possible? Are you comparing your goals to the right relational groups?**

Doing a Reality Check

Given each of the relational orientations, it's important to check in regularly on whether you're calibrating your goals for each success category properly. If you try to gain Happiness by imitating others' consumption, for example, you'll spend lots of money in vain. Ever met someone who had to have what you had? Did it seem to give them the happiness it gave you? Ever had a friend who used to play tennis with you for fun and then went off for two weeks of professional training? When he came back he was so into competing that it was no longer fun: Tennis was now Achievement, and not a source of Happiness, however much satisfaction it gave that person to "win."

So too with charitable giving. You want to give something to an institution you care about, so you volunteer to head the next fundraiser at your kids' school. All the incentives are there for you to turn this into an act of personal Achievement: if you focus on beating last year's goal you'll get lots of recognition and a pat on the back for your generosity. But will you really be cultivating your own capacity to understand and care about the needs of others? Will the kudos get in the way of your experiencing the satisfaction of true generosity?

We know an incredibly generous entrepreneur who is so aware of this problem that he tried to forestall any public acknowledgment when he gave over $40 million to a capital campaign. It was only after he understood that part of the value of the legacy gift was in allowing others to think aloud about how such contributions should shape the future success of the school that he gave in and allowed a ceremony. He also understood that his happiness would not be the prominent personal satisfaction of this event, but that the event itself was of great importance in the school's ability to attract other gifts. Acquiescing to the ceremony was an act of Significance in his ongoing generosity.

Making the Right Comparisons

The feeling of just enough is not just about what you get but about who you are. What level of Achievement is enough depends on whose standard you are comparing yourself to. We know who we are partially from self-knowledge, but also from the mirrors we hold up, the role models and achievements we compare ourselves to.[4] Unlike the days of lifetime employment, when the Horatio Algers of the world experienced real-life mentoring, today we live in a world of virtual mentoring. In the absence of extensive contact with people you admire, it can be difficult to resist comparing yourself to a fantasized media role model. Carefully examining who you compare yourself to in your pursuit of success is a critical insight point. Are you setting the dial on Michael Jordan when you're 5′4″ or can you strive for a more reachable model?

In our survey responses, we saw a striking absence of concrete role modeling among our participants. Instead, their sources of learning about success were their general upbringing, their parents' values. When we asked who they admired as possible role models of success, many left it blank, answered "no one in particular," or picked historical figures who had not been in business.

It's important to bring your goals down to the admired but possible reality. Many people fear to establish a lowered limit for fear of killing their own sense of "can-do" ambition, or they feel they've betrayed an inner standard of excellence. But this fear is addictive. Nothing they do will ever be good enough for their own standards. Self-honesty and a hard look at your relational settings for success can provide a better path to what is just enough. Beware: Lowering your aspirations to a reachable size doesn't let you off the hook in terms of the need to invest time and energy: There is a lower bound on enough! If you don't take a close look at the minimum amount of work or effort you need to put in, you won't do enough in to reach your goal. Hold on. Have we just bought into the workaholic culture? Is anyone having fun here? Not to fear. When you begin to set these goals with control and a view to the whole picture, the satisfactions of success take on a higher level of fulfillment than never to have reached a goal at all—or hit one and missed the others.

Not Jane's Story

Take, for example, Tanisha, an inner-city high school student who worked very hard and had some lucky breaks when she was accepted at a summer music camp and a mentoring program gave her ongoing personal and financial support. Most of the kids there were from fairly wealthy families. Tanisha had lived in extreme poverty. She did not know her father. Her mother was a drug addict and had no steady job. After the first week, Tanisha called her mom. All week she'd been feeling worse and worse about her background. As she saw all the things the other girls had, all their opportunities and social skills, she believed she didn't have a chance in life. She wasn't good enough. She wasn't prepared enough. She'd never make it through the program.

For about an hour Tanisha was on the phone with her mom, complaining, worrying, homesick. Her mom didn't have any answers. When Tanisha got off the phone, she shared some of her discouragement with her cabin mates. Bitterly, one replied, "Yeah, well at least your mom listened to you. Mine won't be in the country for another month."

As the weeks went by, Tanisha heard more and more about the other campers' lives. It turns out they too had unfulfilled dreams, and many felt no support from their families. Tanisha began to believe that she actually had a treasured resource in her family, despite the setbacks her own situation represented. When she later had a conversation about this with her mother, her mom actually began to seek help for her addiction. She told the counselors she believed she could be there for her kid and wanted to do it better.

This is a true story. Tanisha is now in college, on full scholarship. The program, SummerSearch, is dedicated to the long-term success of its participants. Tanisha's insight point about the real nature of whom she was comparing herself too had strengthened her core drivers. She realized that though her situation had its obvious difficulties, she had enough to find success. Her beliefs were tested, found to be somewhat mistaken, and readjusted. She realized she had capabilities whose potential was more than she'd assumed. She found a surprising new resource for success in her strong relationship with her mother. And her mother found a new sense of significance in her own parenting. Knowing these things about who she really was helped her not only survive the camp experience, but thrive in it.

Quick Points: Making Successful Choices

Enduring Success requires:

- Experiencing variety and separate satisfactions.
- Moving beyond the present to prepare for the future.
- Pausing to reflect on the small successes we all experience, and which give us the energy to go on.

Critical experiences provide insight points at which you can:

- Perform both rational and emotional analysis of your situation.
- See the opportunity for growth in each of the four success categories.

Defining enough depends a clear understanding of:

- The relationships that matter to you.
- Realistic standards of comparison.
- The difference between the urgent and the important—both must be attended to.

Chapter 8

Further Calibrations of Enough

Had we but world enough, and time . . .
—Andrew Marvell, "To His Coy Mistress"

How can you determine for practical purposes how much of anything is enough for today? For this week? For your lifetime? After all of our theoretical ruminations end, this remains your basic question. And the keys to answering it will be found in the "dials" you use to adjust the image you see in your kaleidoscope: dials of time, relationships, and limits.

When Jane thought about her relationships with her boyfriend or her boss, whom she greatly admired, or the people in her church, or her artistic friends in the city, she saw her choices about success as multiple *betrayals*. Choosing to winnow any of the targets that were competing for her attention couldn't possibly be done because someone important to her would be left out. But if she didn't make some choices, *she* would be the loser. She was still lacking a diagnostic tool for making these choices: the surprising element of Time in connection with relational reasoning. In this chapter, we look at the two together to show how that uncanny ability called *timing* can be cultivated not only to adjust your relational focus (and all the changes that implies), but also your ability to determine what is *enough*.

Applying Time to Your Calculations

How to know what is enough of each relational stance? Assessing the relative state of each of the success categories in your kaleidoscope can warn you of an imbalance. Applying a differentiated notion of time to the problem can help you broaden the scope of your choices further: you don't have to service all relational stands at once. **What is enough for now, what for later, what is enough for a goal two years down the road?** When you cast these questions in the kaleidoscope context, they do more than parse your ambitions into baby steps, medium steps, and broad strides. Helpful as that is, the dimensionality of time held up to *four categories* transforms your very understanding of the "taxonomy" of the categories and their relational orientations.[1] They suddenly take distinctive shapes in reference to chronology, and as a whole, exhibit rhythmic patterns. These differences of orientation can be cultivated over time so as to contribute to the switching and linking that is central to the patterns of enduring success.

A Herman Miller Story

Mike Volkema, chairman of the legendary office interior manufacturer Herman Miller, reflected on how complex it can be. He told a story about his own struggle to get the right timing and balance of messages for his organization to adopt all the right relational perspectives. Mike believes strongly in the value of personal empowerment and in bringing the whole person to work. He's willing to go out on a limb to create opportunities for people to bring their special talents and perspectives to a problem. But at the same time, it's important that employees not always put their own needs and cognitive view first. A good employee should be able to switch perspectives: to enjoy good design, to care about how others experience an office environment so as to create the right products, to be competitive, to know how to attend to family and friends, and to create a legacy of design and environmental responsibility that will allow future generations to thrive. The four categories!

The problem is, these pieces don't always fit. You have to calibrate them yourself and make sure the rest of the organization also has this success intelligence. Volkema recalled an incident where he really had to think hard about how *I-oriented* his strategic decisions should be. He had observed that the company was wasting quite a bit of time and resources on getting its management together to make decisions. Top leaders were geographically dispersed for a variety of reasons. Too much time was being spent on scheduling conference calls, getting to meetings, canceling calls, and so on. He decided the company should build a common leadership space. It was an innovative and ambitious plan. The building would use the same kind of nonprecious materials that Herman Miller products employed: plywood, glass—similar to the clean designs that Charles Eames first established with his famous chairs. Inside, there would be Aeron chairs and the wonderfully creative Resolve workstations designed by Ayse Birsel. They experimented with a changeable floor plan that allowed "streets" and "storefront corners" to evolve from the way people used the space. The plan had the added advantage of being cost effective. The materials were not expensive, and the design was people friendly. (In our framework, this was a good linkage between Achievement, Happiness, Significance, and Legacy.)

One leader with long experience at the company informed Volkema that he didn't want to move. He'd seen the plan for his new office, but he liked his current location and amenities. This plan was not contributing to *his* Happiness, or the way he thought he worked best. Where was the whole person in that? Volkema was now facing a trade-off between competing orientations. He made the executive decision and moved the manager, explaining the need to focus on efficiency and achievement was urgent. A layoff and market downturn reinforced this view. A few months later, the executive enthusiastically admitted he now loved his office and the increased ease of communication.

Was this an accomplishment of Significance or Achievement? Volkema clearly cared about his employee's needs, but when he faced a choice between delivering perceived value for the employee now or supporting his own sense of what he needed to do to make the company more competitive and solve the communications problems, he came out on the side of Achievement. The real point, however, was that he knew the difference between hoping the employee would value this decision down the road and knowing why he was choosing it for the present. Had the manager not ultimately enjoyed the move, Volkema would have been open to hearing about it and addressing the problem again.

Multitasking the Orientations of Success

When you successfully multitask at anything, your attention only *appears* to be on everything at once. In reality, you are sequencing your focus at lightning speed while maintaining a view of the whole. Let any part of this complex pattern break down and you drop a ball. As we pointed out, people who achieve enduring success switch orientations between the four categories of success constantly without losing track of all the pieces they are trying to accomplish. So do good leaders. **In multitasking success, execution is not just about finessing tasks but about sustaining multiple relational and time orientations as dictated by the special demands of each success category.**

As we pointed out, people who achieve enduring success switch orientations constantly. So do good leaders. They are not wholly driven by their own needs, or by the needs and reactions of others. Like our investment banker, they keep scanning the doorway and watching the power plays at meetings to see what others are doing and wanting, but they also have a plan of their own for what they want to achieve.

Ideally, this plan emerges from their core, and they learn to establish their autonomy within the confines of an organization. But there are special challenges in shifting relational orientations as the leader, because there is a strong proxy role to take into account. **Whether you are the parent or the CEO, not only do you have to cultivate the four orientations for your own choices, you have to cultivate an aggregate set of orientations for a family or organization in such a way that individuals can pick it up and assimilate it in their own lives.** Given the politics of most large organizations and the complexity of anyone's life, it is easy to get sidetracked.

Employees may feel that the orientation of their boss—or conversely, their own advancement—is the only important agenda. Parents may live for their children, children may feel they're being asked to live for their parents. None of these options creates the kind of independence-interdependent team combination that is necessary to innovative and coordinated execution of strategy or leads to a healthy personal relationship.[2] Without these, who would call their activities a real success?

When we studied our research subjects, we noticed that these people didn't have one relational outlook for every problem any more than they focused their energies on only one category of success. **They seem to have developed an intuitive understanding for when it was time to put others' needs ahead of their own, and when it was time to take a break for their happiness and contentment.** This skill is critical to meeting the demands of multifaceted success, and it is also another avenue to an honest evaluation of your own core drives. The parent who never admits to self-orientations is as burdensome to the child as the eternally self-indulgent one. But you cannot be both at once under most circumstances. Time helps you sort and decide which relational perspective is most appropriate.

Relational Orientations: You and I Are Two—Not One

Some of the difficulties of switching and linking success goals touch on a classic psychological problem of differentiation. Who is the I who determines the I-oriented goals? The ability to distinguish the self as an *independent* self can be particularly difficult for a parent. The bonds between parent and child are typically among the strongest you ever feel. This can confuse your ability to critique your own needs around success. You so identify with your child that his or her happiness seems good enough for your happiness. The dropout career mother who says, "I don't need Achievement as long as I'm giving to my child's needs" is rarely so committed to self-sacrifice as she may think. She can be confusing her child's identity and her own, achieving the "in-in" satisfaction of Happiness by proxy and often with devastating results.

Many parents find themselves so confounded by demands of career and family that they drop out altogether from competitive work. Many retirees assume they no longer need something to achieve and become listless or irritably over-competitive on the golf course. A wince factor creeps in: "I coulda done that too. I woulda done that if only . . ."

I-Other Confusion

Some of the greatest problems of calibrating relationships stem from a confusion of interests. When do you know with some accuracy that you understand what will help others, and when are you really speaking to your own needs? It's pretty easy to be cynical about the parent who "has" to go to dinner every night with a client "for the sake of family," and say he's really doing it for himself and his own Achievement. But relational calculations are rarely this cut and dried. Our assumptions about them have to be equally open to what we might call "messy boundaries" between our own self-interest and that of others. The parent who stays out might truly believe that his hard work is an act of giving to the family, a way of supporting their desires and needs. But it may also not be perceived as such by the family itself. The kids might like nothing more than to drop the expensive high-pressure soccer camp and see their dad one more night a week.

One of our interviewees told a particularly poignant story of being caught up in this conundrum. Tom's job and his company's culture required extensive client entertainment and travel. He and his wife were mutually agreed on his decision to pursue this high-pressure career, and the extremely good financial rewards had made it more than possible for her not to work outside the home. (She did, however, continue to be highly competitive in her work on arts education.) As soon as they had children, Tom had set some limits for himself. He would have to travel a great deal of the time. Three or four or five nights a week he would be out before the children awoke and not be back before they went to bed. But Friday nights were always reserved for dinner with his wife, and Saturday mornings were for breakfast with the kids. He would also spend time alone on weekends with each of his four children. One Tuesday morning, he happened to be home at breakfast. His son came down and gave him this enormous whoop of delight. "Dad! Is it Saturday already?" However much the schedule made sense in his overall plan, it looked very different from a five-year-old's eyes.

Rather than live with half-voiced regrets, it is important to recognize these needs and understand how to replicate their emotional and relational calibrations in a time frame and context that still expresses and satisfies your core. Your context may prevent you from being a full-time dancer, for example, but you can still take lessons and improve your muscle tone. While some may argue the career dropout *should* be single-dimensioned and satisfied with self-sacrifice, or that an escape to selflessness will provide true peace, we found that mixed emotions are not necessarily bad. The creative force of these emotions is what drives our ability not only to be for ourselves, but to be for others. There are many who claim the *I-We orientation* is so evolved in humans as to be hard-wired in our DNA.

Enough for Self and Others

Empathy puts you in another's shoes (its literal root, from the Greek *empathos,* roughly translates as "being in another's feeling"). **But just because you understand someone's needs doesn't mean you can service them without costs to them and you.** What, then, is enough empathy? And how do you judge how accurate your empathetic skills are?

Again the kaleidoscope does not solve this problem once and for all, but it provides a natural outlet for addressing the various relationships you feel are part of the good life. Significance stands somewhere in the compromise: Leaders should perceive the real needs of those they care for (or have a duty to), but they also must *create* a new common sense of values to achieve community success.

This solution has a present-future resolution. Children have needs, and so do parents. The parent who understands just how much parenting is *enough now* and when to attend to other needs has gained an ability not only to address the four chambers of their own success, but to lay the foundations for the children's four-square accomplishments. Say you see the importance of limiting human impact on the environment when few people value environmental sustainability. Significance is not just about delivering something that gives back to the earth, but creating this sense in others. Your satisfaction with a successful campaign to protect natural habitat is self-oriented in that it resonates to your core values, but these values, in turn, are about giving to community. **Leaders who can create activities of genuine significance in their organizations and also create a common sense of value about them leave a much greater legacy of success than those who quietly make a pledge to the local charity but have no felt engagement or leadership stake in the outcomes.**

Time mediates the unresolvable differences between choosing for oneself or another. Such conflicts of perspective or interest are inescapable, however much we genuinely we believe that our own self-worth is wrapped up in how well others we are connected to are doing. Though the perspective is integrated, interests are often not so compatible. Time gives you the right frame in which to work through both needs by separating *when* you invest energy from whom you serve in each category.

Corporate Citizenship: Self-Interest or Self-Denial?

One of the great confusions business faces today is what relational posture to take toward corporate citizenship. Is it a self-interested act of competitive achievement or a self-denying act of generosity that increases one's reputation for providing value to the community?[3] In fact, it is both Achievement and Significance. Like many activities, social responsibility straddles more than one category. The problem comes in the packaging. Depending on which stakeholder a company is addressing, it may try to profile corporate social responsibility solely as good business sense or good social sense. **One of the public challenges of leadership today is to create a public sense of business success that gives legitimacy to all four categories of successful activity rather than adopting a one-answer-fits-all approach.** Meet that challenge and organizations create the kind of trust that allows them to say to any one constituency, "We believe we've given (or taken) enough."

Relational Calculations

As you review the chambers of your own success choices, the relational "dial" can provide a critical point of insight about what you've chosen to do and why. Answering this with discernment about the differences in relational orientations between the four components generates a road map: You begin to know where you're going emotionally and can make good adjustments on what is enough to get there. That process is like making an important decision about which city you want to travel to: Depending on the destination, you'll know what to bring for the trip, when you've arrived, and when your trip is over!

As we saw, relational calculations provide a good platform for enough. Applied with a view to your core self-definitions, they help you address important sources of satisfaction and dissatisfaction. For example, did you practice a musical instrument all those years as a child because it was intrinsically important to you to master it, or was it important to your parents? The first would be in your Achievement and Happiness categories, which have internal impacts; the second reason would place this activity in Significance: delivering value for others you care about. Knowing the differences helps you decide what is enough music for *your* sense of a good life. Are you trying to be happy through Achievement? Trying to build a Legacy by inflating your own achievements rather than creating a foundation for other people's achievements? Which would be a more effective approach to Legacy, getting out of the way or helping people along? **The challenge is getting the balance of relational**

needs in proper proportion within the category of success you are addressing.

Relational orientations can be rationally described, but as Daniel Goleman's and Howard Gardner's research on emotional intelligence has suggested, relational skills are developed in real time.[4] You have to practice and experience caring close up in order to deliver expressions of caring effectively and to receive satisfaction from the effort. Otherwise, you can deliver value and still have no chips in your personal Significance chamber. If you think that your winning is really a sign of serving others, you need to re-check your orientation. Donning the Santa suit and raising 10 bucks may not be as big an achievement outwardly, but your act of giving yourself may provide far more internal satisfaction.

Only those who can bring authentic emotion *and* rationality to the calculation of relational orientation really achieve greatness. Just as the categories give a framework for the relational sorting that can lead to a better sense of *enough*, so too can the ability to distinguish the proper time dynamics of each category.

When Enough Seems Impossible

When the assignment of a given activity to a success category is unclear or the relational orientations argue for a different investment of emotional and financial energy, we are in the moments we have called *insight points*. They call out for your interpretation as to the importance of what you are doing, and the nature of what it is you are trying to succeed at. They ask what is enough and why? These moments can be rationally analyzed in terms of a good fit between relational orientation and the goals you set, but there is still the problem of quantity. What investment and how much impact is enough to satisfy your sense of what is right, necessary, and emotionally worthwhile? No one can answer this except you, and humans are notoriously programmed to make poor judgments about what they need.

Behaviorists have confirmed in a multitude of experiments our tendency to choose nearer rewards with smaller payback over larger rewards with delayed payback. We eat too much dessert for the quick sugar high and bemoan the gradual loss of our waistline. We make "just one more" unscheduled business call during our planned vacation. Then one day, you call your wife to say you've suddenly been told by the boss to drive to yet another meeting, after being away for three weeks. And that's the day your wife's response is to ask for a divorce. The boss is terribly sorry and offers you a vacation with your wife if you'll just do this one last thing first.

We will never totally overcome our ability for self-delusion and shortsightedness, and there are usually deep emotional currents driving these behaviors, but enough offers an important corrective mechanism you *can* use to your advantage: it reminds you to stop and think twice:

- Are you doing enough in each of the four chambers on a regular basis?
- Or are the chips all one color and still there is no sense of enough?
- Have you asked why?
- Have you tested whether you've set any concrete limits for yourself?
- Are you switching relational perspectives to test your assumptions?

As we observed in the previous chapter, *just enough invites you to put some outside parameters on your infinite desires*—not just the minimum your family needs, but also the point at which you really feel the specific satisfactions of all four categories. Otherwise you create addictions.

Are Limits Just for Losers and Lazy People?

From the lure of off-road vehicles to "No limits!" advertising slogans, the idea of living without boundaries has a glamour and danger that can be seductive. But it is not always a wise or satisfy-ing way to live.

Corrections needn't be as categorical as you might think. You can even ritualize some of your switching of perspective. Senator Richard Lugar is said to be the only person known to have turned down an invitation to a White House state dinner because it was his wife's bowling night, but Lugar had made this a sacred ritual in the constant shifting of his commitments and energy. Howard Steven-son is a very hard worker and has traveled frequently. His wife and he have a merged family with seven children, now grown. He has always made it a rule to take any call that comes in from his family during work, but to limit the conversation to a few quick points unless it is an emergency. He'll find out what's up, explain his own needs, and either take care of it right then or arrange a specific time to respond later. Were he working for a jealous boss who required total atten-tion and saw everything else as a threat to corporate loyalty, he couldn't achieve this kind of dynamic switching between categories. But more and more progressive leaders are understanding that not only is success in all four categories a sign of a good company, it's a must for today's workforce of dual-career parents and changing val-ues about large institutions and family life. **One of the major bench-marks of any great company should be its ability to ensure that the people with the greatest stake in its activities should also be able to achieve the four categories of success in their own lives and work.**

In our survey of top executives, many interviewees had diffi-culty with the idea of limitation and success. About 85 percent re-ported with varying words that they felt they had to have financial security to be happy; but so far, many of them were still seeking to reach the magic number when they could stop. Millions in assets were still not giving them what they were looking for, and their ex-planation was that they simply hadn't quite gotten enough—if not for themselves then for their children. Meanwhile, they worried aloud over wanting to have many other things in life. At the heart of this difficulty is the idea that limits are a negative thing—even though one of the most secure feelings people have is when they are in situations with predictable limits.

Enough Is Pragmatic, Not Sacrilegious

Even though *never enough* seems an obvious detour from satisfaction, the idea of *just enough* may rub very hard against your sense of excellence and what you feel you should consider as success. It seems almost sacrilegious to think about your aspirations and not try to go for the max. We've encountered many high achievers who feel they have a moral obligation to do this as long as they direct achievement toward the good of the world. But that's turning your success into a religion. It only works as a model if you are a saint or a fanatic.

Howard Stevenson recently met a priest during his travels and began discussing this book with him. The priest asked Howard how he would guarantee that his ideas would go down in history for all time. Howard responded, "I don't. You can't. That's a goal without limits. It presumes there is something beyond time that this activity should represent. What's enough for me is if my ideas are valued and meaningful to the next generation of those I care about and also give me a source of satisfaction in the here and now." The man of the cloth shook his head—he clearly thought Howard was selling out.

Religion, said the great theologian Paul Tillich, is about ultimate concerns, which are often expressed in absolutes. Buddhism stresses universality—becoming one with the universe to the total suppression of the I. Islam and some forms of Christianity turn to the absolutes of legacy, subordinating all activities to the importance of the hereafter. Other denominations stress absolute empathy with the suffering. Protestantism tended to fixate on perfection of the self as achiever, one who works hard in service of the Lord's ways. Our society's secular religion, the enlightenment narrative, suggests an even closer relationship between humans and their place in the universe: understand it and you will understand that it is perfect. As Robert Nozick wryly noted: "It tells us we can have everything worth having, to a superlative degree, and be everything worth being; our nature is already congenial to that."[5]

And so it goes. Taoists seek the absolute of nonbeing. Hindus place the welfare of the whole living world so far ahead of individuals that an absolute interpretation might suggest you should starve. After all, even plants are now known to show feelings when a sharp knife is held near. Philosophers often seek an absolute commitment to truth or to perfect justice. Even the Ten Commandments are not suggestions.

Our better selves, our ultimate values and beliefs, are usually described in the same language of absolutes. Hence our aspirations are readily shaped into never enough. Seek the ultimate, not the limited. So it is with attitudes about success. If you're not seeking to be *all* you can be on one dimension, you won't deserve to make it. Never enough self-sacrificing. Never enough happiness. Never enough winning. Never enough hard work.

But these absolutes are far larger than human capacity and imply there is something horribly flawed in acting human. Christianity expresses ultimate forgiveness of these flaws, but leaves people caught in a challenging paradox of seeking to live out perfect ideals and accepting never getting there. It's hard to discern the appropriate parameters for worldly success. Similarly, Buddhist teachings advise us that the only happiness is to link love and faith to the eternal. They explain that we create our own suffering by succumbing to the selfish cravings of our separate selves. Such standards not only downplay some of our success categories in favor of others, they leave little compromise space for shifting your attention. The ultimate is a place of reverence. It is also the stopping point (you cannot mentally go to someplace outside this spot to contemplate God or whatever form your ultimate concern takes).

We make these points to suggest that if you measure success only against an ultimate standard, you are reaching for a state "like unto death" and condemning your imperfect, human side.

To paraphrase Tielhard de Chardin, whether we are human beings having a spiritual experience or spiritual beings having a human experience, the two are not the same. Why would we apply the same measurements? How do you go from the timeless, nonmaterial world to the messiness and duality of real life? We believe that the kaleidoscope framework helps mediate this process. The components of your self-definition are themselves a mix of aspirational and idealized notions (values, beliefs, unique talents) and fixed realities (emotions, context, some capabilities).

Enough is the transitional idea that gets you from one to the other.

Enough in the Real World

The associations between perfection and the foundations of belief provide a strong incentive to resist the idea of enough, even though religions advocate other forms of limitation. **Enough is not a religion in our framework, and we do not express it in absolutist terms.** It is a practical mediator, a tool for getting to that middle ground between the ideal and the concrete. This middle ground is not mediocrity! Rather, it is the space where there is room for multiple human accomplishments of high caliber.

A positive belief in the value of enough evens out and enlarges the playing field so that there is room for a human, achievable scale without the loss of aspiration. There is room in your life for more than one thing. As the word enough implies, there is both an upward and lower limit on this space. On the one hand, not just any level of accomplishment is enough—it has to compare well to actual embodiments of your ideal standards. But it is also not about limitless power, self-denial, wealth, or talent. Believe the latter and you condemn yourself to the kind of success that is exhausting people and ruining our ability to live together and support community.

The process of applying enough to success is a return to the ancient Greek admonition: *Meiden Agan* "Nothing in Excess." Enough in your life references another ancient ideal, the Golden Mean. This was an ideal but concrete proportionality, capable of reason. Because setting limits is so fraught with emotional resistance and fear of losing out on something, we take time here to provide some basic training on what goes into the calculation.

The Calculations of Enough

You will encounter four critical stages in the process of determining enough, no matter which of the core definitions or categories of success you are addressing. These stages are recognition, evaluation, calibration, and acceptance.

Stage 1: Recognition

Recognition is a process of knowing on a deep level just *what* fulfills your sense of satisfaction in its many forms—and also recognizing what does not. These satisfactions are summarized and distinguished by our four categories of success, embodied by countless activities in each realm of your life. Recognition also involves understanding what will pragmatically contribute to enduring success: your core values, your capabilities, your context, your emotional needs.

Stage 2: Evaluation

Enough provides the ability to probe *why* and *how* something is of importance to you—that is, valued and enduring. Often moments of enduring success are somewhat of a surprise even to the doer precisely because they aren't the biggest or most famous thing they ever did. Like the wealthy person who forgot he liked hamburgers and died hating food, it's easy to overlook the satisfactions that appear in small-scale events—Jonathan's yard sale, for example, or an event in the life of one or our interviewees, Bonnie. She felt that one of her most enduring successes was the time she was able to get her daughter to understand and buy into delaying a shopping trip because Bonnie had an unforeseen work problem. Up until this point, every career/family conflict had left her feeling like a failure in one or the other realm of her life. This time, however, her daughter understood and even helped set up dinner arrangements that evening. On her part,

Bonnie turned off the work spigot the next evening to experience the shopping trip with her daughter. She was able to say with complete confidence, "Neither day was perfect, but this is enough."

The evaluative process is about discerning *why* these moments have the quality of enough, which starts with a determination of which success category they best fit. This is critical to making hard choices between the many moving targets of the good life that beg to be addressed.

Stage 3: Calibration

You can't do everything and you can't do nothing. How much is enough? You can't have everything and you can't have nothing. How much is enough?

Many people operate with no workable calibrations, bouncing their expectations from standard to standard with no coherent way to make a choice. In our survey, one thirty-four-year-old with a $7 million business told us: "Money means far less than it used to. I am creating a billion-dollar business merely to prove that I can. I find that money often makes life less enjoyable in that you tend to overlook the simple things when you have more money."

When it doesn't add up, you rarely feel the effort is worth it. Calibration, or weighing the importance of your specific needs, is critical to coherency. So is calibration of the potential resources it will take to achieve your goals.

Enough sets the thresholds by calibrating against all four categories of success in multiple time frames: enough for now, taking into account having enough left over for tomorrow's goal, and anticipating that what is enough for the rest of your life will evolve and change. In doing this, enough provides the important resource of *optionality*: the ability to create viable choices about the use of your resources, your choice of goals. This condition is essential for adaptability to changing environments—changes in the world situation and in your own emotional makeup. No environment changes the playing field more radically than success itself! Today we are trapped by our addiction to our current state of prosperity. Even if the pollution and overeating don't kill us, the rest of the world may wish to do so.

Stage 4: Acceptance

Enough is an expression of acceptance. A positive experience of satisfaction, to make or do enough. In really feeling "*this* is enough" and knowing why, you find some partial fulfillment of that impossible ideal that you seek from success, which some call the Good Life.

Acceptance comes from fulfillment of various needs: safety, belonging, pleasure, connection, and so forth. As we've shown, no single experience can capture all the pieces of this concept. Enough today is not enough for tomorrow, nor even for a minute from now in some cases. The lightning switches of attention we have already referred to were buoyed by our interviewees' capacity to enjoy the moment. They were present and aware. One might think this was simply a function of happiness, but it goes further. When you feel something really is an accomplishment now (not just something on the way to some far distant goal), you are appreciative of its importance—and can feel that's enough to go to the next thing you need or want to do.

Enough is the transformer that channels your core into concrete goals for all your categories of success. It turns your best visions of yourself and the world into activities with concrete, meaningful proportions. Conversely, an examination of your self-definition, your own inner core, helps you refine your understanding of what is enough for you now and still take into account your future needs. You may not be able to save the whole world today, but you can help one person. Are you doing so? Do you know how much time you should spend at this task? Are your emotions in alignment? Have you explored how much you will need to bring to amassing a fortune, enjoying it, giving it away, using it as a resource for others? Do you know why you choose this mix? If you had only a month to live, would the proportions change? You may not reach your absolute fullest potential, but you can stretch your goals. Is that occurring?

How Much Time Will It Take?

If the success framework is fractal—offering the same template for a yard sale or a major corporate acquisition, and these events occur over many stages in your life, you might think that time frames were interchangeable. But again the four chambers were found to have their own special requirements in terms of time orientation. You increase your chances of accomplishing satisfying episodes in each if you set the correct time profile in terms of goal-setting and impact/payoff.

The axis we've imposed on the kaleidoscope shows the distinctive time orientations of each category.

Happiness, as all the life satisfaction studies have shown, is experienced fully in the present (see Figure 8.1). To experience happiness is to lose all sense of time, whether in the bliss of meditation or a drug-induced ecstasy. Addiction to these states often results in a permanent loss of the sense of time, which is an equivalent to how we describe death. More positively, happiness in its many forms, from contentment to joy to rapture, is a satisfaction in the moment, even as it can be a judgment about the moment. You cannot be happy in the future, but you can be hopeful (optimism and happiness are not the same, though one can link you more easily to the other). You may have a pleasant feeling about the past, but your

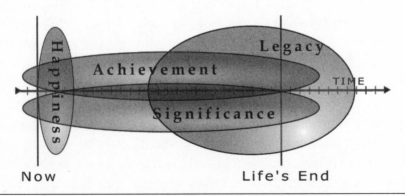

Figure 8.1   The time axis for the four components.

feeling is really in your present *recall* of the past. To remember you were once happy is not the same as being happy.

Again there is a bit of messy boundary problem between this clean time orientation and its relation to your self-definition. Happiness studies have shown that anticipation is a critical factor. If your actual experience is less than your anticipation of it, if you measure it against a standard that is significantly higher on your pleasure standard, your actual happiness is diminished. Does that mean happiness really is about future goal and present impact? We think not, and it is important not to calculate your pleasures on a future-weighted time scale. If happiness is always heavily dependent on something "out there," you are likely to experience disappointment with reality, much as an advertisement can tempt your *appetites* for pleasure but when you taste that new product, it disappoints. When you experience that *frisson* of anticipation, your happiness is actually in the experience of the *frisson!*

Achievement is oriented to a goal that is in the future, but its satisfaction is experienced in the present based on accomplishing something. Take away either part of this time configuration, and your achievements no longer feel like a success. Children who never experience the time lag between a goal and the effort it takes to reach it are denied a deep source of inner satisfaction and self-esteem. Conversely, those who become lost in the world of unreachable dreams suffer an ongoing achievement hangover. Artists and perfectionists are particularly vulnerable to this problem, as are those seeking more material forms of the infinite more! There is always someone "more successful" out there to whom you could compare yourself, and so you never set a goal that you can experience in the now.

Anna Sandor is one of the wisest women we know. Anna had an incredible urge to write even as a young girl, when as a refugee from Hungary, she turned to her journal to record her thoughts. Soon she was composing elaborate stories, fantasies of romance, adventure and challenge. Now Anna writes screenplays. She has twice been nominated for an Emmy, has won the Writers Guild of America

Award, and twice won the coveted Humanitas Award, first for her drama *Rose White*, about a woman who fled Poland in the holocaust and struggled with her identity for years afterward in New York; and once again for *My Louisiana Sky*, her movie about a child with mentally challenged parents. As Anna reflected on success, she noted the terrible insecurity most writers feel. The Humanitas was, she said, an instant of happiness, followed by the horrible fear every time she produced something "they'd finally find out I couldn't really do it." She laughs when she says this, knowing she's a pro, but also understanding that the satisfaction she feels in writing and achieving can be very elusive, and not at all the same as the moments of happiness she feels in having a good meal or attending a concert. She worries about artistic dissatisfaction, which we would trace to setting goals that can never be reached in the present.

She told a story of a friend, a violinist, who created a Grammy Award-winning string quartet that has found more than a modest degree of fame and success. Laura attended a performance. The audience was extremely educated and extremely warm in its applause, and Laura and Anna left the concert happy for the group's success. But the next day, when Anna talked to her friend, he was bitter. He said he walked off the stage having once again lost his wrestling match. It was between him and his demon—the music itself—and as usual, the music won. He was full of self-loathing, knowing he could never quite reach that ideal he assumed was the composer's. And that, said Anna, is the fate of the artist.

It's not our role to determine whether this friend is right or wrong in his success goals, but we use the story as an insight point. If you set goals of such abstract excellence as to be unreachable—the common pattern of artists who only heed the muse that tortures them—success cannot be a positive experience. Achievement goals must offer a present satisfaction. Just enough suggests that for the long haul, you would do better to find a standard that is a stretch, but reachable. Not to confuse it with ultimate beauty, but to secure a future-present mix of goals and satisfaction *out of your own accomplishments* that can keep you going and not destroy you and your family in self-loathing.

Anna accepts that, on the one hand, she will always have an ideal standard of literary excellence that she can never fully live up to. But she has also developed a pragmatic standard that allows her just enough success to feel ongoing satisfaction and pride in what she does. These moments strengthen her core and give her energy for when the writing gets tough, or negotiations with producers becomes wearing.

Significance also straddles future and present times. You focus your generosity on those you care about today and hope to deliver value for their future. In some ways Significance is the opposite of Achievement in that the action is now, the pleasure later, when the results are assessed by others.

On the other hand, **Legacy is a future-future activity.** You spin off legacies from current and past achievements, but their impact will occur after you've finished. Not just after you die. You can leave a Legacy in your high school achievements, or your first job. But its legacy value will be for others, without your involvement. Some people try to experience the impact of their own Legacy *now*—they create a new research lab and then decide perhaps they'd better run it for its first 10 years. Or they imagine the heartfelt gratitude of their friends' speeches at their funeral and then try to elicit that response from them at the next dinner party. Obviously, such efforts fall flat. The first is really another achievement activity, and the second an attempt to gain some acknowledgment of your significance to your friends now. Neither of these is legacy, which is about the foundation for other people's success after you're no longer in control.

If you can't give up the control, you can't create a successful Legacy. If you expect perfection, you can't give up control. Using the time orientation to jerk your preferences out of the present and toward the future—or vice versa—is a good corrective device, but as always you have to stay connected to your self-definition: You cannot be motivated to create legacies and be satisfied in the knowledge of a generative act unless you actually *value* the future. That means believing there is something of value outside yourself and your personal lifecycle.

Rich Success in the Real World

Age will impress many people with the value of Legacy in a way they may never have realized before, but enduring successes start early in adopting these multiple time and relational perspectives. Such is the kaleidoscope picture of the high-achieving high school class president who already has a sense she's leaving a Legacy, who feels she has a responsibility for doing something that nurtures her community and not just her resume, who enjoys herself rather than punishing herself for not being perfect.

Laura saw this balance in the profile of a neighbor of hers. Al Dunning and his wife Clarice lived on a street in Laura's neighborhood in Cambridge for a combined total of 144 years. Al and Clarice not only knew all the local history—they'd been a part of it. As a boy, Al and his buddy had found a tunnel in their basement. They followed it for over half a mile and ended up behind a furnace in Christ Church, across from the Cambridge Common. (The church warden nearly fainted when he heard a knocking on the wall panel near the furnace.) They'd stumbled on a secret tunnel that was most likely part of the Underground Railroad and perhaps earlier-on a smugglers tunnel during the siege of Boston at the start of the Revolutionary War. Needless to say, it was a dangerous place. Al's father and the church warden soundly punished both boys and closed the tunnel for good. But Al kept the story alive as a Legacy in the neighborhood, which through attrition was losing its strong historical ties to the African American community. (Al's house was across the street from the former home of Emery T. Morris, one of the founders of the Niagara Movement, the forerunner of the NAACP, and only a few lots away from the home of Rev. Thomas Wentworth Higginson, colonel of the first African American U.S. regiment, which was lionized in the movie Glory.)

Al had been a maintenance man at MIT for most of his working life. He'd achieved enough financial success to keep one of their childhood homes in spite of rising Cambridge taxes, and he'd had a satisfying career at the university. The job left him plenty of time for his family and friends. Every day he walked his dogs, at least twice, and as he walked, Al maintained the neighborhood. He'd stop and share news. He knew the names of the children on the street. He showed up for neighborhood meetings. He babysat his granddaughters. He never was intrusive, but he always seemed to be making sure the basics were in running order. If a fireplug was damaged, or a road hazard was blocking traffic, Al would make sure the right person knew about it. If a neighbor was having trouble, he'd offer help, or get help from someone else. He became known as "the Mayor of Parker Street."

Some people would look at the rising housing prices in this neighborhood (on average, up 1,000 percent in 15 years) and rising average incomes, and they'd assume the most successful person was the one with the biggest renovation. But Al had consistently been the leading citizen simply by virtue of his being there, showing up, and helping everyone experience a better living standard. When Al and Clarice were about to enter an assisted-living home, the neighbors decided to celebrate the Dunnings and their history on Parker Street with a farewell party. Few people get such a spontaneous send-off while they're still alive. The mother of a former actual mayor of Cambridge even arranged for the street corner to be designated with a plaque in honor of "Al Dunning, the Mayor of Parker Street."

Both Al and Clarice died unexpectedly within six months of this event. At their funerals, their children and grandchildren expressed their gratitude for a legacy not only of wonderful parents, but of the contribution their parents had made to their community. The Mayor of Parker Street's success was not only enduring and satisfying, it ranged the four categories throughout his life.

The Framework Gets You Something
Money Can't Buy

When we walk people through all the "dials" and axis and categories and chips involved in this model, it's easy to lose the larger purpose of the kaleidoscope in its commonsense applications. Understanding the complexity of these dynamics is critical not just to "getting ahead," but to the paths that lead to great achievements and life satisfactions. The richness of success, its enduring value in your life, depends on a healthy dose of accomplishments in every chamber of the kaleidoscope on a regular basis. When success feels "off" or unsatisfying, the kaleidoscope gives you a practical and insightful diagnostic to reexamine the relative picture in each of your four categories and check for the right alignments of emotion, relational orientations, and time frames. Are you putting all your Happiness into an Achievement framework? Is your family's idea of Happiness your idea of Significance? Is your Legacy a source of satisfaction without turning into one more competitive win? Have you calibrated the goals and anticipated the impacts appropriately?

Even the grimmest of moments can offer the possibility of adding chips in all the chambers of your success profile. Some readers may recall a letter that appeared on the front page of the B section of the *Wall Street Journal* in the first month of the Iraq war. Lt. Cmdr. Kevin Mickey had sent a "blog" to his parents about his experiences, which was reprinted in the article. He mentioned he'd had a chance to take a day off and took a brief "fun trip" to the next town. He got a laugh over a newly erected road sign by the highway. It had two arrows. One pointed east and had the word "desert" next to the arrow. The other arrow had a space that read "Insert city here."

This is a wonderful example of being ready for the potential for all four components in your journey. Even in the depths of war, you still have the need to experience Happiness, but you cannot expect it to dominate your efforts nor to be automatically subsumed in your Achievement mission. These categories are potent forces, driven by strong emotional needs. You can't mix them without risk of adverse reactions. If Lt. Cmdr. Kevin Mickey had stopped in battle to chuckle at the road sign, he'd be dead. But his need for emotional release was probably higher than ever before. Juggling, timing, understanding why you're doing something and what will be just enough in each category—these are the skills you *can* control and which form the foundation of an enduring success.

Quick Points: Further Calibrations of Enough

To calibrate your actions you must:

- Define "I" and separate it from "we" without losing your sensitivity to others' needs.
- Set upper and lower limits on your activities.
- Recognize the sources of your satisfactions and realistically assess your unique skills—not accept those imposed from the outside.
- Evaluate specific moments and events to see why they satisfy.
- Understand that setting limits gives you options for other uses of time and other sources of satisfaction.
- Accept that "more" is neither always possible nor always the goal.
- Time stamp your goals.

Chapter 9

Just Enough for a Lifetime

As a naturalist by profession and a humanist at heart, I have long believed that wisdom dictates an optimal strategy for proper steering toward the dream and away from the danger: as you reach upward, always festoon the structure of your instrument with the rich quirks and contradictions, the foibles and tiny gleamings, of human and natural diversity—for abstract zealotry can never defeat a great dream anchored in the concrete of human warmth and laughter.

—Stephan Jay Gould, *I Have Landed: The End of a
Beginning in Natural History*[1]

One of our interviewees was drawing a picture on the tablecloth of how he viewed success. He sketched three boxes, a very large one in the middle flanked by two rather puny squares. Success, he said, was the big box. That's what had preoccupied his mind and his emotions for nearly all his life (he was forty-five). The other two were family and self. "My goal now," he assured us, "is to even out these boxes, to see them as a three-legged stool. But it's very hard . . ."

He's not alone. There is a widespread search for "something more" among successful people today. Jim Warner's study of 200 CEOs primarily drawn from the high-achieving Young Presidents Organization, revealed that 70 percent reported feeling "driven" to achieve financial independence and 60 percent felt ready for a life change for negative reasons: They felt they were losing out on something else.[2] We call this the "success versus" view. Success is a big monument to financial achievement, which is placed in a dualistic trade-off with something else: success versus family, success versus self, success versus society. Choices around success then become a zero sum game: it's about choosing to go after financial goals versus other desires. In this way, we separate success from the ways in which we understand our other criteria for the good life and the way we spend the rest of our time. There is no integration of our needs: success versus. Others go to the opposite extreme, seeking a model that will let you have it all in success. In either case, success easily degenerates into a cost or investment, and the good life into an act of consumption.

In *Habits of the Heart,* the authors sketched out the American view of success, and could have easily been describing our interviewee and his cohorts from Warner's CEO survey. Success is understood as a highly individualistic function of personal choice; economic success is an exercise in self-reliance and freedom to the exclusion of values about social connection.[3] This view fails to relate economic success to our ultimate goals. It sets up a way of thinking about financial advancement that is inadequate—actually, *counter*—to achieving a good family life, positive recognition from others, or a prospering society.

Many people we interviewed expressed difficulties with the conflict between individualistic economic prosperity and community-oriented values in their life. One of the most exciting discoveries in our research was the realization that these dissatisfactions and the pathologies they generated around success could be viewed as *hopeful* signs. It wasn't that ambitious people today have no values about community or family; it wasn't that they have no ambition to achieve greatness. (This would truly have been depressing.) It was that they simply didn't know how to frame success as posing many positive choices in their lives; they didn't know how to assimilate into their choices about success those activities that touch on their core ideas of a good life and their values about self and others.

The problem is not a lack of dreams—if anything, society is overwhelming us with the stuff of dreams—nor even the selfishness that was so evident in a notable few at the very top of the economic boom. It is a problem of having no framework and method for success as a function of multiple choices among

incommensurate (noncomparable) and competing goals. In its absence, people are likely to fall into the success pathologies we mentioned at the outset: either going all out for the one big box of financial prosperity, or choosing the lowest common denominator in all domains so that no goal is big enough to pose a conflict with the others.

Getting Off on More Than One Track

Is there a better way to structure the pursuit of success and the choices you make around it? We've argued throughout this book that it is critical to throw out the "success versus" model for making your choices. The one-target-covers-all is equally limiting. Any activity that promises to get it all at once is playing on a field far smaller than most people's expectations of real success.

Dualistic models will always place you in a "success versus" scenario: either mourning the loss of family and connections or mourning the loss of economic opportunities. Every effort to stimulate your interest in one box will pose a loss in the others. *Coulda. Woulda. Wince.*

If success is about achieving irreducible noncomparable goals, what strategy will help you go after all these pieces? In this chapter, we take up the final critical aspect of the kaleidoscope strategy: Instead of a zero-sum solution, we will suggest a pattern, which we call *Spiraling and Linking,* that extends the choice framework to accommodate and order competing demands on your life.[4] Based on our four categories of success, this pattern makes room for the quirks and foibles Stephan Jay Gould celebrates in the quote at the start of this chapter as a necessary part of the creative life. It is a refreshing view. Far too many people today believe any detour from achieving big goals—even to enjoy their family—is a bothersome or even fatal distraction. We think these multiple tracks are critical to life and to organizations that want to create products and workplaces that are creative in response to human needs. We have already seen in Part Two how the kaleidoscope assigns these various needs a place. Now we'll discuss a strategy to help you go after all those chips!

Our advice is drawn both from theoretical work on decision theory and behavioral studies and from observations from our research. The enduring successes we studied did not tend to adopt a "success versus" worldview (or they reported dissatisfaction when they did), but secured success at many different, related things. These individuals allowed their success to reflect their full range as human beings: deep needs around self and others, pleasure and giving, present mastery and future promises. Were they special examples? Yes, they seemed to know how to achieve this enduring version of success intuitively. But as we have observed throughout this book, this diversity in our emotional makeup can be harnessed and organized in rational ways. You can hold your kaleidoscope up to the light and check out the pattern of chips in the four chambers. You can know yourself and constantly study changes in your own abilities and in your situation. You can be open to surprises that pull the pattern in unexpected ways. You can focus the right emotional, relational, and time orientations on each of the categories you pursue. And you can get more of the conflicting chips with a Spiraling and Linking strategy—if you employ the concept of *Just Enough*.

The Wisdom of Entropy

The kaleidoscope framework, with its four distinct chambers of accomplishment, sorts out the conflicting desires and emotions. Order can be comforting when it's simple, but the complexity of our ordering framework also creates the possibility of great confusion and pain. How do you go after four noncomparable goals? Where do you put your energy? How do you time the direction and amount of your goals for each category? Is your plan for the overall framework stable, or will it shift throughout your lifetime? **As you've probably noted in your own experience, people's needs in each category wax and wane. This pattern is very much like the phenomenon of entropy, which has been noted as the rhythm behind successful innovation and adaptation in the marketplace.**

Today's management theories are well versed in harnessing the energizing power of entropy. In the 1980s, Peter Senge's path-breaking book, *Fifth Discipline*, brought new applications to this long-known idea in the form of feedback loops of a learning organization. Jonas Salk had pointed out the same cycle of decay and renewal in his own understanding of knowledge creation. In 2002, we witnessed a number of fresh views on this problem, from Jim Loehr and Tony Schwartz's *Full Empowerment*, which outlined the biological rhythms of energy entropy, to Jim Collins's *Good to Great*. Two thousand years ago, the biblical writer Ecclesiastes was also advocating a cycle of rest and renewal: "To everything there is a season, and a time for every purpose under heaven."

Why, then, should we throw out all this wisdom about entropy in favor of a freeze-framed "success versus" strategy? In his book *Paradox of Success*, psychologist John O'Neil notes how easy it is to become a prisoner of success.[5] If you are especially good at something, how will you know when should you put it down before you reach burn out and the feeling of no longer being able to enjoy your success? If you've not quite hit the mark, you are driven to try, try again. Greed is the face of this addiction, but behind the mask is a deep need for *control*. Every increment of control leads you to want even more control to get back what you're missing. Little losses of control begin to feel threatening. You get irritated, you get impatient, you make mistakes. Your own success becomes the cause of your failure.

If you're not already addicted to this behavior, you'll probably want to give up in discouragement at the thought of having to deal with four categories that can't completely be kept under control . . . unless you have a better plan.

Accepting Conflicting Desires

A great deal of research has been done on how people set their preferences when goals are in conflict. They tend to choose the near reward over the further reward even if reason tells them they are being foolish. Their passion exerts more control than their reason, making them prey to their own appetites for pleasure.[6] Socrates scolded the Athenians for just this weakness: "Are you not ashamed, as citizens of Athens, the greatest of cities and most renown for wisdom and power, that you care for the acquisition of wealth and for reputation and honor when you neither care nor take thought for wisdom and truth and the perfection of your soul?"[7]

Even if you have a very strong will and reason overcomes your appetite, you may be unwilling or unclear as to how to evaluate a sure satisfaction in comparison to a less sure reward down the road. **Why would you put the near good at risk by going after another one, especially if it requires delayed satisfactions?**[8] Switching categories takes skill and it takes will. You can devise economic incentives for yourself, but in the end your success will only seem worthwhile if you can actually achieve satisfaction in *all* four categories. We're not empirical psychologists, but Laura is a classicist, and she likes to use Homer's epic story of Odysseus and the Sirens to describe how the ancients were able to define and cope with the same dilemmas of success.

After 10 years fighting at Troy and winning fame as a hero, Odysseus longed to go home. This yearning became his One Big Idea. The word for this "longing to return home," *nostos,* was even given the premier position of being the last word in the first line of the *Odyssey,* marking its central importance to the epic. It is the same root from which the milder English word nostalgia (literally: homesickness) derives. But Odysseus was a complicated person, and through ill luck (the angry gods) and his own curiosity he was taken to the ends of the earth, even to Hades, before reaching his beloved Ithaca. At each stage, another aspect of his humanity and heroism are tested to their full. In the Sirens episode, Odysseus has to sail by a rocky outcrop where beautiful women are singing an unearthly melody to lure ships to their doom. He has been warned that they are enchantingly beautiful and their song is irresistible. Inevitably ships are lured to this island and run aground on the shoals.

Odysseus longs to hear the song and he longs to make it home. These desires are mutually exclusive, as he is smart enough to recognize. In a literal depiction of will over sexual passion, he ties himself to the mast (having ordered his crew to stop their ears with wax). As he passes the sirens he nearly goes mad, sobbing and begging his men to turn around. They cannot hear him, he safely sails on.

There are two important lessons here. The first is obvious: Even the most resourceful people in the world have conflicting desires. **You have to anticipate these battles between your passions and be prepared with a strategy to give one up. "Feel" alone will not get you there. It may even send you on the shoals.** But there is another lesson in Odysseus's story that is not as frequently noted but is equally important: Odysseus had one big idea, getting home, but his real depth as a hero comes from the many different ideas and experiences his curiosity engendered. Some of them were lustrous, others quite dark, and many carried the ambivalence of his conflicting aspirations to conquer even Hades and yet remain a homebound husband.

This is what transforms a folktale into a timeless epic: The poet Homer presents a complex hero with multiple goals and deep-seated desires. The unfolding of this portrait occurs in multiple time frames. Some of his heroic pleasures are immediate, others suspended over the entire 24 books of the epic. For this hero, success is the journey itself. (His final recovery of his household is a very dark and ambivalent commentary on the decay of feudal kingships, and like most epics, the ending is not really satisfactory.) To expand on Jim Collins's apt metaphor for greatness, Odysseus had a hedgehog idea but not a hedgehog life.

Strategies for Handling Conflict

If you really want the richness of giving and getting, consuming happiness and leaving something behind, you have to have a plan for dealing with conflicting objectives, knowing that the emotional needs driving them will not all be met at once. Reaching Achievement, Significance, Happiness, and Legacy is not automatic, you can't control it with one idea. Nor can you tie yourself to a mast to navigate between the shoals of success. In fact, as we've argued, these supposed distractions from achievement and satisfactions in winning are not necessarily shoals if you don't let them pile up too high. Attending to these emotional drives on a regular basis gives you the satisfaction to keep going, to stay the heroic course.

How then, will you make your choices on an ongoing basis in order to achieve success for a lifetime? What will be enough in any one category? How long will it be enough?

Our research uncovered three typical patterns for making choices between the four satisfactions of success:

1. The first, which we call the *Collapsed Strategy*, rests on an assumption that one big goal will get you everything, but the experience in real time is that it is never enough.

2. The second approach, the *Sequential Strategy*, relies on satiation to give you the impulse to switch chambers. You divide life into two-decade increments, and go all out for one success goal at a time. This approach has the illogical goal of sticking with something until you no longer enjoy it. Some try to ritualize these choices. To echo a well-known aphorism many people use to describe this pattern, until your twenties you learn, in your thirties and forties you earn, and from fifty onward you return. But this approach forces you to abandon things that remain important to you for a good chunk of your life.

3. The third approach, the *Spiraling and Linking Strategy*, compresses sequential choice into a much tighter time frame. You move between the categories on a daily, sometimes minute-by-minute basis, and in each of the realms of your life. To do this you need discipline, foresight, and emotional versatility. You need to leverage the switching with rhythmical resonance. You need to forge linkages in your strategic thinking about success so as to make transitions easier. And you need good signals for calibrating the amount of time and energy you put into each episode in a category. For this you need a reasoned sense of *enough*.

Collapsed Strategy

We encountered one of the most vivid accounts of a life with regrets during a plane ride. The man in the seat next to us appeared to be highly agitated. He pointedly announced he didn't like to talk to people on a plane. Five minutes later, he was spilling his guts. His story, though an example of extreme achievement and professional status, could have been anyone's:

> When I first started out, right out of high school, I was con-
> sumed by the idea of success, and it was very simple. I thought
> that success was reaching a certain income level, somewhere be-
> tween $20,000 and $100,000. I really thought that. I won't be a
> success until I'm making $100,000. That and having a house
> with large white columns in the front, because when I was a kid,
> one of our neighbors who was successful had big columns on
> their house. For 10 years that's just about all I thought about. I
> started my own business and I'd take any contract that came my
> way. Didn't matter what we did in the business as long as it made
> money. I figured this was the key to everything: money, things,
> happiness, you name it. I even built a house with white pillars on
> it. I now realize it looked ridiculous in that neighborhood.

Essentially, this man—whom we came to refer to as "White Pillars,"—had adopted a collapsed view of success: Achievement was his one big goal, and he was hoping that if his bank account were just big enough, he could somehow attract all the other kinds of joys of life into that category (Figure 9.1). We're all familiar with the moral warnings against such assumptions: Money can't buy everything; one sparrow is not a summer's day. But rather than give up this desire for a simple solution to happiness, many people fervently believe in a fancier version: if you're efficient and work smarter, you can have it all from one thing. You can get "flow"— that perfect suspension of time and consciousness that marks effort-less mental and physical synchronization, or that perfect synergy you sometimes feel in working on a well-coordinated team. You can "balance" a high-powered career and school-age kids with time-shifting. If you don't, you're just being stupid or inadequate. Don't you know it's important to go for win-win?

Such advice easily slips into destructive collapsed assumptions. Your attention to your own advancement is mistakenly assumed to

Trying to have it all through focus and choice
Problems

 One activity rarely fulfills complex goals.

 Different skills and emotions come into play.

Different people who matter have different judgments about the nature of success and the real benefits.

Total focus often creates collateral damage.

Figure 9.1   Collapsing success into one category.

serve others well, your mental state "should" be happy. You "should" be admired by others for having done something significant. The pieces are there in theory, but their different dynamics make it almost impossible for one to get you the other three. "Flow" expert Mihail Csikszentmihalyi has repeatedly warned against mistaking the dynamics of flow for a steady state of synchronization and maximum performance. However coordinated you may be, flow is an occasional phenomenon that can only result from separate, more discrete efforts.

White Pillars made a mess of his life with this strategy. As it turned out, he did make his $100,000 before age thirty, but by then other things were going sour:

> Sure, I had a family, kids. But I really didn't think about them at all. I'm ashamed to say that, but it's true. Then my wife divorced me and I didn't want to lose touch with my kids and I began to adjust my schedule. By this time I'd also begun to think about the job a little more. Why was I taking such stupid contracts? Why didn't I better myself? So I looked around for a contract that would build something everyone would admire. And I found I was really into it, I got interested in architecture and later on city development. I remarried. I joined a few boards and attended all the right parties and I had status.
>
> But my kids still were monsters with me, and they got into a lot of trouble. Well not all of them, but one of them. I'm still bailing him out, and it's scaring me.

Sequential Strategy

When White Pillars hit a wall at age thirty, he turned his attention to Significance. But he couldn't quite escape his addiction to money and Achievement. Others try to overcome this backsliding by turning their backs completely on Achievement and adopting what we call a Sequential strategy (Figure 9.2).

Sequential strategies methodically take the idea of delayed gratification to an extreme. It's the pattern of choice for many young people today, especially the so-called dot-comers who saw promises of fast riches just down the road. You work hard at Achievement, slaving away from grade school into your thirties or forties. Then you close that chamber and move on to Happiness, to play with your money and enjoy being a millionaire. When your happiness is

Waiting for satiation before moving on
Problems

 When will you decide to move on and leave the satisfactions behind?

 You have continuing emotional needs for the satisfactions provided by earlier activities.

 What is enough for now is unlikely to be enough of forever.

 There is always more.

 You may miss opportunities that will never come again since spouses, children, friends, and others will not and cannot wait.

Figure 9.2   Approaching success categories sequentially.

satiated, you close that chamber and concentrate on Significance—you magnanimously give something back to others, say through work in a nonprofit. Then you try to create a Legacy of your experience through a book or teaching. **If the Collapsed strategy is chaos theory at its nightmare extreme (every event holding the promise of multiple interpretations but none of them satisfying in real time), the Sequential pattern is particularly descriptive of Newtonian solutions: life is atomized into discrete pieces, to be addressed individually in a linear approach.**

At age 30, White Pillars tried this strategy but it could not make up for what he'd lost. At sixty, he turned his life around. Ten years earlier, he'd invested in a visionary project that threatened to throw him into bankruptcy when his market turned down. As he put it, there's nothing as humiliating as being on a board, going to the fund-raiser, and knowing everyone in the room is talking about you being broke. It gave him pause. He realized that he really wanted to see his big development project through not just to win the biggest pile of money, but because he wanted to do something that was really valued in the community, that changed the community for the better, that made an important difference. His financial recovery wouldn't be enough without this aspiration. He stuck it out, continually adding to his investment when he had the opportunity, changing the development plans to work with the community and get permits more quickly. The market did turn around. Today this project is referred to as a landmark renovation of a distressed area and is compared to some of the most ambitious city plans in the United States.

In recent years, White Pillars also began engaging in truly creative acts of philanthropy. One of them was the establishment of a college program for inner city students to get professional business degrees. He was already working with another community college to enlist other retirees at his retirement community for some active duty. He scoffed at the ones who were now addicted to their golf to the point of contributing nothing in the world, and noted that most of them had turned golf not into leisure but into their next competitive game. It was a bit sad, he thought. Wasn't that what he'd originally wanted?

"What made you change?" we asked. He stared as if we were crazy. "Isn't it obvious? Death. You hit sixty and you suddenly realize you're not always going to be here."

When your desires compete, Sequential solutions are absolutely necessary to getting more than one thing. The problem is with the time frame: **Slugging through a decade of work with empty chambers of Happiness, Significance, and Legacy creates its own failures.** Families are destroyed. Your ulcer objects to the treatment. Your own fixation on winning crowds out your ability to see what others you care for need. If you try to make all this up in the second half of your life, you may find you've irreversibly lost the chance. Some deal with this by defying biology: Starting a new cycle of parenting in their sixties, for example, and this time being there for the kids. Not everyone is so lucky physically or financially. (Nor have they thought of having a sixteen-year-old in the house at age seventy-five.)

You Can't Put the Good Life on Hold

No chamber sits on hold emotionally, nor does any one chamber stay filled forever. Many of the chips in your kaleidoscope will fade in color. You need to renew your satisfaction in these areas in real time, not by remembering that *one* day you really achieved or that *one* day you and your family really connected. But in renewing them, you have to work the framework all over again: Your capabilities change with age, as does your context. The business strategy that brought fame and fortune in the 1980s is passé in the new millennium. You have to renew your curiosity, your caring, your moments of contentment. You can't do this if you artificially impose a rigid barrier between each success category of your life. You have to create channels for movement between them and know, when you are attending to one category, just what is *enough*.

We learned this lesson most clearly from some of our intervie-wees who had experienced retirement. Those who'd saved up all their life for this moment of pleasure by never experiencing happi-ness had no idea what to do with themselves. They only had achieve-ment skills. They had no community, and few social skills beyond those that could be bought with a corporate title. They often drove their spouses crazy. On the other hand, those who tried to keep up their former pace and make one more grand killing in the market-place often found themselves not quite so satisfied about going to work, taking on the next problem. They feared that they may have lost their fast ball.

Those who seemed most balanced in retirement had invested healthy doses of activity in all four categories over their lifetime. Marsh Carter was a case in point. When he felt his capabilities were no longer appropriate for State Street, he announced his retirement:

> I decided it was time to leave. I'd been CEO for nine-and-a-half years, and that seemed about right. I'd achieved the major strate-gic goals we'd set when I came, even though we had a great set-back for the first three years because of the market. This had clearly been a success (compound annualized growth rate of op-erating earnings was over 17 percent, of operating revenues over 25 percent). Why did I leave? My priorities have always been clear, even though I've had to struggle sometimes to do what's right. And it was time to go.

This statement is about as clear a picture of understanding and acting on your personal limits of enough as we have seen. Carter's life is also an illustration of the fact that reaching enough in one area does not mean you have cut off other areas of activity and exploration. As we mentioned earlier, it wasn't but a few months before Carter was serving the state of Massachusetts by heading the commission investi-gating security at Boston's Logan Airport. He's been teaching a class on leadership at Harvard University's John F. Kennedy School of Government and MIT's Sloan School. Meanwhile, he and his wife, Missy, are spending more time with their grandchildren and both of them have become even more active in their charitable work. **They didn't wait to develop these interests and skills however. Carter was quietly doing voluntary teaching for years before he retired, fitting it into a busy schedule without fanfare. Missy has a long-time relationship with inner city schools. In an eloquent description of her choices she explained, "you choose to put your efforts in that place where God calls you: in that space between your own talents and the world's great needs."**

Spiraling and Linking Strategy

The pattern described in the Carters' pursuit of a meaningful life and a satisfying success is one of radical acceleration of the time frame in which you move sequentially between the four categories of success without trying to collapse them into a framework requiring only one set of emotions and orientations. In other words, you have to pay frequent attention to all four chambers of success, in all realms of your life. This is what our interviewees did so well: They could focus and yet switch. They could switch and yet link, so that what they did for their happiness was not entirely disconnected from their values about family, work, or community. The linkages, however, should not be confused with some secret formula that collapses the different dynamics of each category into a one-size-fits-all scheme. They still have to bring different perspectives to the categories—sometimes in quick succession. Linkages help them get there, as when you master a technological problem and instantly see an application for a consumer need. You are still bringing different goals and orientations to these two things.

When people employed this strategy, they could get various kinds of satisfaction from an episode without shrinking their emotional or relational universe. In other words, they got *more* from their pursuit of success by setting limits on how much attention they paid to any one category (Figure 9.3).

Ironically, they did this by imposing limits, by knowing what was enough. Marsh Carter knew when nine-and-a-half-years

Success Feeds Success

 Achievement yields feelings of competence that allows you to give to others without feeling diminished.

 Significant activities gets the giver emotional support from others.

 Experiencing happiness gives you repose that restores energy.

Legacy activities give meaning beyond the here and now.

Figure 9.3   The spiral of enduring success.

was enough as CEO: "I've seen too many CEOs outstay their time. Right now, everyone says my leadership was a success."

Carter's observations on this decision are telling: "There are other things I want to do. I've always been a bit of a free spirit, even though I'm very disciplined. I could always do more, but I've found I had to keep within the limits."

Carter is describing the same talent that fueled Jonathan Fernandez's yard sale. It's the same thinking that brought Sarah to the conclusion to start her own business: knowing that you could do more, you have the discipline and foresight to switch directions. It's what George Lodge discovered he needed in order to fulfill his political goals. You know you've done enough on course A, now it's time for plan B. Both can be a success, but that, as Carter says, takes discipline. Such choices are not usually an unalloyed emotional high. They need rational support.

If you expect you can make a switch simply by waiting until your enthusiasm for something is entirely dead, which is essentially a strategy of satiation or failure, you (1) waste time, (2) make yourself vulnerable to addiction, and (3) kill something in yourself. The real trick is to work with your many different passions, disciplined by the reasoned exercise of enough. When it's done well, as one of our executives noted, it almost feels as if you've acquired a new sort of genius.

This model implies a very different educational approach than most of us learn, one that cultivates diverse intelligences and the skills for reckoning incommensurate choices. You don't wait until you're fifty to give something back, you start as a child. You don't cultivate one talent to its precocious extreme, you experiment with many emotional and intellectual competencies. Indeed, when we read the college surveys about life goals, we are struck with the idealism this generation has expressed. The problem for them is in feeling they have been compelled to delay these impulses till they fill their achievement chamber with lots of money and independence.

If Jane Only Knew

This was Jane's problem. She had been building a well-rounded and capable life, and yet she was despondent. Equipped with talent and moral values, but by no means a martyr personality, she believed that she shouldn't settle for an unsatisfactory job that made her a great deal of money but crowded out her other needs. She felt she *should* be able to find a job that collapsed all her desires into the pursuit of money. In the absence of an obvious answer (and she was honest enough to see that no job promised all these things), she was suffering from indecisiveness. Ironically, this was driven by all the pieces of success that should bring you to enough—with one important exception. Her overall strategy was to assume that she could collapse the pieces into one big idea rather than parsing her very different passions and lifestyle desires into multiple pursuits over time. **If she could just set some limits on her expectations for any one activity, she'd actually open her choices to get more from her life.**

When Jane thought about her needs, she saw that they already touched on all four categories of success. She felt satisfaction in giving, in achieving, in the pleasures of hiking, music, and city life. She hadn't thought much about Legacy, but she was wrestling with the biggest generativity question of all: whether and when to have children. The problem was with the larger picture. There was not a single frame that would contain all these pieces. She kept having to leave something important out of her life plan. The pain of her indecision was understandable. **The emotional chambers of success sit in a nonlinear relation. The effects of activity in one have a disproportionate effect in that chamber and on the others because they are interrelated.** The satisfaction she felt from her real achievements was diminished because of her feeling of loss and neglect around the other goals she attached to a good life.

Jane had to discipline her desires. She had to anticipate the general parameters of enough for each of her passions. Spiraling and linking within the kaleidoscope framework could help her get there. Identifying enough for each chamber in different time increments—

enough happiness for the moment, for tomorrow for the future; enough achievement for today and what's enough challenge for the year—would set the dials at reachable levels. But only if she could go after each one sequentially and yet fast enough to take care of the moving targets. To do this, she had to see the big picture of success as a movable feast of *ongoing,* somewhat conflicting satisfactions rather than a set of perfectly complementary static goals. It would be like the difference between a grand tour to 10 separate cities and a snapshot of the Parthenon. However beautiful the static picture, you could never get enough from it to test your skills, experience repeated surprise, connect with others, and leave something behind.

Skillful sorting of her desires into the right category was essential. When she assessed her skills in church music and the opportunities in that field, it became clear that she could never reach a level of achievement in sacred music that would feel competitively satisfying and financially rewarding. Music did not belong as the main chip in her achievement chamber. But in choosing software, or a similarly well-paying job for which she had or could build capabilities, she needed to set a level of achievement that allowed her to put it down and pick up her music on a regular basis—at least several times a week, preferably working with a choir. Notice that these are not impossible goals. They do imply, however, that she needed a job that didn't involve travel, something that had prevented her from making a commitment to volunteering at her church. She had to identify what would be enough to really satisfy her needs without looking for perfect financial independence, perfect control over her life. Because, as is now abundantly clear, there is no such thing.

This plan would mean changing the conditions of her job, which was very hard for Jane to contemplate. Her fear of taking a risk was enormous. Moreover, she hadn't built her capabilities to support this decision. She had no backup plan and no money in the bank. Why not take a year, save up a few months salary, and spend the time looking for another situation, knowing what you're aiming for? It's easy for a year to slip by, the spending to outstrip the savings, and putting off that great passion of your life. Having an understanding of which chamber the main pieces in your life best fit helps you stay the course. It reminds you to check on whether the chambers are being neglected, which you've made no progress on filling up with fine colored chips of your various accomplishments.

You also have to experience satisfactions in the here and now to keep the passions alive. Jane's first step was to reserve time for her music practice and religious devotions every day, even if volunteering at a church was a year away. Finding a more stable job would also make it easier to decide when to have a baby. What she would have to give up, however, was the fantasy that there was some magic point at which money would fill her Achievement and Happiness expectations to the brim and make the choice for her. That would only lead into a frustrating desire for the infinite more. She had to give up her dependency on satiation.

Success Is a Lifetime Process

The idea of just enough helps you make this break from an addiction to security or total independence (or the improbable combination). No one really gets perfect independence or security. So how do people live without it? They experience the satisfaction of mutuality, of a friendship, of teamwork (Significance). They open themselves to enjoying the day through a sense of appreciation (Happiness). They compare themselves to a realistic situation that is close to their own and yet challenges them to score some wins and grow (Achievement). And they take pleasure in making a success be of lasting value to others (Legacy). They also are prepared to see the success journey as a lifelong process, not something to get over with so you can really live.

One extremely driven achiever we know was suffering under a demented schedule. It was ruining his health, and yet his project deadline was literally a year away. We forced him to meet us for lunch and sat outdoors with a simple sandwich. "What," we asked, "would you most like to do when you finish?" He sighed. "Go to the country," he said, "and do nothing. Just enjoy the view. Then spend some time with my kids." We pressed a little harder. What is it you like so much about the country? "Oh, the trees, and the breeze, and just taking a break." He broke off, catching our smile of amusement. We glanced up at the trees. Looking around at the setting he broke into a grin, "Like right now." The breeze and view were available then and there, but he was cutting himself off from his own satisfaction. His big idea of Happiness was so large that he didn't realize that right in front of him was just enough nature and time off to feel real satisfaction and renewal now. When he realized this, he said, "That's okay. I'm fine. This is just enough for today." **As the oft-quoted Ralph Waldo Emerson once said: "We are always getting ready to live, but never living."**

Experiments in preference and motivation have confirmed that smaller gains in the present are more tolerable when they are seen to have a place within a larger picture of future gains. When you see that you have four critical pieces to your ideas of what success delivers, and that setting a limit on one gives you immediate access to another, it's easier to switch before you've reached satiation. Just as it's easier to set aside a second helping knowing a great dessert is on its way. It's also easier to switch when you know you'll be going back to that satisfaction in the near future. But you have to leverage your energy through present satisfactions. Say you work in a poorly paying job where no achievement is well-rewarded, and you never feel a sense of mastering an important problem. The satisfaction level is so low that you'll have trouble switching achievement goals either because you feel you can't quit until you get a prize or because you've been stunting your capabilities to do it any other way. This is the horrible poverty trap that many people find themselves in: given the low pay and higher costs of living, no effort seems enough to feel a sense of financial progress. Resignation into temporary pleasures takes over unless you calibrate your goals to the four components in proportions you can actually experience and build toward. **The key is to take a small step now!**

That's not the same as saying achievement should always result in happiness as we define it, but rather that when you feel the satisfaction of achievement, it should forge a linkage to another category, such as the experience of happiness. You don't have to love every minute of the job itself, you've made room mentally to stop and enjoy a break. Savor it and you are emotionally prepared to go back to your work with enthusiasm. Such linkages increase switching when they are positioned carefully. When, for example, New Belgium entrepreneurs Kim Jordan and her husband Jeff Lebesch followed their dream to start a microbrewing company, they forged a strategy that would link their passion for good beer, good fun, and environmental responsibility.

It all looks seamless to an outsider. The company's innovative and extremely pleasant factory in Fort Collins gets by without air-conditioning and produces 300,000 barrels of prize-winning beer a year. Their employees vote major changes together with a thumb-ups "We do it" or a thumbs sideways "We want to hear more before agreeing." They sponsor bicycle races and goofy games like the Sunshine Wheat tractor pull, where water-sprinkler tractors are attached to six packs of Sunshine Wheat Beer, one of the New Belgium brands. They have a firm commitment to minimizing resource consumption.

You could mistake this combination of activities for some magic bullet of happiness that combines fun and profit with social responsibility—until you see the thought and work that powers all the fun: The employees bring hard work and dedication to the brewing process. The team agonized over their personal financial sacrifices that went into a decision to go in with the city to buy a monopole and generate wind power, or a new five-pond biological process water treatment facility, from which, among other things, they will generate enough methane to run a co-generation plant. It was no small sacrifice despite the logic of the decision when last year, employees voted to give up their bonuses to fund this effort.

CEO Kim Jordan feels tensions in the company's growth. As she put it, "How do you resist the plod of corporate death?" She knows the terms of achievement are changing as the company gets larger. How flat an organization can they sustain and still pursue growth? But instead of taking the obvious course of growth for granted as the ticket to even more prosperity, more happiness, more social responsibility, Jordan is taking a serious look at her mix of goals and wondering if a change of strategy would be better for the company.

Would it make more sense to construct a firm around many little businesses rather than one large one? What would be best for the ideals the founders brought to this business? What would be best for her and her family at this stage of their life? What would allow employees to grow their own capacities for success?

This thinking has caused the New Belgium people to be open to revolutionary changes in the business and new thinking about organizational design: just as they were open to how you could create an environmentally sustainable brewing process at headquarters that would also serve as a showplace for visitors to test the product! Just as they were open to change when Jeff ventured to step down as co-CEO in order to do less management and more product and engineering experimenting. Kim's also working on legacies: as newly appointed head of an industry board, she is challenging that group to adopt industrywide standards on environmental impact. She brings a special emotional versatility to this process: hardnosed and competitive at one moment, she also talks about values like love. When they put that word in their mission statement, one manager objected it was too soft. She responded, "I know you're uncomfortable with this, but we're keeping it." Today the mission is quite comfortable in describing beer drinking as "liquid love," an experience of pleasure and balance. For seven years, New Belgium has had a poster board in the factory where people leave notes that read: To: X From: Y: I appreciate you for: Z. This in a firm where the average employee is a twenty-seven-year-old male.

The Dynamics of Switching and Linking

The pattern of switching and linking within a kaleidoscope of success goals resembles multitasking but is most like the concept of *bounded instability*. The pieces of success work best in an interrelated design, creating more power than each on its own, but it is not a simultaneous process. Peter Ueberroth's surprising break for ice cream in the middle of our interview is a good example. The context for both activities was work: The ice cream came from a client. The parameters of this break were well defined. If you are in a job that motivates solely on greed and sees all competitors as enemies, don't expect people to send you ice cream. It's very hard to put aside that competitiveness to link up to activities of significance in your work life. Corporations that achieve enduring success never do so on a reputation of greed and ruthlessness.

Well-developed product and service strategies are both the result and driver of the linkages we describe. They rest on an intrinsic interest in solving certain kinds of problems and self-interested rewards for doing that (a good profit) but also on knowing the customer well and caring when the customer is poorly served. When you see your product as having the potential for a productive interrelation of these goals, you have linkage. But you cannot avoid the need for versatility and switching. When you are in an important price negotiation, the difference between the two interests and mental frameworks will be apparent.

To summarize, *just enough is an enabler and a motivator, the key to letting go and moving on*. Just enough is a dance in which you beat a magical path from the desirable to the possible. Defining "enough" lets you leave something not because you're disgusted or you've hit a wall, but because you know there is something else you want satisfaction from and you won't get it unless you leave this thing behind.

Just enough transforms limits into a positive choice. The well-designed small garden may be far more pleasing than a list of disconnected land holdings. The more toys you have the more time you have to spend on picking them up. There is a paradox here: by setting a limit to your expectations in any one area you can actually have a richer experience overall.

Just enough gives fulfillment in real time. We are so conditioned to assume that every success target should be about breaking through the limits that we forget the second part: if you don't reach a temporary stopping point you can't experience satisfaction. As John Stuart Mill advised in defining happiness: It's about "not expecting more from life than life is capable of bestowing."

Enough is not a conservative impulse (as in "I'm perfectly content, nothing will ever change, and I'm glad"). It's a progressive notion of knowing what you want to accomplish or have more of in the future, but within limits. It helps you go after what you really want.

You also know it when it's absent: if you haven't cultivated a sense of enough, the *wince factor* comes in. You experience fear that if you put this down, someone else will pass you. You envy the one who has more on some dimension. Beware! There is always someone to whom you could unfavorably compare yourself. Without a sense of limits you could lose all appreciation for what you do have or can have. **It's not just about the "what I haves" versus what you have. It is about the "what I find satisfying."**

If you are looking to expand your own capabilities and stretch your accomplishments, the only viable way to work the sequence of four satisfactions is with regularity and adroitness. Just enough is not exactly a turnkey psychological tool, but something close to it. We observed that just by entertaining the idea that enough is a competitive philosophy, people triggered their emotional capacity to change and to enjoy. As such, enough is paradoxical: it brings focus to your effort through limits, but allows you to experience *more* satisfying accomplishments.

Checking and Using Your Feelings

All of these qualities are particularly difficult for high achievers. You can reinforce switching with mechanical reminders to check your schedule against the four categories regularly. As you tune your sensitivity, take notice of the signs of satisfaction. You know you've developed an intuition for just enough if:

- You look forward to something else rather than stay "stuck" on one thing emotionally or literally.
- You feel satisfaction and recognize the nature of it.
- You can give up control.
- Your legacy is operating independently.
- Those you care about are thriving.

- At the end of the day, you reach your goals.
- The goals were measurable, and meeting them brought a sense of fulfillment.
- You have bigger goals for tomorrow.

You continue to *feel* positive after working on something: excitement, pleasure, concern, pride, even sorrow can be positive if it reflects an expression of emotional caring. (Just watch out for the evil twins: envy, wrath, gluttony, avarice, total control.)

Comparing the Strategy to Juggling

We wondered why so many people seem so devoid of the capacity to exercise a reasoned sense of enough, so we began to listen carefully for signs in the messages society and, in particular, businesses are voicing. Among the many factors we noticed were the widespread incentives in advertising and motivational literature that play on a fear of losing out on the "best things in life," reinforced constantly in media celebrations of maximized behavior on one dimension. There's a lot of pressure to spend your time looking over your shoulder: If you aren't a success by tomorrow, the market will be against you, age will be against you, all those other maximizers will beat you out. When you look at the world plausibly depicted by Michael Lewis' *Next*, with its profiles of younger and younger people exercising intellectual and economic authority, it's hard not to conclude that if you don't cash out by thirty-five you've lost your chance at success and at life. **None of this thinking cultivates an ability to set limits on what you are doing now for the sake of the larger picture in your theoretical kaleidoscope.**

If limits still seem like a cop-out to you, or the Switch and Link unclear, think of the kaleidoscope strategy as juggling. It would be far easier just to compress four balls into one big one, but the point of the exercise would then be lost. You have to keep all the balls going by giving them sequential energy. You have to anticipate. You have to know just what is enough energy to give a ball momentum without throwing the whole pattern off. And you have to keep your eye on the falling ball. This is precisely the opposite approach to conventional success advice that stresses maximizing your strengths. If you go for the ball that's always at the top, you'll drop all the others. Table 9.1 shows some of the typical linkages that help you experience the satisfactions that help you define the parameters of enough, and by contrast, those that limit your success.

We could go on with the iterations in Table 9.1, moving over different realms such as work, family, or community, but you get the idea. Select your goals with the understanding that by linking their accomplishment to goals in the chambers, you enrich not only your contribution toward making a difference, but the satisfaction you get from success. Multiplying the chips you create in each chamber can be as easy as extending the time frame in which you measure success. Not just what did you accomplish, but what new thing has been created and where does it take you next? One of the more surprising and satisfying success stories out of Silicon Valley was not the sudden wealth of a few hundred millionaires,

Table 9.1 Satisfactions that follow from linkages.

Positive Linkages	Disconnects
A + S = Delivered value and social. Result: Legitimacy, recognition, admiration, help when you are in need.	A − S = Selfishness. Result: Isolation, mistrust, nobody cares about you. Enemies pile on when you fail.
A + L = A record that inspires others to greater heights of achievement.	S − A = Disappointing ideologue.
	L − A = A sense of entitlement.
H + A = Energy, optimism. Result: Self-confidence.	H − A = A waste of talent. Result: Low self-esteem and often parasitic dependence.
	A − H = A sad winner.
S + L = A movement about which eulogies are sung.	S − L = Good idea without social force.
	L − S + Jealousy of the future.
H + S = Generous compassion.	H − S = A recluse.
L + H = A feeling that life has been well lived without having to keep living it forever.	L − H = Fear of death.
	S − H = Martyrdom.

but how many entrepreneurs of Indian-descent were transferring their knowledge to establish successful software startups in India.

Every high achiever we've studied or read about seems to have a built-in "next problem" they link to. What will you create from your creation?

Ken Hakuta: Success over a Lifetime

Here's how one person's profile of switching and linkage looked in real time over several decades. Ken Hakuta is more than the wonderfully creative inventor of "Dr. Fad," a children's television character who brought the wonders of science to his public television show for about 15 years. Ken loves science, loves entertainment, loves children. He's also an entrepreneur, and when he saw an opportunity to make money he took it: a silly little toy he spotted in Japan, which he eventually called "Wacky WallWalker," made him a substantial fortune. When Ken saw that he and the market were reaching enough with WallWalkers, he started another company, an online herbal distribution business. Meanwhile he had developed a deep attraction to Shaker furniture, which he acquired from time to time. It gave him pleasure both for its aesthetics and its rich cultural heritage of work, simplicity, and reverence. When the largest collection of Shaker furniture in America threatened to be broken up for sale, Ken seized the opportunity and purchased the whole thing. But he didn't hoard it for himself—he organized an international tour of the Shaker collection, known as the Mount Lebanon Shaker Collection. He researched the topic and underwrote a book on Shaker furniture, both to create a legacy of knowledge about this craft and also to interest other buyers and donors to the collection. This took him to a position as the only Asian American director on the board of the Smithsonian American Art Museum. Meanwhile the herbal business went bust in the dot-com meltdown. Ken hung on but a cold calculation of cash flow and venture money made it clear the game should be ended.

We met with Ken about six months after he'd shut down his business. It had been very discouraging, especially because he had

had to lay off good young entrepreneurs. Watching him in real time, however, was a life lesson in switching and linking with a reasoned sense of enough. Working out of his home and temporarily funded from his savings, Ken answers the door to receive one of his former employees. They discuss a new idea for a possible next business. He turns and points out a Shaker piece, admiring the beauty and asking his guest to appreciate the aesthetics. Now it's time out for a moment with the gardener—there's an interesting problem with some mulch that has been delivered, and he's interested for two reasons: There's a management lesson here if he can master it and also he's curious about the horticultural value of the material that's been brought in. Is this something they might want to invest in when they start the next business?

The phone rings. His son is calling from his college dorm and wants to check in on a lead for a summer job. Ken excuses himself for five minutes and goes in the next room. We hear laughter, and when he returns we share a moment to talk about our dreams and joys in raising our college-age children. But none of this is his main activity. Work is still a large part of Ken's life, but now it's work on a legacy. So far we've tended to describe legacy as something about yourself, but in Ken's case he was building his *uncle's* legacy. Nam June Paik has been a brilliant pioneer in video art, achieving great fame and some fortune from the effort. But he is old and never thought about what would happen to his work when he was gone. Unless Ken or someone else makes all the arrangements for its continued preservation and exhibition, a great artistic collection will disappear. To make this happen, Ken is deeply involved in legal complications over the ownership and rights to these videos. He spends his time solving these problems, communicating with his uncle and the family, and enjoying the many wonderful moments he has with the film and with his family.

Ken has an inner assurance and deep sense of values that seems immune to discouragement. But it's not without a reasoned effort. He is fully conscious of the power of appreciation in his life—what we would call the four satisfactions. When we ran into him about six months after this interview, he was still working hard on the video art museum. He assured us it was very stressful at times, but that he was completely certain it was what he should be doing. "If I can just pull this off," he said, "it will be enough." On our last visit he had just returned from Korea where a museum had been built to house some of the works.

Ken Hakuta knew what was enough achievement for himself, and he knew it would take many repeated efforts to create the legacy he wished for his uncle's work. Part of his great strength and success in our opinion, is his self/other orientation and the ability to shift with great frequency between his own pleasures and curiosities and his concern for others. If you freeze framed him, you'd conclude he was very self-centered or very self-sacrificing, depending on which moment you froze. He lives both selves with a passion in an ongoing way.

People like Ken Hakuta seem to make the transitions intuitively, but when you ask them about their activities, they see a logic; they see a big plan; they report different kinds of satisfactions. They regulate these things through a reasoned sense of enough. Switching and linking are skills that can be cultivated through reasoning, as long as it stays connected to the emotional complexity we have identified as critical to success.

The Dependency Effect of Never Enough

Without the switching and linking skills you lose both the pragmatic and motivational passion for achievement. Like an addict, you become dependent on never enough: Never enough time. Never enough information. Never enough security. Never enough innovation. The controversial producer, Michael Ovitz, may represent one of the most extreme examples of this.

Mike Ovitz

For years Ovitz was the "titan" of Hollywood, managing and producing top programs and running the top talent agency in Hollywood throughout the 1980s and 1990s. Then he hit a series of monumental setbacks in his projects, but still he persisted. In the face of financial difficulties, he is said to have amassed a staff and overhead expenses of $50 to $60 million per year, spreading his investments over 70 different projects. When Ovitz recently tried to raise new capital, he was unable to raise the $150 million he needed for a television division. According to the an article by Bernard Weinraub in the *New York Times,* Ovitz had become his own worst enemy. Wrote Weinraub after extensive interviewing: "A man who occupied a powerful perch has, over time, made prominent enemies. In a single year, Ovitz had been recruited and subsequently fired from the president of Walt Disney, taking a $100 million severance package for his pains. Apparently the investors had had enough."[9]

Joseph the Taxi Driver

Laura recently encountered the most dismal person she'd ever met, a cab driver in New York City. This man, call him Joseph, was treating her to a litany of his troubles—which were considerable. He didn't make enough money. An immigrant, he didn't like New York. He didn't like driving a cab but he didn't have an education. He'd joined the cab company at age 57 so he was going to have work two extra years beyond the normal retirement age of 65. That made him resentful, tired, and fixated on his health, which he assured her was very poor. He was from Central America, the eldest of six sons, and his father had volunteered to send him through high school. But since there were no jobs in his country, he'd declined in favor of driving a truck. Later he came to America. Had he ever tried to finish his education here? Go to night school? Impossible. Maybe one course just to try it out, near to your house in Brooklyn? No can do. Sleep is essential. Kids? No kids. The woman he married couldn't conceive and she'd left him 20 years ago.

It's possible that this man was suffering from posttraumatic stress disorder or some other depression. Clearly, he'd not had many breaks in life, at least from his view. But two things struck us as relevant to our study of success: First, he was the *worst* cab driver Laura had ever seen. A rotten driver with no attention span, he was losing money by the minute. He missed every opportunity to change lanes and then got frustrated when he was stuck. He took the worst route in terms of traffic. This was not his best skill. He was banking on the wrong activity. And second, even with all his handicaps, he had more choices than he believed.

He could indeed have tried a small change in his life, such as one night school course. He might have made some friends there, or improved his English enough to negotiate a better deal with his landlord. His evenings were clearly spent alone, but all around him were opportunities to join in and help others.

That's the good news and the bad news: you have many more choices around success than you may imagine. But as we've already pointed out, most people, in the face of many choices, find themselves more stressed and confused.

Bob Anderson

By contrast, consider a long-time friend and entrepreneur, Bob Anderson. For years Bob was a successful entrepreneur who richly valued his family and his church. Just as he began to share these loves with others by founding a new organization on leadership and values, he experienced some health problems. They would require a radical change of his lifestyle, and presented a special challenge in that he was about to close his first new deal in a startup business in venture capital. Bob has shown an incredible adaptability to these changing contexts, even though he will be the first to say that he is not the most flexible personality in the universe. His faith, his experience, and his perspective—in other words, his core self-definitions—have helped him adjust his goals and develop new stress management skills so that he is channeling his attention into each of the four chambers *in workable amounts.* He readjusted the dials and already has completed several of his work and nonprofit goals and is refocusing on the next targets. It is very satisfying.

You Have to Recognize Enough

To keep the critical balancing pattern that we've observed among these high achievers, it's important to have a good comprehension of the function of enough.

First of all, how do you know it? Signs of enough from our interviewees ranged from an appreciation of the emotional rewards involved in an accomplishment (much like the life satisfaction measures, these tended to be of fading but ongoing quality) to the evidence that they were able to put something down without feeling deep regret about having done so. If you sensitize yourself to these benchmarks, you will regard the day as a success, at least in that realm. **When some efforts fall short of satisfaction or elude rational goal setting, you have a diagnostic for change. Either the goals were wrong, you were wrong, or they were never measurable on a scale of satisfaction.** Some of these things are in your control. Others a function of context. Say it was just a bad day. Surprises came up. Priorities changed—those are typical moving targets in the landscape of success. There are always distractions. You have to be able to adjust your goals and aim at the next right one.

The second point about enough is that *the four chambers of success help you reach it.* Each acts as a counterweight so that, like a seesaw, it takes less effort to switch directions when there are weights on both ends. To keep up the right momentum it's important to reassess your big picture and how you are weighting all four chambers on a regular basis.

A Life in Dynamic Balance

The proportionality between the categories of success that satisfies you at age twenty will rarely be the same as that which you seek at age fifty. As many of our interviewees and students observed, most people tend to weight achievement more heavily than legacy and significance in their early twenties. As they gain in financial and professional strength, they may cut back to spend more time on significance and happiness, only to turning the majority of their effort to legacy in their fifties or sixties. These passages have their own insight points, but they do not imply a one-dimensional goal.

Some of the most enduring and admired people we know are still achieving in their eighties, still giving of themselves, and very much enjoying the process. They've done so by fine tuning their idea of what is enough for each stage of their life and building their core from each new episode so as to create an even stronger platform for the next stage. This is the spiral of enduring success.

Victor Fraenkel once pointed out that those who survived the Holocaust did not tend to dwell on the meaning of life but asked themselves what was required of them for the day. In the same way, we think that while the big picture is important, the real key to success is not in framing one big target and shooting at it, but in the ongoing question of what is required to grow all your chambers of aspiration and need for now, in light of tomorrow, and with a view to building a full life. Would that be enough?

Constructing Your Kaleidoscope

What is your pattern? The dynamics laid out in the kaleidoscope framework generate infinite questions to help you see your underlying desires and get what you want. What emotions are driving an activity in one component? Are you addicted to a unidimensional framework out of fear or pleasure seeking? Are your current capabilities great for one chamber but inappropriate for other forms of the good life that you seek? Could you fly back from a business meeting to bring a birthday cake to a friend who thinks that's the most important gift in the world? What do your friends and family need to know about supporting *your* needs? Could you tell them when and why you need to spend time at something for the sake of one of your four categories of success? Is there a mismatch between your values and beliefs and your context? Have you anticipated the constraints that one activity will put on another domain of success? Are they irreversible or can you anticipate and correct for them now?

These questions all stretch the possibilities for using the success framework to its fullest extent. Success has an organic unity that challenges and fulfills. It's worth the effort to go for just enough. While we suggested at the start that the kaleidoscope framework presented here is an initial summary based on our observations and research, but has not been empirically tested, we wondered ourselves how far this structure would take us (Figure 9.4). Was it transferable and meaningful to other cultures?

We tested our initial assumptions with a group of CEOs in Brazil, who sat down together to talk about their ideas of enduring success. Three were born in Brazil, one was from Mexico, and two were from the United States. Each of the accomplished executives echoed critical aspects of our framework. Bill Rohner, then president of Caterpillar Brazil, talked about the importance of the relational dials in his work: "You have to be constantly alert to who you compare yourself to and how context can change it. One day Caterpillar was number one, then suddenly it was comparing itself unfavorably to the success of Japan, only to correct and once again assert its winning position in the marketplace."

Francois Nadas was managing director of Bloomberg's Latin America operations at the time of our discussion. In his thirties, he's constantly questioning how his values differ and resemble American preoccupations with control and materialism. He's incredibly excited at the growth he's experienced in his job, and yet he wants to keep his life in balance. He does so, he reports, out of a feeling that he has to be *building something every day*. With uncanny maturity, he adopts a multiple time frame for this observation: "I am always asking myself, what did I build today for the future?"

John Mein, then president of the American Chamber of Commerce, noted how much people's idea of success varied with the time of their life, and contrasted this to what he felt was a very dangerous preoccupation in the business world to imitate someone else's idea of success.

Albert Holzhacker runs a surgical equipment manufacturing firm. An engineer, he wanted to stress the multifaceted sources of

Managing the Dynamics for Life
Early Career

Achievement builds the base or possibilities, but involving others and experiencing joy is a great part of youth.

Changing Through Time
Mid Career

Mature leadership creates achievement, but great achievement requires investing in others' needs. Legacies are created as we go.

The End Game
The Golden Years

In the golden years, achievement goals may shrink, happiness about your life and satisfaction from the positive impact you have had on others who can build on your values and accomplishments become stronger measures of success that endures.

Figure 9.4   The dynamics of life.

one's ideas on success. "This is a rational and animal feeling, success. You want not only to be a winner, you want to *feel* a winner. It's a relation between external and internal, material and spiritual." Albert is drawing on this wisdom as he advises and helps out with an educational project in Brazil.

All of them were concerned with the education of the next generation of business people. How could schools and companies avoid creating the kind of selfish monsters that represented the worst of free enterprise? All are important leaders in their field without being celebrity successes. All took the time to meet and discuss an academic research project on the tired old subject of success. Commented Micael Cimet, president of EDS Latin America and someone's whose incredible career we've followed for more than half a decade since he attend INSEAD's management program, "You know, when you asked me to come and talk about this, I thought the focus of your study was a bit too conventional. But when I thought about your initial question, what do you really mean by success," I realized, "This seems so simple, but it is really profound."

Quick Points: Just Enough for a Lifetime

When you seek Enduring Success, you have to face some profound realities:

- You have conflicting desires.

- One activity will not give you everything you want.

- Approaching your goals in decades-long sequence will cause you to miss opportunities and leave your continuing emotional needs unsatisfied as you pass to the next stage.

- The key skill is spiraling and linking your activities.

- Enduring Success requires constant attention to the four categories of success—and remembering that the mix will shift as you mature.

Epilogue

Solon of Athens (reputedly the wisest man on earth) went to visit Croesus, king of Sardis (reputedly the richest man on earth). Croesus showed him around and then asked him, "You are said to be the wisest man. I can't help but ask, who do you think is the happiest man you have ever seen?"

Solon looked around and then replied, "An Athenian named Tellus."

—The Story of Croesus and Solon, Herodotus,
The Histories, Book I.28-45

As Jane found after only a few short years of success in her job, the money and recognition were great but did not satisfy her completely. There was more to life, she thought, but she despaired of ever having enough freedom to find this richer experience. Jane was already turning the profitable habits of a high achiever into a lifetime pattern, assuming there was only one way to go about success: the same one she'd always followed in school and at work. Discovering how the four categories of success could give her a way to direct her desires to serve her church, win in the business world, and have a child was a revelation and a joy. She was clearly more energized when she rethought her choices within this new framework.

We would like to be able to add to the lore of happy endings and tell you Jane worked out her dilemma. But we do not know that. Jane continued on her walkabout as planned, but as we parted she earnestly expressed her thanks for giving her these new tools. "Keep doing this," she urged us, "it's really important."

We did hear echoes of Jane's story in many of our research conversations, and we have reason to believe that the more detailed solutions suggested here represent what *can* be a structuring of Jane's ambitions and values that provides a happy ending. But it will not be, nor should it be, the neat solution for all of her career and life problems. The search for success is an activity for a lifetime. The prospect of finding new chips for your kaleidoscope and new linkages for your loves and your ideas enlivens every part of your life— not just the part where you go to work with a new set of tools and score new victories there.

We hope you will come away from this book with a fundamental understanding of our two major themes and the cognitive tools for using them in gaining your own success. The first is our caution against the assumptions of celebrity and thinking that what you expect from success can be gained by putting your all into the One Right Target. This is a critical problem today, and one that is often exacerbated by the way business leaders are educated. In their seminal article on shareholder maximization, Michael Jensen and W. Meckling argued that managers are agents whose first obligation is to pursue interests of the shareholders.[1] The apparent logic is that, given the inevitable divergent views among these owners, the default goal should be share price maximization. In their opinion, any exercise of managerial discretion not attributable to maximization incentives would be an exercise of bad faith.

Though these authors intended to argue for responsibility and restraint, their one-target paradigm of maximization has been perverted into a neurotic, unstable behavior model without any balancing mechanisms. Maximization has lost its link to sustainability. Now it's simply about going beyond whatever extreme has already been established. You just keep ratcheting the knob up higher and higher until the machine breaks.

This is what happened for many of the high-tech businesses that boomed out shareholder wealth through the late 1990s far beyond the companies' capacity to sustain a return on the capital invested through profits. This is also what happened for the many absentee parents who discovered too late that their teenagers had "gone underground," isolating themselves from emotional attachments to the family. Our educational systems emphasize the same pattern, celebrating the maximizers and suggesting that children must maximize every subject, every sport, every minute of their time.

Our second theme is that everyone needs to construct a success framework. In our kaleidoscopic metaphor it must encompass a set of chambers representing the good things you seek from success. Our categories—Happiness, Achievement, Significance, and Legacy—classify what appear to be people's irreducible desires around success. In honoring all four of them, you create the necessary balancing device for ambitions that threaten to exceed any sustainable social or emotional capacity. Not static balance, but a dynamic movement of switching and linkage over time. To do this, we have methodically dissected the driving forces and relevant perspectives of each category and also suggested the critical importance of knowing how to find and apply "just enough" to secure your goals and yet move on to the others in each category.

Finally, we would like you to remember this: You can't control every outcome, so invest your energy in the controllable. You can't change your body type, but you can control your eating. You can't predict the market a year from now, but you can set up diversification that yields strength and sustainability. These disciplines are not only important for your personal enjoyment of the good life, but for the reconnection of success to the social ends you seek.

These lessons are critically important today when the economic environment seems out of control. Robert Reich, in his book *The Future of Success*, reported that he was seeing a deep sense of frustration and dissatisfaction among leaders.[2] They long for the days of unquestioned authority and feel constrained about what they can say and do as leaders.

Leadership experts from David Gergen and Joseph Nye to Rosabeth Moss Kanter have all questioned whether the world's moral and economic instabilities are a sign that we are entering a new stage of leadership. The problems of immorality at the top have been so widespread as to place a premium on leaders we feel we can trust; and yet the power of formal authority, such as a CEO's power to resist short-term pressures on stock price, seems very constrained, however

moral he or she may intend to be. We want leaders who can coura-
geously resist corrupting, short-term incentives. But tied as these outcomes are to having to court favor with a fickle and increasingly
greedy set of constituencies, it can be a daunting task.

The mantra today is that courageous leadership gets rewarded
in the marketplace. Quiet leaders, such as those featured in Jim
Collins's *Good to Great*, Warren Bennis's *Geeks and Geezers*, or
Rakesh Khurana's *Searching for a Corporate Savior*, seem to be more
prepared for the long haul. How do we understand these lessons
within the context of diverse goals that go far beyond institutional
power to our very definitions of the good life? In the last five years,
we've seen more than a dozen top companies rocket to financial
heights only to abruptly turn and burn out. In some cases, the financial and legal debris they leave behind has critically injured the nation's economy, people's jobs, and our ability to build coalitions.
Meanwhile, the marketplace has in many cases irrationally rewarded
these failures of leadership with golden parachutes and increased
stock options.

So, too, political agendas seem to be recognized on only one dimension, to the loss of the nation's larger cluster of ideals around
life, liberty, and the pursuit of happiness. Bush spoke of a "perfect
success," in Iraq as if there were such an end point to war, in which
all ends are tied up at a finite date. Our viable forms of leadership
are particularly unclear. John McCain and Ross Perot made good
mileage politically but, as David Gergen pointed out, it is far more
difficult to succeed at going beyond individual celebrity to build institutional legacies from their support.

We see the same sense of constraint and burnout in individuals
as we see in the conflicts of national leadership and trace much of it
to the inadequacy of applying celebrity and maximizing paradigms
to today's abundance of personal choice. We are dazzled by an increasing number of options about what to do at a given stage of life,
where to work, where to invest, what to purchase, who to vote for.
At the same time, none of these options fully satisfy us. The state of
dissatisfaction has larger consequences than in the past because it's
easier for many people to switch affiliations: Divorces have become

socially and legally devoid of obstacles; golden parachutes make it easier for leaders to exit a firm; alternative financial instruments and increasing control over your own investments make it easier to exit a given stock; incredibly global sources of information via the web offer shopping alternatives in everything from your kitchen appliances to your religious practices.

None of these conditions are necessarily bad in and of themselves, but they have created a deep sense of instability that, for many people, has increased their experience of indecisiveness or exhaustion. The gains we see in terms of choice have not necessarily led to an increase in our satisfaction any more than they have led to a more stable sense of reliable leadership in business or politics.

What is more, there is good reason for this instability and the fear it generates. We are faced with highly contradictory forces in our culture and economy, torn between a desire for increasing freedom and independence about our life choices and a need for more coordination of our resources in order to compete effectively. The new consumerism appears to be the perfect example of this conundrum. Perched on the Wal-Mart-Gucci axis, consumers go for low prices at businesses that have achieved massive consolidation of purchasing and delivery strategies, and where possible indulge themselves with extremely individualistic upscale treats. No wonder our sense of standards is shaky at every level: economic, moral, and even in terms of structuring the leadership of an organization.

Just Enough presents a flexible standard that we feel provides a strong new framework for getting out of the success malaise. It offers a coherent framework for exercising choice and focusing energy around deeply important human and social needs. By recognizing the complex components of our own self-definition and understanding our main categories of choice and satisfaction, we can begin to anticipate and structure a way through the contradictory forces that comprise the good life and good society. Happiness, Achievement, Significance, Legacy—how will you restore these concepts to a healthy level in your life and in your society?

In asking this question, we are not trying to dull your appetite for a life of great ambitions, merely to prepare you to discern what will really dazzle your soul for the long term. As Mark Twain noted in *Roughing It*, "I learned . . . that gold in its native state is but dull, unornamental stuff, and that only lowborn metals excite the admiration of the ignorant with an ostentatious glitter. However, like the rest of the world, I still go on underrating men of gold and glorifying men of mica."[3]

The orientations of the four categories have something to say to each of the major generations today, but it remains to be seen whether a new generational worldview will develop. Perhaps it will be called the Linking Generation, a group of individuals and leaders who can move between opposing needs with regularity without losing a larger consistency of design. We saw this pattern in the opposing domains of activity that drove the successful conclusion of the first Tylenol poisonings in 1980s. Many dozens of decisions had to be made by Jim Burke at Johnson & Johnson that positioned self-interest against social need, only to be resolved by attention to all these urgencies sequentially. Public safety was prioritized before profit, but the company returned to a profitable strategy as soon as these conditions were fulfilled. It couldn't seek perfect protection of consumers—other taintings of this and other products have occurred since—but the company found a responsible level of enough in the recall and packaging to regain consumer trust and serve the needs of all those who used their products (the first line of their Credo). Doing this was an exercise not only in public leadership but even more so in employee development. The way Tylenol was handled gave employees a sense of commitment and energy to recapture market share that left a legacy in business behavior for years afterwards.

Finding Enduring Success

That larger design of satisfactions and desired ends is what we've called *enduring success*. Our challenge is for you to find your particular pattern of enduring success, using the framework suggested here. In an understandable desire to keep things simple, we too easily learn to silence the existence of choice in our lives, going instead for the simple strategy: what's been won before by someone else. Nothing succeeds like success.

Take a chance: We won't promise a fairy tale ending, but we will promise a direct line to your own satisfactions over time and a more likely pattern for securing them. We've structured this approach much like a play where the audience is given a choice at critical junctures in the plot. In our framework, success is:

- Achievement matched to your desired goals.
- Happiness in the here and now.
- Significance through making a difference to others.
- Legacy in the form of leaving something behind that will continue to build others' capacity for success.
- An understanding of yourself—your values, emotions, context, and capabilities—that makes your efforts not only more likely to be accomplished, but important and worthwhile in your own mind.
- A series of choices touching each of the categories with regularity in all realms of your life.

As we promised at the start, we have offered many "prompts" in the form of insight points to explore this framework in detail, but only you can decide the ultimate plot that will describe and build your kaleidoscope.

Finally, we would like to leave you with the *rest* of the story of Croesus and Solon, with which we began this final discussion of success. Written centuries ago, in another culture and another time to mark the birth of the democratic state in the Western world, Solon's lessons for the man who truly was "as rich as Croesus" have resonant echoes for us today:

Solon of Athens (reputedly the wisest man on earth and "father" of Athenian laws) went to visit Croesus, king of Sardis (reputedly the richest man on earth). Croesus showed him around and then asked him, "You are said to be the wisest man. I can't help but ask, who do you think is the happiest man you have ever seen?"

Solon looked around and then replied, "An Athenian named Tellus."

Croesus answered sharply, "What is your reason for this choice?"

Solon: "Two good reasons. First, his city was prosperous and he had fine sons, and lived to see children born to each of them, and all these children surviving. Secondly, he had wealth enough by our standards, and he had a glorious death. In battle with a neighboring town, Eleusis, he fought for his countrymen, routed the enemy, and died like a solder; and the Athenians paid him the high honor of a public funeral on the spot where he fell."

So Croesus asked, "Well, who was the *second* happiest man you've ever seen?"

Solon replied, "Two young men of Argos, Cleobis and Biton. They had enough to live on comfortably; and their physical strength was proved by their athletic success but even more by the following incident. The Argives were celebrating the festival of Hera, and it was most important that the mother of the two young men should drive to the temple in her ox-cart; but it happened that the oxen were late from the fields. Her two sons then harnessed themselves to the cart and dragged it along, with their mother inside, for nearly six miles till they reached the temple. Afterwards they had a most noble enviable death, a heaven-sent sign of how much better it is to be dead than alive. The crowd that witnessed this event crowded round, congratulating them on their strength, and the women kept telling the mother how lucky she was to have such sons. So the mother, in pleasure at this recognition, prayed to Hera to grant Cleobis and Biton, who had brought her (Hera) such honor, the greatest blessing that can befall mortal man.

"Then the ceremonies, sacrifices and feasts were performed. The two boys fell asleep in the temple, and they never woke again. The Argives had statues made of them, which they sent to Delphi as a mark of respect."

Croesus was becoming more and more vexed. He said, "That's all fine, but what about *my* happiness? Is it so contemptible that you won't even compare me with the common folk you mentioned?"

Solon answered, "My Lord. I know that God is envious of human prosperity and likes to trouble us; you have questioned me about the lot of man. Listen then. As the years draw on there is much to see and to suffer that one might wish otherwise. Take seventy years as the life span; those seventy years contain 25,200 days, without counting intercalary months. Add a month every other year to make the seasons conform. And you will have thirty-five additional months, which will make 1,050 additional days. Thus, the total days for your seventy years is 26,250, and not a single one of them is like the next in what it brings.

"You can see from that, Croesus, what a chancy thing life is. You are very rich, and you rule numerous people; but the question you asked me I will not answer, until I know that you have died happily. Great wealth can make a man no happier than moderate means, unless he has the luck to continue in prosperity to the end of life. Many very rich men have been unfortunate, and many with a modest means have had good luck. The former are better off than the latter in only two respects, whereas the poor but lucky person has the advantage in many ways. Though the rich have the means to satisfy their appetites and to bear calamities that the poor do not have, the poor, if they are lucky, are most likely to keep clear of trouble, and will have besides the blessings of a sound body, health, freedom from annoyances, fine children and good looks. Now if a man so favored dies as he has lived, he will be just the one you are looking for: the sort of person who deserves to be called happy.

"But mark my word: until he is dead, count no man happy. Till then he is not happy, but only lucky."

Now What?

While Solon's caution turned out to be true for Croesus, his advice left this ruler helpless to charge. The happiness that Croesus sought in wealth was impossible. In seeking Solon's judgment, Croesus missed the point: **Happiness is inside you—it is not a competitive goal.**

On the other hand, had Croesus taken Solon's stories to heart (and if he had read this book!) he would have seen that these examples were anchored in the four categories of which we have written. He would have understood the concept of **Just Enough** achievement of wealth and power, and thus might have avoided the destruction of his empire that lay ahead of him. He could have appreciated his situation and extended his accomplishments toward activities that satisfied him in a way his wealth never offered. He might have found significance through committing his economic and social wisdom to paper and in training his children to be wise rulers. Through that, he would have found true legacy. Even the statues that exist depicting these great people are apparently figments of later generations' imagination.

In researching and writing this book, we found ourselves in the grip of having to determine **Just Enough**—what would be enough information to get our ideas across, and what would be just enough knowledge for us reasonably to expect you to take back into your life? After consideration, we hope you will take away and put in play the following ideas:

- Enduring success requires happiness, achievement, significance, and legacy.
- Your emotions demand satisfactions of many kinds, very often.
- Your unique combination of values, beliefs, capabilities, and emotions will play out in a particular context that will determine what you should do to be and feel successful.
- You can and must learn to define **Just Enough** with time and relational goals attached: enough for now, enough for today, enough for this year, and enough for your life and for others you care about.
- The mix will vary as life changes occur, but all four sources of satisfaction are available to you.
- Even though someone may surpass you on a single dimension, with this strategy the odds are in your favor for a more enduring success.

Notes

Chapter 1. Stress! Excess! Success?

1. Daniel Goleman, Richard Boyatzis, Annie McKee, *Primal Leadership: Realizing the Power of Emotional Intelligence* (Boston: Harvard Business School Press, 2002), p. 40.
2. William James, "Letter to H. G. Wells," *The correspondence of William James,* ed. Ignas K. Skrupskelis and Elizabeth M. Berkeley (Charlottesville: University of Virginia, 1992); cited in Bergen Evans *Bartlett's Familiar Quotations* (New York: Delacourt Press, 1968), p. 667.
3. Joan Didion, *Slouching Toward Bethlehem* (New York: Delta, Dell, 1967), p. 123.
4. Del Jones, "Not All CEOs Live High Life," *USA Today* (February 12, 2003), p. 1A.
5. Juliet B. Schor, *The Overworked American* (New York: Basic Books, 1992), p. 21.
6. See George Ainslie, *Breakdown of Will* (Cambridge, United Kingdom: Cambridge University Press, 2001), p. 181ff, for a summary discussion of the relation between prediction, empathy, and the loss of the "self."

Chapter 2. The Dangers of Going for the Max

1. Phyllis Berman, "Buyout Buccaneer," *Forbes* (July 23, 2001), p. 64.
2. David Owen, "Sorenstam's Got Game in Reality and Virtually," *New York Times* (May 25, 2003).
3. Jack Welch interview with Ray Suarez, *NewsHour with Jim Lehrer,* PBS (September 16, 2002).
4. Lawrence Eisenberg, "Caine Scrutiny," *AARP Magazine* (April 2003), p. 53.
5. Annetta Miller, "The Millennial Mind-Set," *American Demographics* (January 1999), p. 60.
6. Marjorie Garber, "Our Genius Complex," *Atlantic Monthly* (December 2002), p. 72.
7. Macolm Gladwell, "The Talent Myth: Are Smart People Overrated?" *New Yorker* (July 22, 2002), p. 28.
8. Statistics are from several sources and compiled in Michael Lewis, "In Defense of the Boom," *New York Times Magazine* (October 27, 2002), p. 44.
9. Jerry Useem, "Have They No Shame?" *FORTUNE* (April 14, 2003), p. 57.
10. Rakesh Khurana, *Searching for a Corporate Savior: The Irrational Quest for Charismatic CEOs* (Princeton University Press, 2003).

11. Carol Hymowitz, "The New Fast-Trackers Work Like Maniacs and Then Take a Walk," *Wall Street Journal* (February 22, 2000), p. B1.

12. PricewaterhouseCoopers: Venture Economics; National Venture Capital Association Moneytree Survey, 2002. www.pwcmoneytree.com/vec/news-ve/2003.

13. See note 12.

14. Erika Brown, "The Midas List," *Forbes* (February 17, 2003), p. 88.

15. Jim Collins, "The 10 Greatest CEOs of All Time," *FORTUNE* (July 7, 2003).

Chapter 3. The Satisfactions of Just Enough Success

1. John Dryden, *An Essay of Dramatic Poesy* (Oxford: Clarendon Press, 1896).

2. Personal interview with Peter Ueberroth, Newport Beach, California, June 12, 2002.

3. Peter Ueberroth, *Time* magazine cover (October 17, 1983).

4. The authors did not interview Mr. Eastwood personally for this profile but relied on many public accounts of his career.

5. Lillian Ross, "Nothing Fancy," *New Yorker* (March 24, 2003), p. 45.

6. See note 5, p. 45.

7. See note 5, p. 41.

8. Julie K. Norem, *The Positive Power of Negative Thinking* (New York: Basic Books, 2001), pp. 82–84.

9. Jim Loehr and Tony Schwartz, *The Power of Full Engagement: Managing Energy, Not Time, Is the Key to High Performance and Personal Renewal etc.* (New York: Free Press, 2003).

10. Warner reported 70 percent felt "Driven to financial" independence, 50 percent felt they were "Not using my talents," and 39 percent reported "No romance or sexual passion." See www.oncoursein.com.

11. Howard Gardner, *Frames of Mind: The Theory of Multiple Intelligences* (New York: Basic Books, 1983).

12. John R. O'Neil, *The Paradox of Success: When Winning at Work Means Losing at Life* (New York: G.P. Putnam's Sons, 1993), p. 125.

13. Jack L. Groppel, with Bob Andelman, *The Corporate Athlete: How to Achieve Maximal Performance in Business and Life* (New York: John Wiley & Sons, 2000).

Chapter 4. Your Success Profile

1. Richard W. Stevenson, "A Trusted Friend Leads Bush Campaign Fund-Raising Effort," *New York Times* (June 21, 2003).

Chapter 5. Who Are You? And Why Are You Doing That?

1. Leston Havens, *Making Contact* (Cambridge, MA: Harvard University Press, 1986), p. 21.

2. Jonathan Lear, *Happiness, Death, and the Remainder of Life* (Cambridge, MA: Harvard University Press, 2000).
3. See Chapter 1, note 6.
4. Robert N. Bellah, William M. Sullivan, Steven M. Tipton, Richard Madsen, and Ann Swidler, *Habits of the Heart: Individualism and Commitment in American Life* (California: University of California Press, 1996).
5. See Chapter 3, note 10, p. 133.
6. James Collins, *Good to Great* (New York: HarperBusiness, 2001), p. 195.
7. Robert Nozick, *The Examined Life: Philosophical Meditations* (New York: Simon & Schuster, 1989), p. 156.
8. See Chapter 1, note 6, p. 12.
9. See Chapter 3, note 9, pp. 82ff.
10. Mihaly Csikszentmihalyi, *Flow: The Psychology of Optimal Experience* (New York: Harper Perennial, 1990); Martin Seligman, *Authentic Happiness: Using the New Positive Psychology to Realize Your Potential for Lasting Fulfillment* (New York: Free Press, 2002).
11. Theresa Amabile, *Creativity in Contex* (Boulder, CO: Westview Press, 1996).
12. Howard Gardner, Mihaly Csikzentmihalyi, and William Damon, *Good Work: When Ethics and Excellence Meet* (New York: Basic Books, 2001). By good work the authors mean "work that feels good and does good things."
13. Joseph Campbell, Betty Sue Flowers (Editor), with Bill Moyers, *The Power of Myth* (New York: Doubleday Company, June 1991), pp. 151–155.

Chapter 6. Complex Patterns in Real Life

1. This information is drawn from Katharine Graham, *Personal History* (New York: Knopf, 1997).
2. See note 1, p. 19.

Chapter 7. Making Successful Choices

1. Howard H. Stevenson, with Jeffrey L. Cruikshank; research assistance by Mihnea C. Moldoveanu, *Do Lunch or Be Lunch: The Power of Predictability in Creating Your Future* (Boston: Harvard Business School Press, 1998); Chapter 1, note 6, pp. 38–40; see also Charles Taylor, "Inescapable Horizons," in *The Ethics of Authenticity* (Cambridge, MA: Harvard University Press, 1992), for the ethical consequences of this problem.
2. A. O. Scott, "The Hungriest Critic of Them All," *New York Times* (June 29, 2003), section 2.22.
3. Daniel J. Kindlon, *Too Much of a Good Thing: Raising Children of Character in an Indulgent Age* (Mirama Books, 2001).
4. See Chapter 5, note 12, for an interesting discussion of "the mirror" and Chapter 1, note 1, p. 7.

Chapter 8. Further Calibrations of Enough

1. For a similar use of time to expand the discipline of self-management from something about self control to self-discovery, see Thomas C. Schelling, *Choice and Consequence: Perspectives of an Errant Economist* (Cambridge, MA: Harvard University Press, 1984), p. 74–77, where he applies time to understand the nature of addictive behaviors.
2. For practical difficulties of communication under such confusions of role, see Chapter 5, note1, pp. 160ff.
3. For multiple examples of the moral problems these "trade-offs" pose, see Amitai Etzioni, "Order and Morality," in *The New Golden Rule: Community and Morlaity in a Democratic Society* (New York: Perseus Books, 1996).
4. See Chapter 1, note 1 and Chapter 3, note 12.
5. See Chapter 5, note 7, p. 250.

Chapter 9. Just Enough for a Lifetime

1. Stephan Jay Gould, *I Have Landed: The End of a Beginning in Natural History* (Three Rivers Press, 2003), p. 396.
2. Jim Warner, *Aspirations of Greatness* (New York: Wiley, 2002).
3. See Chapter 5, note 4, p. 22ff.
4. For an excellent review of nonlinear dynamics and their application to organizations, see Susanne Kelly and Mary Ann Allison, *The Complexity Advantage* (New York: McGraw-Hill BusinessWeek Books, 1999), pp. 11–19.
5. See Chapter 3, note 13, pp. 123ff.
6. See Chapter 1, note 6, for an excellent review of this literature.
7. Plato, *Apology* 29D.
8. See Chapter 1, note 6, for an excellent summary of this problem.
9. Bernard Weinraub, "Hollywood Giant Comes on Hard Times," *New York Times* (August 10, 2001).

Epilogue

1. "Theory of the firm: Managerial behavior, agency costs, and ownership structure," *Journal of Financial Economics* (1976), pp. 305–60.
2. Robert B. Reich, *The Future of Success* (New York: Alfred Knopf, 2001).
3. Mark Twain, *Roughing It* (New York: Harper & Row Publishers, 1962).

About the Authors

Laura Nash is Senior Research Fellow at Harvard Business School. Pursuing a wide range of contemporary issues in business, she is author or co-author of seven books, including *Good Intentions Aside, Believers in Business,* and *Church on Sunday, Work on Monday.* She was president of the Society for Business Ethics in 1998. For the past 20 years, she has taught and consulted on corporate values. She has a doctorate in Classical Philology from Harvard University.

Howard Stevenson is Sarofim-Rock professor at Harvard Business School and Senior Associate Dean for External Relations. He has been a business entrepreneur and a professor at Harvard since 1968. He is an author of numerous cases and books on entrepreneurship as well as *Do Lunch or Be Lunch,* reflections on predictability. He has his doctorate in Business Administration from Harvard Business School.

Index